THE CONSCIENCE OF
THE STATE IN
NORTH AMERICA

CAMBRIDGE STUDIES IN THE HISTORY
AND THEORY OF POLITICS

EDITORS

Maurice Cowling

G. R. Elton

E. Kedourie

J. R. Pole

Walter Ullmann

THE CONSCIENCE OF THE STATE IN NORTH AMERICA

BY

E. R. NORMAN

Fellow of Jesus College and
Assistant Lecturer in History, University of Cambridge

CAMBRIDGE
AT THE UNIVERSITY PRESS
1968

Published by The Syndics of the Cambridge University Press
Bentley House, 200 Euston Road, London, N.W. 1
American Branch: 32 East 57th Street, New York, N.Y. 10022

© Cambridge University Press 1968

Library of Congress Catalogue Card Number: 68-10473

Printed in Great Britain
at the University Printing House, Cambridge
(Brooke Crutchley, University Printer)

FOR PATRICIA

This book was supported by the N.A.T.O. Fellow-ships programme, established 'in order to throw light on the history, present status, and future development of the concept of the Atlantic Community, and of problems which confront it'.

CONTENTS

PREFACE

'Antipathy against persons of different persuasions', Bentham once wrote, 'is one of the last points of religion which men part with'. Scarcely, perhaps, a pleasing remark, but it applies cogently enough to the struggles which accompanied the adjustment of the ancient framework of the confessional state to the religious and ideological diversities of modern society. The New World enjoyed no exemption. This short study is not a history of religion in the United States and Canada; nor is it an account of the relations of church and state. It is an interpretative introduction to those relations, in the light of similar experience in Britain. Many of the illustrations will doubtless be familiar to specialists in the fields concerned, but they are reintroduced here to give substance to a central proposition: that the redefinition of the relationship of the state to religious belief, since the middle of the eighteenth century, has followed an essentially similar though chronologically uneven course in the United States, Canada and the British Isles. Since a certain degree of vagueness pervades such knowledge as exists in Britain about the history of religion in North America, accounts of some sequences which might otherwise appear superfluous to an American reader are here offered in the hope of establishing common ground.

I am grateful for the kindness and help of many, and especially of Mr Stephen Otto in Toronto, Dr John Macauley of Kansas State University, Bishop James Pike of the Centre for the Study of Democratic Institutions in Santa Barbara, Dean Newman Bracken of Toronto, Mr Steve Brown of Zanesville, Ohio, and Mr John Vernon of the Cultural Relations section of N.A.T.O. This book has been greatly assisted by generous grants from the managers of the Smuts Fund. I am also especially indebted to Dr William Brock and Dr Jack Pole, who read the manuscript and suggested several amendments. EDWARD NORMAN

Jesus College, September 1966

1

THE NEUTRALITY OF THE STATE

> But the true issue was this: whether the State, in its
> best condition, has such a conscience as can take cogni-
> zance of religious truth and error.   GLADSTONE

It is curious that the United States, Canada, and the British Isles,
with a shared heritage in which so many common elements are
acknowledged, have generally been dismissed as essentially dissimilar in one important aspect of their histories: the relations of
church and state, of religious belief and public life. In this sphere
historical interpretation has largely managed to refrain from anything approaching a comparative view. No coherent unity of
experience seemed apparent. In fact the three countries have been
regarded, in this respect, quite simply as incomparable. Early
commentators occupied the ground by ascribing the American
separation of church and state to the vigorous common sense and
unique conditions of the new nation. The survival of religious
establishments elsewhere was usually described as a penal result of
moral deficiency in the civil institutions of the countries afflicted.
Where British or Canadian experience revealed features which
were at all comparable with their own early separation, Americans
(when they were aware of them) have immediately supposed,
not that those other countries may in some things have sustained
developments which paralleled theirs, but that *any* redefinition of
the religious and governmental spheres must ultimately have derived from the example which they had offered to the world.

The American experience, in this question, has been regarded
as unique. So categorical has the assumption been, and so effectively has it prevented the consideration of alternative explanations, that some evidence must at the outset be adduced to indicate
its real existence. Nineteenth-century commentary shows that

The neutrality of the state

European observers were as guilty of misplaced emphasis as the Americans themselves. Thus de Tocqueville attributed the extraordinary absence of religious contention in the United States to the singularity of her arrangements for the separation of church and state. He did not hesitate to affirm that during his stay in the country he had not encountered 'a single individual, of the clergy or of the laity, who was not of the same opinion upon this point'.[1] John Howard Hinton, an English visitor, wrote in 1851 of the disestablishment of churches as 'an absolute creation of the new world'.[2] Philip Schaff added the authority of his testimony, and his opinions have left a particularly enduring mark on subsequent historical interpretation. Schaff came to America as a Lutheran pastor. He at first supported the union of church and state on principle,[3] but this view faded as his 'Americanization' advanced.[4] By 1888, when he published his great *Church and State in the United States*, he had come not only to singularize the American religious achievement, but to eulogize it too.[5] Bryce is also responsible for adding authority to the belief that the divorce of church and state was the most distinctive quality about American religious experience. 'Of all the differences between the Old World and the New, this is perhaps the most salient', he wrote.[6]

Nearly every modern American version has merely been an elaboration of these early conclusions. Thus Sanford H. Cobb, in his *Rise of Religious Liberty in America* claimed a 'unique solution of the world-old problem of church and state—a solution so unique, so far-reaching, and so markedly diverse from European principles as to constitute the most striking contribution of

[1] *Democracy in America* (1835–40) (Oxford, 1955 edition), p. 238.
[2] *The Test of Experience; or The Voluntary Principle in the United States* (London, 1851), p. 40.
[3] *America, A Sketch of the Political, Social and Religious Character of the United States of America* (New York, 1855), p. xiii.
[4] See Henry W. Bowden, 'Philip Schaff and Sectarianism: The Americanization of a European Viewpoint', in *A Journal of Church and State*, VIII, no. 1 (1966), 97 ff.
[5] *Church and State in the United States* (New York, 1888), p. 42.
[6] *The American Commonwealth* (New York, 1913 edition), I, 763.

America to the science of government'.[1] Nor did he leave it at that. There were, he wrote, in the American separation of church and state, 'features unparalleled in the rest of Christendom'; which were, furthermore, 'a peculiarly American production'.[2] Other writers have arrived at strikingly the same conclusion and the stream of unanimity has continued to the present time. 'Separation of Church and State is one of America's greatest contributions to modern religion and politics', wrote E. F. Humphrey.[3] 'The pattern evolved under the constitutional guarantees of religious freedom has not only worked well in this country but has served as an example to the rest of the world', wrote Anson Phelps Stokes.[4] 'We are therefore dealing', he added, 'with a movement of international historical significance: the bringing about, and mainly through the United States, of constitutional religious freedom.'[5] 'The most important difference between the religious life of England and that of America', wrote Willard L. Sperry, 'is the continued existence in England of the Established Church, and the total absence in America of anything like an establishment.'[6] Leo Pfeffer, writing on the legal recongnition of churches as volutary associations, declared that 'it was the United States alone that conceived and proved the workability of the idea'.[7]

There was, during the first half of the nineteenth century, when the American Republic stood almost alone in the separation of church and state, ample enough justification for supposing that it symptomized a great new world departure in religious and governmental experience. But a comparison with the experiences of Canada or Britain will not allow such a view to stand unqualified. All the opinions cited above presuppose that questions concerned

[1] *The Rise of Religious Liberty in America* (New York, 1902), p. vii.
[2] *Ibid.* p. 1.
[3] *Nationalism and Religion in America, 1774–89* (Boston, 1924), p. 359.
[4] *Church and State in the United States* (New York, 1950), I, xlvi.
[5] *Ibid.* p. 647.
[6] *Religion in America* (Cambridge, 1945), p. 6.
[7] 'The Case for Separation', in *Religion in America, Original Essays on Religion in a Free Society*, edited by John Cogley (Cleveland and New York, 1958), p. 59.

3

with the relationship of church and state remained more or less stationary everywhere else in the nineteenth century, or that, if they tended at all towards a redefinition, they did so under the inspiration of the American example. In reality, however, it was the American experience which was derivative: it expressed a development, in favourable circumstances, of forces which were essentially and enduringly British in origin and conception. In the Republic's northern neighbour, the British North American provinces, and in Britain itself, common elements were independently at work to produce the same end: a redefinition of the relationship of church and state. Chronological variations and regional differences have tended to obscure the process, it is true; but the forces making for its ultimate success, and the nature of their assault upon the old confessional state, were everywhere essentially the same. They were of two sorts.

First was the fact of religious pluralism, suggesting to the dissenting churches that the ancient religious exclusiveness of the state might be overthrown and 'religious equality' established in its place.[1] This did not imply the total separation of religious belief and public life, and most dissenters would have been inexpressibly shocked by the idea of real secularism. Their aim was disestablishment; the removal of the privileged and exclusive state churches. They assumed that in the resulting equality of all sects before the law, the state would itself continue to profess Christianity, but in non-sectarian terms. Their aim was therefore a limited impartiality of state action. Yet this was, at least originally, conceived to involve nothing so far-reaching as the notion that the state might eventually come to exercise only a measure of neutrality between believers and unbelievers. The separation of church and state in the federal constitution of the United States was not originally intended to disconnect Christianity and public life; it was a device to prevent the supremacy of one sect over another.

Paradoxical as it may seem, it was the tradition of church estab-

[1] See Franklin H. Littel, *From State Church to Pluralism* (Doubleday Books edition, New York, 1962).

lishment which provided the most cohesive element in the common religious experience of Britain and America. The establishment principle crossed the Atlantic, and even the large numbers of dissenters who settled in the thirteen colonies during the seventeenth and eighteenth centuries were not opposed to the union of church and state—though they were unable to assent to the actual arrangements in Britain. With the exception of the Quakers, and of Roger Williams's experiment with separation in Rhode Island— for which he got into trouble with his dissenting brethren—the Nonconformist immigrants set up state churches of their own wherever conditions allowed it. The establishment principle was readily exported, that is to say, because an overwhelming majority of men still believed in the confessional office of the state. So there occurred the establishment of the Congregational churches in New England, and of the Church of England in all the other colonies except Rhode Island, Delaware and Pennsylvania. But during the eighteenth century it became apparent that the colonial establishments suffered from the same difficulties which were already beginning to be felt in Britain. The growth and diversification of dissent was sapping their authority by making them numerically dubious agencies of the conscience of the state. The American Great Awakening, in the mid-eighteenth century, drew still more men away from the official churches. Its counterpart as a popular religious movement in Britain was Methodism, and actual links between the two revivals were provided in the persons of Whitfield and Wesley himself. Large numbers defected to the new evangelical denominations. It was religious radicalism which ultimately profited; for religious pluralism, as always, was the beneficiary of revival. The swelling body of dissenters, in both Britain and the colonies, found themselves excluded from the privileges of the official religious life of the state, and this meant a large measure of exclusion from public office too. There then occurred, to put it simply, the greatest change; and it occurred in Britain and the British North American provinces as well as in the thirteen American colonies, although the rate of acceleration was somewhat greater in that last place. For a majority of the dissenters surrendered their belief in the exclusively confessional office of the state, and sought not to *replace* the religious establishments, but to *overthrow* them. 'Religious equality' was what they now demanded, and in a way which raised it to the level of dogma. The change was at first dictated by practical considerations, however. The dissenters were so subdivided among themselves that no one church was large or powerful enough to replace the existing recipients of state favour and protection. The Baptists and Quakers were early and more ideologically-inclined opponents of established religion. Now they were joined by most other types of Nonconformist, though in varying degrees of conviction and according to locality. The change occurred first in the thirteen colonies, then in Canada and Britain itself.

Everywhere, the immediate problems in overthrowing the established churches were immense. Since the dissenters correctly saw the question as one of opening up the full benefits of the British Constitution to themselves, they turned to political radicalism as the obvious instrument to hand. Opposition to the claims of the Church of England allied well with radical politics for another reason too: the unreformed and disproportionately endowed condition of that institution gave it high priority on the lists compiled by reformers of institutions. Even in Congregationalist New England the political radicalism of the second half of the eighteenth century was given new edge by the growth of articulate dissenting groups. This added to an existing store of radical ideas, for in New England the Congregationalist clergy were themselves the guardians of political concepts inherited from the seventeenth century constitutional conflict: of opposition to divine right and the royal supremacy in religion, and the maintenance of the contract theory of government. 'Out of reading and discussion, preaching and practice, there had grown up a body of constitutional doctrine very closely associated with theology and church polity, and commonly accepted by the New Englanders', Alice M. Baldwin has written; 'most significant was

6

the conviction that fundamental law was the basis of all rights.'[1]
Yet even in New England, dissenters from the Congregational
establishments, especially the Baptists, were agitating for the
divorce of church and state as a measure of constitutional reform.
In the colonies with Church of England establishments this agitation existed at its most popular expression, and it was there that
radical religious demands enjoyed their first successes.

In the American colonies an advanced and well-cultivated radicalism imparted a sophistication to the dissenters' requirements.
The break with the Crown in 1776 provided just the *tabula rasa*
the dissenters could use to usher in the rule of religious equality.
In the First Amendment to the new federal constitution, church
and state were separated. This was largely due, it is true, to the
work of Episcopalians and Deists, and indicated as much their
own philosophical and practical objections to the establishment
principle as it did any real desire to concede the principles of
dissent. Even in this, the handful of leaders involved were unrep-
resentative of the general opinions prevailing among Episcopalians.
The real issue was being settled in the new states of the Union,
however. In some there were disestablishments contemporaneous
with the birth of the new nation; in others, the achievement of
disestablishment came—only after much disputation—during the
next fifty years. These separations were the victories of militant
dissent. Some vestiges of public confessionalism were cleared away
by state legislatures during the nineteenth century, and some survived, even to the present day. Both theoretical and legal connexions of the American state and non-sectarian Christianity were
allowed to continue because it was inconceivable that they should
not: they were popular where they were recognized, and assumed
to be part of the national heritage where they were largely mixed
with the general cultural deposit. Having satisfied themselves
with an early and formal separation of church and state, the
Americans left the constitutional position unchanged until 1934,

---

[1] *The New England Clergy and the American Revolution* (Duke University Press,
1928), p. 168.

when the Supreme Court ruled that the federal separation must apply to the individual states through the operation of the 'due process' clause of the Fourteenth Amendment of 1868.[1]

The growth of religious pluralism, and its effects, were as marked in the British North American provinces as in the thirteen colonies to the south. Pluralism existed among the early settlers; it was suggested by the Catholic population of Quebec; and it was reinforced by the arrival of the Loyalists and by nineteenth-century immigrations. Here, too, there were Church of England religious establishments: in the Maritimes, in Upper Canada, and, though rather vaguely defined, in Lower Canada as well. And here, too, the dissenters allied with radical politics to fight for religious equality. They enjoyed no favourable upheaval, like the southern rebellion, to assist their endeavours. But their radicalism could imply a comparable need to re-draw the relationship with the Crown if concessions were unforthcoming. In 1851, for example, the Methodist leader, Egerton Ryerson—a moderate—wrote a paper on the clergy reserves question for the guidance of the Imperial Parliament. 'What the Canadians ask, they ask on grounds originally guaranteed to them by their Constitution', he declared, 'and if they are compelled to make a choice between British connection and British constitutional rights, it is natural that they should prefer the latter to the former.'[2] This was a reproduction of the American case against Britain.

The dissenting militancy of the Maritime provinces and Upper Canada, was not derived from the Americans, however. It was an exaggerated version of the experience of Britain itself. Demands which were becoming increasingly familiar in early nineteenth-century Britain—assaults upon the privileges of the established church, claims for a redistribution of her property, and then for complete voluntaryism, and the cry of non-sectarian education—

[1] *Hamilton* v. *Regents*. See Murray A. Gordon, 'The Unconstitutionality of Public Aid to Parochial Schools', in *The Wall of Separation between Church and State*, edited by D. H. Oaks (Chicago, 1963), p. 80.

[2] E. R. Stimson, *History of the Separation of Church and State in Canada* (second edition, Toronto, 1887), p. 79.

all these had an early flowering in the favourable circumstances of colonial life. And lacking the strength to resist dissenting pressures in the local legislatures, these demands were generally conciliated, piece by piece: a cumulative process considerably advanced by the grant of Responsible Government to the Canadas, following the Durham Report, in 1840. State churches were not actually disestablished. They evaporated as establishments when their privileges and properties were withdrawn by government action. There has never been a formal separation of church and state in Canada, and there was no mention of religion in the constitution of Canada—the British North America Act of 1867. By the middle of the nineteenth century, separation had become an accepted principle in Canadian official life, though government support for church social and educational work has continued in Quebec on denominational lines, and is evident in most of the other provinces in non-sectarian fields.

In Britain, the established Church of England and Ireland, and the Presbyterian establishment in Scotland, were similarly subjected to the pressures applied by the agencies of religious pluralism. It was about the time of the American Revolution that dissenters' agitation for concessions increased in Britain—their restiveness being related to the contemporaneous revival of political radicalism, and the scrutiny to which existing institutions were increasingly liable. During the first half of the nineteenth century, these demands became more effectively expressed. This was largely due to the fantastic growth of dissent. Evangelical nonconformity was proving more than adequately competent at winning converts from the urban and rural poor, and the Act of Union with Ireland, passed in 1800, added some four million Roman Catholic dissenters to the area governed from Westminster. Theological differences of opinion were splitting up the Scottish Church, and this too, was making for a steady increase of dissent. Yet the forces behind the maintenance of the religious establishments were formidable, and opposition to the sort of political radicalism which was everywhere made the vehicle of the dissenters' demands was much more effective than in Canada or the American colonies. The battle for religious equality was therefore much harder. The dissenters' successes, on the other hand, were very striking. In 1844, after a struggle with the courts over the question of Crown control and patronage, the established Church of Scotland split down the middle, with one half seceding to form an independent body. This was a triumph for the voluntary system in religion, even though Dr Thomas Chalmers, perhaps the leading secessionist, was opposed to voluntaryism on principle. In the Act of 1869 the Churches of England and Ireland were separated, and the Church of Ireland was disestablished and disendowed. Ireland, indeed, in her religious complexion, enjoyed a relationship with England similar to that of Quebec with the other North American provinces. Irish Catholicism became involved with political radicalism to a refined degree. By the mid-nineteenth century the hierarchy were loud in their eulogy of that very principle which the Vatican so roundly condemned: a free church in a free state. The contrast was marked with Quebec, where the Catholic clergy sought as much state aid and protection as they could get; but it allied the Irish bishops with their counterparts in the United States, many of whom were of Irish origin anyway. Further successes of British dissent came in the 1860s and 1870s, when the Imperial Parliament withdrew state aid from most of the colonial churches—each instance greeted by the dissenters as yet another precedent for England herself. By Parliamentary legislation of 1914 and 1919, the Church of Wales was disestablished and disendowed. Each of these disconnexions of church and state was accomplished quite independently of any resort to American example.

Militant dissent was therefore successful in securing the separation of church and state in half the British Isles. But what of England itself? The position was far from static, even though the church establishment has actually survived to the present time. Parliament, having ultimately bowed to the majority principle as a qualification for establishment in the cases of Ireland, the colonies, and Wales, applied it in England too. The religious census of 1851 revealed that the Church of England still enjoyed an absolute majority over all other Nonconformist bodies—just—and it has continued, since that time, to remain the largest single church in the country. Yet most of the demands of the dissenters were conceded. They were presented to the legislature through some of the most powerful and effective organizations of public opinion in the nineteenth century, like the Liberation Society (for the freedom of religion from state control), the Protestant Dissenting Deputies of London, the Education League, and the incredibly articulate Nonconformist press. At first there was a good deal of difference of opinion among the English seekers of religious equality. Some hoped for state concurrent endowment of all the churches, others held back from common action through mutual suspicions, and still others, like the Methodists, because of sheer conservatism. But by the second half of the nineteenth century most dissenters—even the Irish Catholics—had enrolled themselves under the banners of complete separation between church and state and the universal application of the voluntary system of endowments. A sympathetic political arm was provided by important sections of the Gladstonian Liberal Party.

With the combined forces of a growing religious pluralism hammering away at the state church, and radicalism demanding its abolition on grounds of political justice—just as in the American colonies and the Canadas—the privileges and constitutional safeguards of the Church of England were gradually withdrawn by a cumulative process of piecemeal legislative enactments. In 1828 the Test and Corporation Acts were repealed, and Protestant dissenters, previously allowed to sit in the House of Commons and to hold local and national office under the Crown only by the passage of annual indemnity measures, were now admitted to these benefits in their own right. In 1829 came Catholic Emancipation: the Parliamentary oath was amended so that those elected could take their seats without having to swear to the idolatrous nature of Catholicism. In 1858, Jews were admitted to Parliament.

Following the celebrated Bradlaugh case, freethinkers were able to take their place in the House without the commission of hypocrisy or perjury, under the Affirmation Act of 1888 and the Religious Disabilities Removals Act of 1891. These acts together struck a very severe blow at the establishment principle as then being practiced, for the legislature, which exercised an erastian control over the Church of England, was now, constitutionally, no longer composed solely of churchmen—nor even of Christians. After 1824 the Parliamentary grants for established church building ceased. Practical concurrent endowment of other churches also ended—the English *Regium donum* (to Presbyterians) stopped in 1852, and in the 1869 Act the Irish *Regium donum* and the Maynooth grant (to Catholics) were discontinued. Gladstone quite early came to see the implications for the establishment principle in such reforms. In 1838 he wrote: 'There may be a state of things in the United States of America, perhaps in some British colonies there does actually exist a state of things, in which religious communions are so equally divided, or so variously subdivided, that the Government is itself similarly chequered in its religious complexion, and thus internally incapacitated by disunion from acting in matters of religion.'[1]

The most dissident of the English dissenters were out to bring the logic of this diagnosis to fulfilment. The establishment's monopoly of higher education was shaken with the foundation of the secular London University in 1836, and its monopoly over marriage ceremonies was broken after the Marriage Act of the same year. A series of Burial Acts after 1852 recognized the right of dissenters to their own forms of service. Religious tests were abolished in the universities of Scotland in 1853, and at Oxford and Cambridge in 1871. In 1855 a 'Liberty of Worship Act'[2] finally surrendered the state's right—albeit by then an empty one—to prosecute dissenters for meeting in unrecognized places of worship. In 1857 the jurisdiction of the Ecclesiastical Courts in divorce and matri-

[1] W. E. Gladstone, *The State in its Relations with the Church* (London, 1838), p. 73.
[2] 18 & 19 Vict. c. 86.

monial cases was abolished. In 1860 the endowed grammar schools were opened to dissenters. In 1866 an oath restricting many offices of state to Protestants was withdrawn. In 1868 compulsory church rates, a hugely unpopular taxation in support of the state churches, were ended. In 1870 a system of non-sectarian state primary schools was created, and the establishment's practical monopoly of education was destroyed. In 1936 commuted tithes were finally extinguished. This is an impressive list of modifications to the establishment principle won by dissenting pressure, and it is only the barest outline.

What these reforms amounted to, in fact, was the withering away of the ecclesiastical parts of the constitution. The achievement was not easily accomplished, nor was it complete: men were aware of the process at work, and each measure was strongly contested by the ultra guardians of establishment. Most of those in Parliament who passed these acts were also supporters of the establishment principle; they made timely concessions to remove threats to the whole system, and on each occasion they refused to contemplate the discussion of the principles concerned as a whole, taking their justification, as they declared, from the grounds of expediency. Once begun, however, this movement did not prove so amenable to control as the legislators had imagined. So many small fragments of the fabric were given away to preserve the main structure, in fact, that eventually there was not too much left. The fears of the ultras turned out to have been truly based. Certainly the Churches of England and Scotland survived as established institutions, and still in occupancy of the national religious endowments in the shape of cathedrals and church property. The Sovereign is still obliged to be a member of both Churches, and head of one of them. The bishops still sit in the House of Lords as spiritual peers, and are still appointed by the Crown. But there the reality of the establishment ends. The British state may still have a conscience in constitutional theory—though even that is riddled with inconsistencies—but in practice it acts as a neutral arbiter between the competing elements of a religious pluralism. Service and institutional chaplains are appointed from all faiths, as they are in North America. Religious education in the state schools is non-sectarian. Religious broadcasting in the public corporation is shared among the Christian denominations. The final toppling of the established churches was never actually accomplished, but that should not obscure the truth that the state has long since dispatched strict national confessionalism with its own legislative hand. The establishments are now constitutional anomalies. It is difficult, therefore, to subscribe to Sperry's belief that 'the most important difference between the religious life of England and that of America is the continued existence in England of the Established Church, and the total absence in America of anything like an establishment'. A more accurate assessment was made a hundred years previously, by Alexander Mackay, a British barrister who had travelled extensively in the United States. Believing that the connexion of church and state was destined to disappear in Britain, he wrote: 'The connexion in England now depends for its continuance upon the conservative feeling which instinctively rallies round an existing institution, no matter how unnecessary soever it may be, or how ill-adapted to the circumstances of the time.'[1]

Nor is the modern Church of England able to exert, on its own, any really successful political pressures, despite its formally established position and its representation in the House of Lords. As each year passes its influence in this sense diminishes still more, although interdenominational groups, such as the Sabbatarians, or the anti-abortion law reform lobbies, may on occasions provide formidable musterings of opinion. And those sorts of pressures are anyway paralleled by religious groups in the United States and Canada. In the former, issues like artificial birth control, prohibition, civil rights for Negroes, and religious observances in the public schools, are all argued on the political scene by church-related bodies. The larger denominations are represented by

[1] *The Western World, or Travels in the United States in 1846–7: Exhibiting them in their latest development, social, political and industrial* (Philadelphia, 1849), II, 244.

14

agencies in Washington, which have placed the task of influencing legislation on a permanent basis.[1] The most active of these, though it is by no means the most representative, is POAU (Protestants and Other Americans United for the Separation of Church and State). The American Catholic Church, however, maintains the most systematic political interest, which in the present century has usually expressed itself through the National Catholic Welfare Conference. In Canada, too, the churches concern themselves with political issues like education, liquor licensing, Sunday observance, and welfare, and in these they exercise periodic pressures on the provincial and national Parliaments. Quebec is especially noted for the success of Catholic representations. And the western provinces have, in the present century, furnished an example of the growth of a national political party out of a religious movement. Social Credit arose during the economic depression of the early 'thirties through the evangelical theology of William Aberhart's religious broadcasts.

This, then, in outline, was the legacy of religious pluralism common to Britain, the United States, and Canada. Everywhere state churches had been set up with penal laws to protect them against dissent. Everywhere the multiplication of dissenting churches had produced a religious diversity which laboured to tear down the penal laws. These bodies rendered the established churches anomalous by outgrowing them in numbers. Yet it was not this pluralism *per se* which threatened the state churches, but the alliance of dissent with radical constitutionalism. Fundamental and common law concepts of liberty were as applicable in the religious sphere as in that of political rights, and the dissenters were everywhere able to set their demands into a context of general political radicalism. Because the most obvious and most abused link between church and state was endowment, the main attacks were centred on the exclusive application of national religious property and on instances of public taxation for the benefit of the official churches.

[1] Leo Pfeffer, *Church, State, and Freedom* (Boston, 1953), p. 202.

15

The neutrality of the state

The militant representatives of religious diversity were rather more successful in North America, and at an earlier date, than they were in the British Isles. But the second force making for a redefinition of the relations of church and state was considerably more advanced in Britain. It was the growth of state collectivism. In Britain the church had come to assume a number of social and administrative functions which were comprehensive enough in an uncomplicated society which had a governmental system limited in its scope and therefore circumscribed in its competence. Yet the new elements which issued from the eighteenth-century industrial and rural changes were, by the end of that century, producing new types of social problems which, during the nineteenth century, were recognized as such by defined reforming groups and were ultimately brought within the legislative sphere. Known experts and 'scientific administrators', evangelical philanthropists, Benthamists, and some brands of radicals, in revealing and giving publicity to intolerable social evils came eventually, and often reluctantly, to call upon the agency of the state to interfere in private contractual relationships and secure reforms. By a piece-meal process of *ad hoc* government action there was being created, by the mid-century, a chaos of boards, permanent commissions, and inspectorates, to ensure the enforcement of regulations and administrative provisions framed by legislative enactments in efforts to improve the conditions of factories, mines, and shipping, in the health of towns, to prevent the adulteration of food, and to deter poverty. In the age of *laissez-faire*, the machinery of state collectivism was accumulating behind the scenes. For these reforms were achieved without a coherent theory of government action. The state was called upon to upset vested interests and to interfere in contractual relationships because it was the only agency with the power and neutrality to do so. Social welfare, in the broadest sense, was becoming the concern of government.

During all this legislative activity, however, the rôle of the Church in society remained virtually unchanged. Imprisoned within the old parochial boundaries, governed from cathedral cities which the industrial revolution had largely by-passed, and intransigent upon the benches of the House of Lords, the state church was left with its old view of its place in the social order. As the state was breaking through to new solutions to the new social questions, the spheres of activity which were once left to the competence of the Church—and this meant most forms of welfare and large areas of local government—passed directly into the hands of governmental agencies. But it is important to notice that the apparent *diminution* of the Church's sphere of social action was largely illusory: it was not *its* activity which had diminished, but the competence of the state which had vastly increased. The rôle of the Church remained more or less what it had always been. It had failed to produce a significant and corporate response to the social problems of the new age, and it remained basically irrelevant to them. It is true that the part of individual Christians in preparing the state for particular reforms—like the factory legislation—was very considerable. And the scramble for 'Church Extension', headed by Bishop Blomfield of London, led to increased concern about the evangelization of the poor. But this did not suggest any conceptual alteration in the Church's view of its social function—it was merely an attempt to secure the wider diffusion of the old one. Compared with the immensity of the task of tackling the conditions of the towns and factories, the efforts of the Church were relatively slight.

The impact of the enlarging area of state activity on the sort of functions traditionally fulfilled by the Church was immense. Contemporaries, largely unaware of the cumulative effects of individual pieces of governmental action, believed that it was the discord between Church and dissent which allowed the greater agency of the state in welfare—and especially in education. Quarrels between Church and Chapel did certainly provide some occasions of state intervention, since only the state enjoyed the neutrality which could overrule both. This was especially true after the political reforms had opened the legislature to Protestant Nonconformists, Catholics, Jews, and finally freethinkers. And the jealousies of Church and Chapel provided a connexion between the rise of religious pluralism and the growth of state collectivism. For the sort of reforms which dissenting pressures secured in the interests of religious equality had the effect of replacing the offices of the Church with the agency of the state. Thus the Marriage and Registration Acts of 1836 required the creation of government administrative machinery to provide an alternative to the jurisdiction of the Church. It was, of course, in the field of education that the dissenters' grievances prompted a huge increase of state welfare: the network of state schools set up after the Education Act of 1870. But the basic reason for the redefinition of the Church's social function did not lie in the disputes with dissent, but in the sheer immensity of the task of 'social improvement'—an immensity which became apparent to nineteenth-century reformers only after they had set their hands to the plough. In the previous century, men had still argued that the solution to crime and social disruption lay in the wider diffusion of Christian precepts. In the nineteenth century, on the other hand, other men set up police forces to achieve the same end. The difference relates a great transformation. For the Church had not 'lost contact' with modern society and its peculiar problems and needs, as is so often said. Contact had never been established in the first place. The Church had simply missed out in a crucial phase of the growth of the modern state.

If the rise of state social competence 'disestablished' the English Church from many of its traditional social and administrative functions, in the United States associated problems occurred rather later. A comparable scale of industrial change did not appear until later in the nineteenth century, and by then the influence and orthodoxy acquired by the exponents of free contract, strict *laissez-faire*, and even 'social Darwinianism', exercised a partially successful break on the evolution of state collectivist machinery. In quite a real sense, and in contrast with Britain, the fields of social welfare continued to be the preserves of the churches. Public education developed to an advanced point, it is true, and there were government welfare institutions; but the rôle of the churches in providing hospitals, refuges for the poor, and a multitude of charitable organizations, did not really begin to be superseded by the state until the present century.[1] It is no coincidence that a new phase of church and state problems opened in America during the present century, when social welfare became an important part of both federal and state activity. The long period in the nineteenth century when the problem of church and state relationships seemed to have been settled by constitutional separations was thus in a sense due to the absence of government concern in the crucial areas where they meet. At the present time, most private religious welfare agencies in America are Catholic or Jewish. They continue to enjoy the same sort of state support which charitable organizations receive in Canada and Britain, on the argument for retrenchment that they provide social services which the state would otherwise have to duplicate for the sections of society concerned. It is this argument which is presently being questioned by supporters of the strict separation of church and state.[2]

It is now possible to venture a summary of general propositions. In Britain, Canada, and the United States, the rise of militant religious pluralism and the creation of state welfare machinery, have alike prompted a radical redefinition of the relationship between religious belief and public life. State confessionalism has been eclipsed in all three countries: the same causes issuing in very similar effects, despite the growth of constitutional variations and differences of political experience. Starting from a common British constitutionalism, all three have retained common law, and with it a shared inheritance of precepts of political justice which, very broadly, formed the ideological basis for the transition from state confessionalism to something approaching state neutrality. So far from being essentially dissimilar, the United States in fact anticipated, due to her favourable political and social circum-

---

[1] For a brief discussion of this question, see Philip Wogaman, 'The Changing Role of Government and the Myth of Separation', in *A Journal of Church and State*, v, no. 1 (1963), 61 ff.

[2] *Ibid.* p. 71.

stances, a series of measures concerned with the relationship of church and state which were in the pipe-line for Canada and Britain too. Some are in the pipe-line still.

The establishment principle can be said to operate where there is a connexion between the law and religious belief. The state 'confesses' religious belief and provides for its propagation. Where this connexion is sufficiently articulated, the religious beliefs of an entire church may become incorporated and protected at law: then it is possible to speak of a church establishment. Such an intimacy of relationship has generally been sealed by the state endowment of the church concerned, and in a fully confessional state this is done to the complete exclusion of all other churches, though it has been customary in civilized modern countries to extend full toleration to those left outside. Where, however, a number of churches are in a position to claim that no *one* of their number has either the doctrinal justification or the numerical following to constitute a sole establishment, it is possible for the state to protect and endow them all, equally or unequally. This can even be accomplished whilst the state retains a single established church—though at the risk of making it appear anomalous. But there are difficulties about 'concurrent endowment', as this stage is called: it weakens the state's own confessional potential by the acceptance of multiple religious opinion, and in practice general endowment has been only a temporary arrangement prior to the eventual separation of church and state. In modern Switzerland alone does it appear to have worked tolerably. The exponents of radical separation have been the 'voluntaryists'; men who adhered to the belief that all connexion between the state and religious belief is corrupting and compromising to both alike, and whose name, originally a sobriquet, was suggested by their principle that all religious bodies should maintain themselves by the voluntary financial offerings of their own voluntary membership. The voluntaryists have not been too consistent, however, for in supporting, for example, Sunday observance and anti-blasphemy legislation, and in agitation for state patronage of temperance reform, they

The neutrality of the state

have been subscribing to the establishment principle in its simplest expression. They have called upon the arm of the state to protect morality and religious belief. In extreme voluntaryism, on the other hand, the state logically becomes wholly *secular*. All connexion between the law and religious belief ceases, and the state propagates a secular moralism of its own divining. But there is a stage some way short of that; a stage which fully recognizes the claims of believers to believe, and of sceptics not to have to believe: this stage is the *neutral* state. No preference is given to one set of beliefs over another, but the state has abdicated moral responsibility, and, whilst having no connexion with religion, it has none with irreligion either. It is held to be incompetent in such questions; it has lost its conscience. It is therefore neutral between all ideological positions. Now it is certainly impossible for any state to enjoy a complete moral neutrality, for all law implies prior ethical evaluation. But it is towards the adoption of a practical neutrality in practical questions, insofar as it is possible, that North American and British modifications in the relationship of church and state, during the last two hundred years, have tended. It has been much more nearly realized, perhaps, in the United States. It is certainly more conscious there. In the Supreme Court's ruling on the Everson case of 1947, Justice Black interpreted the federal constitution as requiring all American government to be 'neutral in its relations with groups of believers and non-believers; it does not require the state to be their adversary'.[1]

It is important to emphasize that although the United States, Canada, and Britain were redefining the relationships of church and state along comparable lines, the movement was in fact largely a parallel one. Developments, especially between Britain and the United States, were almost entirely independent of one another. They shared the same background and started with the same ingredients: their subsequent similarity was not

[1] *The Supreme Court on Church and State*, edited by Joseph Tussman (New York, 1962), p. 212. For a discussion of the doctrine of state neutrality in America, see Wilbur G. Katz, *Religion and American Constitutions* (Evanston, 1964).

21

the result of mutual emulations. It indicated instead a working out of inherent tendencies along quite different chronological scales.

Actual British knowledge of the American religious scene was, to say the least, thin. In 1899 Bryce wrote that 'little is known in Great Britain of the ecclesiastical and religious history of the United States',[1] and the last half-century has seen little change. During the revolutionary period, the American churches expressed ecclesiastical autonomy by formulating their own church constitutions. With some exception in the case of the Catholic and Episcopal Churches, they remained substantially independent of external influences. Attempts at establishing links between British and American churches were noted failures. Bishop Selwyn's proposal for an organic union between the Episcopal churches of England and America, made at the time of the Lambeth Conference in 1878, found no support from either side of the Atlantic. Robert Baird, an American Presbyterian minister who earned a deserved reputation for his surveys of contemporary religious history in the mid-nineteenth century, was quite emphatic about the impossibility of transatlantic links. 'It cannot be disguised', he wrote of such an unsuccessful venture, 'that the very attempt which we have made to bring the churches of America and Europe, and especially of Britain, into more friendly and fraternal relations, has ended in putting them further asunder.'[2] In 1831, with the founding of the Congregational Union in Britain, a deputation was appointed to visit the United States and establish a formal relationship with their co-religionists there. The despondency of their report can speak also for the experience of many. 'Churches that are in all essential points one', they remarked of British and American religious bodies, 'have nevertheless been so absorbed in their own estate, and so little animated by the spirit of their Founder, as to remain not only without fellowship, but

---

[1] In his preface to L. W. Bacon, *A History of American Christianity* (London, 1899).
[2] Robert Baird, *The Progress and Prospects of Christianity in the United States of America* (London, 1851), p. 46.

almost without the privity of each other's existence.'[1] An American branch of the British Evangelical Alliance, formed in 1847, wilted within a few years, and was never really extended beyond New York City anyway.[2] This was a very clear indication of the religious disengagement of the two countries. Early in the century, British evangelicalism had sustained a great influence in the United States, inspiring benevolent and bible societies on the current British pattern.[3] Lyman Beecher and others copied the idea of the voluntary society from British evangelicals and employed it in America as a vehicle for social and missionary work during the 1820s and early in the 1830s.[4] This type of united evangelical endeavour broke up in the United States later in the 1830s, displaced by narrowly sectarian undertakings. This, too, lessened religious contact across the Atlantic. The question of slavery also did much to keep mutual regard at a minimum: British evangelicals, fresh from their own successful campaign, could not understand why many American Christians refrained from making the existence of their governments intolerable until slavery should be abolished. Americans, for their part, were suspicious of those English Nonconformists, like the Methodists, who still retained, at least until the mid-century, respect for the union of church and state.[5] There was, it is true, a flow-back from America to Britain of early Primitive Methodism, and post-bellum revivalism stimulated popular British evangelicalism. But the only real exception to the religious disengagement was the mid-nineteenth century Mormon mission in Britain, as a result of which there were some 55,000 converts who left to settle in the United States. That, at any rate, was a tangible enough link with one aspect of American religion.[6]

---

[1] Andrew Reed and James Matheson, *A Narrative of the Visit to the American Churches by the Deputation from the Congregational Union of England and Wales* (London, 1835), II, 290.   [2] Baird, *op. cit.* p. 41.
[3] C. I. Foster, *An Errand of Mercy. The Evangelical United Front, 1790–1837* (University of North Carolina Press, 1960), pp. 63, 107.
[4] Winthrop S. Hudson, *The Great Tradition of the American Churches* (New York 1963 edition), p. 72.   [5] *Ibid.* p. 45.
[6] See P. A. M. Taylor, *Expectations Westward. The Mormons and the Emigration of their British Converts in the Nineteenth Century* (Edinburgh, 1965).

The neutrality of the state

British observers in the nineteenth century frequently commented on the American experience of voluntaryism, and at first sight this might be mistaken for a close knowledge of the actual facts of religion in the United States. Dissenting journals constantly referred to the benefits flowing from the separation of church and state there. Observers generally were favourable or unfavourable to American voluntaryism according to the position each adopted towards the continuation of established religion at home. The supporters of the voluntary principle usually held the field. 'To us it seems very clear that religion has assumed an attitude and made a progress in the United States, which, under a system of ecclesiastical establishments, would have been not only improbable but impossible; and that the churches which were once established, have their share in the general prosperity, and owe their existence, as vital bodies, to the very fact of their disestablishment.'[1] Thus wrote John Howard Hinton, in *The Test of Experience; or The Voluntary Principle in the United States*, published in 1851. 'America has in this respect set an example which other nations ought to ponder and to follow', he added.[2] Mackay was typical in pointing to the United States as the only country where the voluntary system was sufficienty implanted to reveal its true character. 'There are many, judging of it from the phase which it assumes in this country [England], who object to it, on the ground of its apparent tendency to run into fanaticism and to carry that fanaticism into politics', he wrote with some accuracy: 'In a country divided between the voluntary principle and that of an established church, the tendency to over-zeal and fanaticism is much increased by the conflict which is waged between the two principles.'[3] But it is important to notice that when British reference was made to voluntaryism in America, it was inevitably to prove the validity of opinions already formulated in response to domestic conditions. This fact underlay otherwise deceptive observations. When in 1844, for

[1] *The Test of Experience* (London, 1851), p. 90.
[2] *Ibid.* p. 124.
[3] Alexander Mackay, *The Western World, or Travels in the United States in 1846–7* (Philadelphia, 1849), II, 247.

example, *The Christian Witness*—a Congregational magazine—asked its readers, 'Can the British Churches have a better model than America presents?',[1] resort was *not* being made to American experience to learn something new; it was to confirm domestic prejudice.

There was, between Britain and the United States, a reasonably wide exchange of religious literature during the nineteenth century, although it was mostly devotional or anti-Catholic in content.[2] 'Some American reprints of English religious books, particularly of works of a practical character', as Baird noticed, 'have had an immense circulation.'[3] American works were also printed in England, but on a much less ambitious scale.[4] Ideas also crossed the Atlantic but they were theologically entertaining ones, rather than questions concerning the relations of church and state. The impact of the Oxford movement and its subsequent legacy of ritualism was surprisingly marked in the United States. The American Episcopalians, indeed, anticipated Oxford theology in some respects, under the leadership of Bishop Hobart, and when the *Tracts for the Times* arrived in the country they fell upon an existing high church controversy.[5] Eventually those ideas were to achieve an orthodoxy in the American Episcopalian Church. In British North America too, and especially in Upper Canada, the Oxford movement reproduced a pattern of controversy. There its leading exponent was Bishop Strachan. 'Nothing is more evident in Canada as in England', remarked the *Christian Guardian*, a Methodist paper, in 1842, 'that there is a struggle between Protestantism and Puseyism, which is Popery in its minority, daily adding to its age and strength.'[6]

[1] London, 1844, I, 21.
[2] Clarence Gohdes, *American Literature in Nineteenth Century England* (Carbondale, Illinois, 1944), p. 45. For comment on the exchange of anti-Catholic propaganda, see below, chapter 3, section 2.
[3] Robert Baird, *Religion in America* (New York, revised edition, 1856), p. 342.
[4] *Ibid.* p. 344, *note.*
[5] See W. W. Sweet, *The Story of Religion in America* (New York, enlarged edition, 1939), p. 384; L. W. Bacon, *A History of American Christianity* (London, 1899), p. 307; and R. Baird, *op. cit.* p. 445.
[6] Quoted in S. D. Clark, *Church and Sect in Canada* (Toronto, 1948), p. 123. See also, W. E. Elgee, *The Social Teachings of the Canadian Churches, Protestant*

The neutrality of the state

Relations between Britain and the British North American provinces were, for obvious reasons of political association and constitutional unity, very much closer on religious questions than those with the United States. Many of the churches were at first administratively linked with their British parent bodies, to whom they looked, even after the achievement of their autonomy, for financial assistance and a supply of ministers and school-teachers. The Parliamentary debates at Westminster on burning topics like the clergy reserves, meant that during the first half of the nineteenth century at least, Canadian religious questions were well-known to informed public opinion in Britain. The publication of the Durham Report in 1839 also gave wide currency to Canadian religious problems. Since the surrender of the clergy reserves to 'spoliation' was regarded as a precedent for radical and dissenting assault upon the home religious endowments, that particular issue, the most important in the Canadian relations of church and state, received a wide and notorious canvass in Britain. There were also personal links between the Upper Canadian radicals, with their dissenting allies, and English radicalism—especially during the 1830s and 1840s when the Canadians enjoyed a Parliamentary mouthpiece in Joseph Hume and his radical circle. The great religious disputes of nineteenth-century Britain were all faithfully reproduced in Canada.

Between the churches of the British North American provinces and the United States, on the other hand, relations were surprisingly unimportant. Revivalism easily crossed the border, and there were frequent exchanges of clergy; but Canadian cultivation of its own identity, and a dislike of the republican institutions of the south, especially after the War of 1812, gave such contacts as existed with the United States a low degree of influence during the nineteenth century. Churches with origins in the south, like the Episcopal Methodist, tended to move towards an early independence from southern control. The separation of church and

(Toronto, 1964), pp. 198–9; and J. S. Moir, *Church and State in Canada West* (Toronto, 1959), p. 4.

26

state in the British provinces was not a device copied from their southern neighbours: it resulted from successful and piecemeal agitations for religious equality undertaken by colonial radicals and dissenters who stood wholly in the British tradition.

The developments and redefinitions in the relationship of church and state were, then, largely upon parallel lines—but this fact has been distorted by local variations in the conditions of the three nations. These were slight in most things, and on the whole produced differences of chronology rather than of content. Yet local variations have been strongly emphasized by those who uphold the view that American experience, in this field, has been unique. It is certainly true that Britain and Canada had nothing to compare with the drastic ecclesiastical disorganization wrought by the slavery issue in the United States. In the mid-century, the American Methodist, Baptist and Presbyterian churches divided on geographical lines into southern and northern, pro- and anti-slavery schisms. But many features popularly supposed to have imparted determining peculiarities to American experience in fact had their counterparts in Britain and Canada. There have been impressive studies of the influence of frontier conditions on the revivalism and sectarianism of American Christianity, both from the standpoints of history[1] and of the sociology of religion.[2] Several points can be made here. Revivalism was not a peculiarity of the frontier, although it soon became chronic there. Nor was it especially an American phenomenon, though in his last book Professor Perry Miller described how it came to be considered 'a uniquely American ritual' in early nineteenth-century American commentary.[3] The Newlight Revival, at the end of the eighteenth century, rapidly infected the Maritime Provinces, and revivalism remained a feature of religious experience in Canada. In Britain the excitements of the open-air meeting and the camp-fire became familiar in the second half of the eighteenth century. 'Such visitations are

[1] P. G. Mode, *The Frontier Spirit in American Christianity* (New York, 1923).
[2] H. Richard Niebuhr, *The Social Sources of Denominationalism* (New York, 1929).
[3] *The Life of the Mind in America*, 'The Intellect of Revival' (London, 1966), p. 13.

not rare amongst ourselves', wrote Mackay in 1849; 'but it is seldom that they attain anything like the appalling influence which they sometimes gain in America.'[1] Ten years later, in 1859, the excesses of the great Ulster Revival were to nullify his qualification. Missionary extension overseas, especially in the colonies, had also allowed British Christians of all denominations to experience 'frontier' challenge for themselves. The keen interest in these ventures, and the voluminous missionary literature, familiarized the problems encountered when planting religious organization in the wilderness. Indeed, it would probably be no exaggeration to say that the British public knew as much of 'frontier' religious conditions as did the east-coast Americans. Quite a lot, that is to say; but at second-hand.

Sectarianism is another well-publicised feature of American religious experience which has manifestations elsewhere, though perhaps on a lesser scale. For sectarianism, as Philip Schaff remarked, 'is not really an infirmity of America only, but of all Protestantism'.[2] Many of the more esoteric of the sects which flowered in the United States had their origins in Britain—like the Shakers—or in other European countries. The great American denominations are nearly all of British origin: the Baptists, Methodist, Presbyterians, Episcopalians, Congregationalists and Quakers. Even the Catholics were assimilated to a distinctively British-Irish version. Lutheranism was, of course, European; and there have been indigenous North American denominations like the Disciples of Christ and Christian Science. American inventiveness has only revealed itself in one distinctly new religion, however: the Church of the Latter Day Saints. But in small sects it has excelled. Some have been exclusively Negro, like the 'Church of God and Saints of Christ', founded in 1896 at Lawrence, Kansas, by a cook on the Santa Fé Railroad. All have in some degree partaken of the quality of 'churches of the disinherited'. Yet it

[1] Alexander Mackay, *op. cit.* II, 254.
[2] *America, A Sketch of the Political, Social and Religious Character of the United States of America* (New York, 1855), p. xiv.

should be noticed that sectarianism has never been typical of American religion as a whole: denominationalism has been the normal pattern. Furthermore, the conditions which produced the flowering of the sects among the poor and along the frontier were not wholly absent in Britain. Population shifts attendant upon early industrialization, or depopulation in parts of Ireland, Wales and Scotland, produced conditions ripe enough for the disinherited to coalesce around sectarian expressions of worship and organization. These conditions were not too dissimilar from the religious desolations of the American or Canadian frontiers. There were plenty of men in nineteenth-century Britain who found themselves outside the traditional ministrations of the churches. Some were swept up by revivalistic fervour and swelled the growth of nonconformity; but many others remained outside, and eventually found an outlet for their incipient hopes of a better world in working-class politics. When it came to experience of 'the second frontier'—the industrial cities—Britain had an advance on the United States and Canada.

The American schisms over slavery, the fragmentations into small sects, and the waves of immigrants who introduced eastern European Orthodox Christianity and Judaism, did not in themselves produce any elements which were radically to interfere with the parallel developments in the British and North American redefinitions of church and state relations. In fact, they merely added to an existing religious diversity which, by the mid-nineteenth century, had been institutionalized as the chief characteristic of the religious life of all three countries. American religious pluralism was simply reinforced by foreign infusions. The newcomers were rapidly assimilated, and were soon staking their own claims to a place in the religious equality. Nor did the European and Asiatic origins of many of the later nineteenth-century immigrants disturb the broad cultural unity of Britain and North America. 'Whatever is found with us, has its counterpart there', the English Congregational deputation had noticed in 1835, after their visit to America; 'In habit, in literature, in language and religion, we are one.'[1] Some twenty years later, Baird remarked that both were 'Protestant countries, and their population is essentially and naturally of the same origin; for both are Anglo-Saxon, and partake in the main of the same characteristics'.[2] The first, part of this observation, which was broadly accurate, has been rendered obsolete by later immigrations, but the second has remained true. Will Herberg has stated the reality clearly. 'Our cultural assimilation has taken place not in a 'melting pot', but rather in a 'transmuting pot' in which all the ingredients have been transformed and assimilated to an idealized 'Anglo-Saxon' model.' He added: 'Despite widespread dislike of various aspects of British life, our relation, cultural and spiritual, to our British heritage is vastly different and more intimate than is our relation to the cultural heritages of the later immigrant groups, who with their descendants compose a majority of the American people today.'[3]

In the question of church and state relations this essential unity of experience finds an expression, despite the constitutional dissimilarities of Britain and the United States. Bryce, who noticed the same sort of process at work which Herberg later analysed, correctly attributed it to what he called 'that essential affinity between the minds and characters of two peoples which causes the development of their intellectual and religious life to move upon parallel lines'.[4] Precisely how the separations of church and state actually occurred in the United States and Canada ought now to be described in outline. Sequences of events which, when treated independently, seem to afford few common features, will clearly show, when narrated side by side, that their leading dissimilarities are not social or political, or even constitutional, but merely chronological.

---

[1] Andrew Reed and James Matheson, *A Narrative of a Visit to the American Churches* (London, 1835), II, 287.
[2] Robert Baird, *The Progress and Prospects of Christianity in the United States* (London, 1851), p. 65.
[3] Will Herberg, *Protestant-Catholic-Jew, An Essay in American Religious Sociology* (revised edition, New York, 1960), p. 21.
[4] In his preface to L. W. Bacon, *A History of American Christianity* (London, 1899), p. vi.

2

THE SEPARATION OF CHURCH
AND STATE

From the middle years of the eighteenth century, British dissenters, both at home and in the thirteen American colonies, gradually organized themselves, if at first rather haltingly, for attempts to remove the legal disqualifications from which they still suffered. Far as yet from the radical militancy of their successors, they sought only their full rights, as they understood them, under the Constitution. From these years they were moved by a new sense of injustice born, it is true, of no deterioration in their position at law, but from awareness of the strength resident in numbers. These men relied upon an interpretation of civil liberties which echoed to them from the constitutional conflict of the seventeenth century and from the ideas of toleration which had then received a somewhat frustrated airing. In the American colonies this tradition of historical interpretation was even stronger, and it is not surprising that it was eventually there, and not in Britain itself, that dissenters first struck down the badge of their inferiority: the established churches. The rebellion against the Crown and the need to formulate new instruments of government provided them with an occasion which was too providential to miss.

Now in view of all that has been written about the unique achievement of disestablishment in America, two points should be made about the outcome. First, the federal separation of church and state in 1787–91 was not intended to encourage the disestablishment of churches in the various states of the new Union—and it did not do so. Where disestablishments occurred, they were in response to agitations already set in motion. Secondly, although some states seized the chance provided by the political upheaval to sever the connexion of church and state, not all did so. The

The separation of church and state

Congregational establishments of New England lasted well into the nineteenth century, and that of Massachussetts was not wound up until 1833. Thus in America the movement of the dissenters for disestablishment and religious equality, beginning coherently around 1760, took some 70 years to complete. This length of time is frequently overlooked. It is thrown into perspective by a rough calculation of the time expended on similar achievements elsewhere. In Ireland the Catholics' campaign against the state church really only become serious politics after 1820, when the first brave spirits began to scrutinize the realism of their Church's insistence on the union of church and state—even if the church was a Protestant one. Disestablishment did not come to Ireland until 1869: that is, fifty years later. In Upper Canada the time was even shorter; from 1817, when the question of the clergy reserves first came before the provincial legislature, to 1853 when they were finally secularized—only thirty years. Considered from this angle the achievement of the American states seems rather less unique and a trifle less dramatic.

I. SEPARATION IN THE UNITED STATES

When the Declaration of Independence was signed, the Church of England was the established religion in all the middle and southern colonies except Pennsylvania and Delaware, where there were no official connexions with single churches but where general Christian beliefs were protected at law. The Congregational Church was established in the New England colonies, Rhode Island alone excepted: there the tradition of complete religious freedom had deposited a legacy, not of complete freedom, but at least of impartiality between Christian denominations. The privileged position of the state churches had not remained monolithically isolated from reform. By 1776 the swelling religious pluralism had already arrayed formidable opponents before the establishment principle in America. Everywhere ameliorative legislation was removing the most galling of the exclusive rights of the state churchmen.

32

Dissent was already nibbling away at public confessionalism; yet there must be some qualification when generalizing about 'dissent'. Conditions and attitudes displayed considerable variation. In New England it was, of course, the Episcopalians who were the dissenters. They did not agitate for disestablishment: it was against their best interests to do so, for it would simply have filled in the case of those in the south who dissented from their own establishments. They were content to seek some relief by attacking the compulsory payment of church rates to the Congregational churches,[1] but in this their real attack upon the establishment principle was greater than they supposed. Taxation for exclusive religious purposes is one of the primary bulwarks of establishment, and its removal is a severe theoretical modification of the relations of church and state—as the English Nonconformists' movement for the abolition of church rates, finally successful in 1868, was to demonstrate. But in general the American Episcopalians in the New England colonies were not to be classified as typical of dissent. Nor were the small numbers of Roman Catholics: they took no active part in the campaigns for disestablishment, although they were grateful beneficiaries of the greater freedom of religion which ensued. The Methodists were on the whole still, as in England, at one with the Church of England in maintaining the establishment principle. It was in fact largely the Baptists and the Presbyterians, rapidly multiplying in the western frontier districts of the colonies, who led and characterized the dissenting agitations. The Baptists especially—lacking a history or tradition of establishment, and democratic in organization—were typically the spearhead. They fought official religion impartially; in the Congregational and Episcopal colonies alike. Variations in colonial conditions made it all the more remarkable that dissenting pressure came to exhibit common features everywhere. Like the growth of colonial radicalism, to which it was related, extensive communication between the churches of the different colonies, and shared journalism, increasingly worked to

[1] S. H. Cobb, *The Rise of Religious Liberty in America* (New York, 1902), pp. 464–6.

create an inter-colonial body of opinion on the particular issues in question.

The thirteen American colonies formed an almost ideal setting for the scene of the earliest successful campaign against the confessional doctrine of the state. The colonists' general grievances against the Imperial Parliament were essentially, as McIlwain suggested,[1] inspired by strongly contended precepts about the nature of British constitutional and common law liberties. It was very decidedly as claimants to constitutional rights that the colonists first sought a redefinition of their relationship to British executive authority, and only later, this proving unsatisfactory, actual independence. The concepts of fundamental law and full religious liberty were crucially important in the structure of their arguments, Here the dissenters generally found themselves as radical in politics as in religion. First they tried to strike down the remnants of the penal legislation which protected the established churches. Next, finding the political scene increasingly sympathetic and rather plastic, they pressed home the attack by demanding the absolute removal of the official status of the established churches.

It was the coincidence of political *and* religious polarization between churchmen and dissenters, especially in the colonies where there were Episcopal establishments, which eventually gave reality to the dissenters' aspirations. Shortly before the start of the revolutionary war the Governor of North Carolina noticed that in the disputes of church and dissent in his colony 'there is no less apparent schism between their Politics than in matters appertaining to religion'.[2] The New England Congregationalist ministers, who supported the rebel cause when it came to arms, were also contributors to the general fund of political ideas. They used the custom of election sermons as the vehicle of radical political theory, carefully preserved from the English struggle of the seventeenth century. 'There is not a right asserted in the Declaration

[1] C. H. McIlwain, *The American Revolution: A Constitutional Interpretation* (New York, 1923).

[2] Quoted in C. H. Van Tyne, *England and America. Rivals in the American Revolution* (Cambridge, 1927), p. 60.

of Independence', it has been said, 'which had not been discussed by the New England clergy before 1763.'[1] In England too, at the end of the eighteenth century, dissenters traced their claims for religious equality to the previous century's upheaval; a few, like Priestley, reaching very advanced positions. Indeed, during their struggle the American rebels enjoyed the sympathy of many Protestant dissenters in the British Isles.[2]

The Church of England, of course, had the disadvantage of being largely on the unpopular and losing side. There were other causes of its unpopularity, and these were seized upon by dissenting propagandists. There was a widespread assertion that many of its clergy practiced immoralities. It is impossible to evaluate the charge, but certainly it was true that in the absence of an immediate authority to remove corrupt pastors, those who succumbed might remain in their cures for years, a scandal to churchmen and dissenters alike. A very small number of bad clerics could brand the majority quite easily.[3] By the time of the rebellion the Church of England, largely innocent of supervision and effective organization, was at a disadvantage. Whereas the other Protestant churches had experienced a new sense of effectiveness, and had created the means of expressing their political and religious demands, the Episcopalians—without even a bishop—simply had to leave it open to individual members to decide what action to take in the revolutionary situation. Some variations resulted. In the southern colonies the Church of England clergy were often divided between loyalist and rebel, whereas in the north, amidst a mass of Congregationalism, they were pretty solidly loyalist. The Methodists tended to a similar distribution, and most stood by the local preferences of the Church of England, from which they were,

[1] A. M. Baldwin, *The New England Clergy and the American Revolution* (Duke University, 1928), p. 170.

[2] Carl Bridenbaugh, *Mitre and Sceptre, Transatlantic Faiths, Ideas, Personalities and Politics, 1689–1775* (New York, 1962), p. 327.

[3] *The Fulham Papers in the Lambeth Palace Library*, American Colonial section, Calendar and Indexes, compiled by W. W. Manross, (Oxford, 1965), pp.xxi-xxii.

indeed, still scarcely separated. There were more Episcopalian rebels in those colonies which had the smallest numbers of dissenters,[1] and in the south a good majority of the Episcopalians were on the rebel side.[2] Van Tyne, who made a statistical survey of some 400 leading rebels, found that eighty per cent of them were dissenters—although it should be noticed that he included New England Congregationalists among the majority.[3] It is also clear that some seventy-five per cent of the loyalists were members of the Church of England.[4] Many of the most sophisticated revolutionary leaders were, if only nominally, members of the Church: Washington, Madison, Henry, Franklin, Morris, Jay, Duane and Hamilton.[5] Churches of non-British origin were divided over the rebellion. The Dutch Reformed Church generally supported the insurgents: it too, like the Congregationalists and the Baptists, had a republican seventeenth-century background. Most of the German Lutheran churches, on the other hand, reflected the passive obedience doctrines so particularly highlighted in the parent body, and sided with the loyalists. The small groups of Roman Catholics, while generally inactive, were frequently sympathetic to the rebel cause. These Catholics were usually of English extraction, and the Irishmen whose participation in the rebellion was a marked feature, were northern Presbyterians of radical stock. Catholic acceptance of the revolution was largely an exercise in enlightened self-interest: it is unlikely, to say the least, that many of them established a link, as has been suggested,[6] between the principles of the revolution and scholastic philosophy.

The Church of England establishments also laboured under

---

[1] W. W. Sweet, *Religion in the Development of American Culture, 1765–1840* (New York, 1952), p. 14.

[2] W. H. Nelson, *The American Tory* (Oxford, 1961), p. 90.

[3] C. H. Van Tyne, *op. cit.* p. 75.

[4] *Ibid.* p. 76: from estimates based on Sabine's lives of the loyalists.

[5] E. F. Humphrey, *Nationalism and Religion in America, 1774–89* (Boston, 1924), p. 47. See also '*In God we Trust*': *The Religious Beliefs and Ideas of the American Founding Fathers*, edited by N. Cousins (New York, 1958).

[6] By Theodore Maynard, in *The Story of American Catholicism* (New York, 1946), p. 117.

political disadvantages during the revolutionary period. The colonists were still conscious of a need to attack the concept of Divine Right: this attack was a part of their ideological inheritance, and had entered deeply into the political texture. Now it was unfortunate for the Church of England that its formularies appeared to uphold just those teachings on the nature on monarchical power which the dissenters had come to regard with diminishing enthusiasm. In England itself, of course, the rise of Parliamentary competence, and the increasing independence of the executive from the Crown, had rendered the Church's teaching archaic: no one really believed in Divine Right. But in the colonies, under dissenting pressure, the Church was easily made to appear the upholder of theories which in reality no one continued to embrace. Churchmen, on the defensive, tried to explain exactly what rights the Crown did have. In the realm of politics this was difficult enough; but in the realm of religion it was intolerable. The question had first been formulated over the problem of a colonial bishopric. Opposition to the various schemes came strongly from the dissenters. Their seventeenth-century terms of reference told them all that was necessary about bishops: they were all like Laud. The creation of an American bishop would have been a clear demonstration of the prerogative rights of the Crown, expressed through the Royal Supremacy. It would also have revealed the power of Parliament over the colonial Church, and this was popularly taken to suggest the propriety of Parliamentary competence over much else—taxation, for example.[1] The fear that a Church of England prelate might be exposed to America was a powerful cause of misunderstanding and bitterness between churchmen and dissenters, and between the colonists and the mother country: an aspect of the causes of the rebellion which is well-known. It must be made clear, on the other hand, that there was plenty of opposition to the bishopric scheme from members of the Church of England themselves. Some sections of the laity entertained the strongest antipathy to the idea of ecclesiastical

---

[1] C. H. Van Tyne, *op. cit.* p. 69.

discipline,[1] and throughout the entire colonial period they were left unvisited by any competent authority—the vague control of the Bishop of London extending (where it extended at all) only over the clergy.

It is interesting, in fact, to notice the large measure of religious freedom which prevailed in the American colonies before their independence. The surviving penal laws against dissenters were rarely, and in some places never, enforced. There was no restriction on religious discussion, and it was this which had allowed so great a consciousness of religious diversity. The point is worth bearing in mind. As those too sunk in ignorance and misery, like the later eighteenth-century victims of industrialization in England, were too unlearned and too brutalized to realize quite how badly off they were, so in some countries the religiously oppressed had no chance even of understanding what religious freedom meant. This was not the case in America. British constitutional liberty, though limited by subsequent standards, had given the colonial dissenters a very adequate experience of religious freedom. Having tasted blood, they knew how to recognize the appitite for more of it. The established churches, in this sense, were swept away because they were too liberal.

It was in Virginia that the classic struggle—Pfeffer called it 'the epoch-making struggle'[2]—for disestablishment occurred, and a brief summary can exhibit features present in most of those other colonies where the connexion of church and state was fractured during the revolutionary period.[3] The events in Virginia were clearly a result of the growth of dissent: the appearance of a strong religious pluralism, especially in the western districts of recent settlement, where the establishment's parochial system proved unequal to the task of retaining control of scattered

[1] *The Fulham Papers in the Lambeth Palace Library* American Colonial Section, ed. W. W. Manross (Oxford, 1965), p. xvii.
[2] *Church and State in the United States*, by A. P. Stokes and L. Pfeffer (revised and abridged, New York, 1964), p. 65.
[3] For the fullest account, see H. J. Eckenrode, *The Separation of Church and State in Virginia* (Richmond, 1910).

pioneer communities. As in the newly growing industrial towns of Britain—a contemporaneous phenomenon—dissent captured many of those who found themselves outside the traditional parish boundaries. Many more lapsed from religious observance altogether. The Church of England in Virginia continued to derive most of the benefits of an establishment, however, especially as it still enjoyed a majority in most of those eastern areas where political and social influence lay. Acts of the colonial assembly had provided the Church with glebe-lands for the support of the clergy, and vestries had been empowered to levy tithes to pay their stipends. The vestries were themselves open only to those prepared to take the oath of Supremacy. They were closed corporations. The establishment enjoyed legislative safeguards: laws for the regulation of dissent, for compulsory attendance at state churches, and religious tests for public office. Presbyterians and Baptists were especially numerous in Virginia, and it was they who led the dissenting attack on these privileges.[1] Between 1763 and 1768 the penal laws were subverted and then repealed, and legal religious toleration was achieved.[2] Not content with this, the dissenters, in alliance with radical politicians, began a series of agitations against the continued existence of the establishment itself. With many Episcopalian laymen at least distantly tinged with Deism, and at any rate becoming mildly dubious of the compatibility of enlightened rational politics with the need for laws to protect religious privilege, the dissenters had a good chance of persuading the assembly. The Episcopalians were also sharply divided over the colonial bishopric question, and this was an issue which tended, in Virginia, to merge with the general campaign for religious equality.[3] With the events of 1776 the anti-establishment men struck. At the Virginia Convention they secured the exemption of dissenters from the payment of tithes, and all remaining penal laws were removed. In October 1776, after the Declaration of

[1] J. H. Mecklin, *The Story of American Dissent* (New York, 1934), p. 231.
[2] E. F. Humphrey, *op. cit.* p. 372.
[3] Carl Bridenbaugh, *Mitre and Sceptre*, p. 320.

The separation of church and state

Independence and with the assembly of the first republican legislature in Virginia, they poured in petitions which went still further; praying now for the actual disestablishment of the Church of England, and, like that from the Presbytery of Hanover, quoted below because it is not untypical, urging the total abolition of religious privilege and briefly laying out some theoretical objections to the establishment principle.

Dissenters from the Church of England in this country have ever been desirous to conduct themselves as peaceable members of the civil government, for which reason they have hitherto submitted to various ecclesiastical burdens and restrictions that are inconsistent with equal liberty. But now, when the many and grievous oppressions of our Mother Country have laid this continent under the necessity of casting off the yoke of tyranny, and of forming independent governments upon equitable and liberal foundations, we flatter ouselves, that we shall be freed from all encumbrances which a spirit of domination, prejudice or bigotry has interwoven with most other political systems ...It is well known that in the frontier counties, which are justly supposed to contain a fifth part of the inhabitants of Virginia, the dissenters have borne the heavy burdens of purchasing glebes, building churches and supporting the established clergy, where there are very few Episcopalians, either to assist in bearing the expense, or to reap the advantage...all of which are confessedly so many violations of their [the dissenters'] natural rights...In this enlightened age, and in a land where all of every denomination are united in the most strenuous efforts to be free, we hope and expect that our representatives will cheerfully concur in removing every species of religious, as well as civil bondage...We beg further to represent, that religious establishments are highly injurious to the temporal interests of any community. Without insisting upon the ambition and the arbitrary practices of those who are favoured by government, or the intriguing, seditious spirit which is commonly excited by this, as well as by every other kind of oppression, such establishments greatly retard population, and, consequently, the progress of arts, sciences, and manufactures...[1]

In reply to petitions like this, the Episcopalians and Methodists produced counter-petitions of their own, maintaining the estab-

[1] Printed in E. F. Humphrey, *op. cit.* p. 78.

lishment principle. The resulting debates in the assembly, as
Jefferson remarked, 'brought on the severest contests'.[1] But a
good majority of the legislators were churchmen, and progress
was delayed. This was in spite of the belief, which was well-
advertised in the new state, that over a half of the population were
dissenters. The justification of established religion was still not
seen, however, to be an affair of majorities, despite the theorizing
of Archdeacon Paley in England. A new campaign to whittle
away still more of the outworks of the establishment was therefore set in motion by the Virginian Baptists. In 1780 a Bill for
dissolving certain select vestries was passed, and in 1784, after a
tedious struggle, a new marriage Act legalized ceremonies per-
formed by dissenting clergymen. By then all forms of direct state
financial support for the Church had come to an end: but on an
understanding, conceded by the churchmen in the assembly, that
concurrent endowment of all churches, and not voluntaryism,
would follow in some legislative provision yet to be framed.
When at the end of 1784 the assembly incorporated the Church of
England, it was allowed to retain its occupancy of the glebes and
church buildings.

The attempt to establish concurrent endowment proved abortive. A Bill was framed to provide all the Christian denominations with public funds secured by a 'General Assessment'—an
allotment of taxes for religious purposes to whichever church
the individual taxpayer might signify. This was, of course, an
extension, on a broader basis, of the establishment principle. It
gave no preference to the Church of England, which was still
legally established, but it did cement a firm connexion between
church and state in the form of religious endowment out of public
funds. For this reason, Episcopalians favoured the scheme, and so did
the Methodists. The Presbyterians, mostly sprung originally from
the Scottish established Church, were also quite happy to receive
state support provided general religious equality was guaranteed—
just as they were content to receive sums from the clergy reserves

[1] E. F. Humphrey, *op. cit.* p. 378.

in Upper Canada during the 1830s. The Baptists, however, purists in their voluntaryism, led the opposition to the 'General Assessment', and in October 1785 the Bill was defeated by three votes. Instead, Jefferson's Bill for 'Establishing Religious Freedom' was passed: this marked the end of the establishment proper, but a connexion between the state and the Church of England survived, for the Church still retained the use of the national religious endowment in the form of property. This last vestige was removed in 1802, when the Episcopal Church was disendowed following a vigorous campaign by the dissenters.[1] Glebes were removed from its control as they became vacant and the proceeds of their sale went into a fund for poor relief and other secular purposes: ecclesiastical property donated or used before 1777 was left in the possession of the disestablished Church. As with the later examples, in Upper Canada and Ireland during the nineteenth century, legislators with a majority in favour of the establishment principle had in fact voted the end of the state church in order to conciliate the demands of militant dissent. In Virginia, the process of separation had lasted from 1763 to 1802. This was forty years: rather longer than the time subsequently taken by the same process in Upper Canada.

In most of the middle and southern states the same leading features characterized the separation of church and state. There, too, the process was typically a protracted series of measures diminishing the legal securities and privileges of the establishments, and ending at last in formal legislative severance. The state constitutions which replaced the old colonial charters incorporated the principles of separation by guarantees which amounted to religious equality. Variations reflected local differences in the intensity or organization of dissent, or in the extent to which the establishment had been recognized as a real grievance. In the old Catholic colony of Maryland, for example, which A. W. Werline examined, the dissenters were never so formidable a body as they were in Virginia, since they lacked both leadership and organization, and

---

[1] D. J. Mays, *Edmund Pendleton, 1721–1803* (Harvard, 1952), II, 337–8.

since the Church of England had strengthened its own position after its legal establishment in the colony.[1] As a result the new state constitution of 1776 recognized the right of the Church of England to exclusive support out of the public funds—the establishment principle—even though the assembly declined to make any actual appropriations from the taxes and so put the principle into effect. This was a sign that the establishment's days were numbered, but meanwhile the new state continued to legislate about religious questions, and on its own initiative.[2] Elsewhere in the southern and middle states disestablishments were more summary and were usually built into the new constitutions. It is interesting that sometimes the establishment principle itself was not struck down, but only the possibility of state preference for one church over another which might violate the guarantees of religious equality and freedom. Thus the constitution of North Carolina, adopted in 1776, declared only 'that there shall be no establishment of any one religious church or denomination in this State in preference to any other'.[3] In other states the establishments similarly ended with the new constitutional guarantees of religious equality, and only vague attempts were made to redefine the relationship of religious belief to the state.

In New England, where the clergy of the state churches had been clearly on the rebel side, the ending of the constitutional relationship with the Crown implied no particularly disrupting effects for the Congregational establishments. During the revolutionary period it was the Baptists who had led the campaigns for religious equality in New England, but their efforts were considerably less successful than in the other colonies. The Congregational churches were stronger and certainly more popular than the Church of England. It was through the agency of the Warren Association, composed of Baptist churches throughout New England, that the northern movement for disestablishment par-

[1] A. W. Werline, *Problems of Church and State in Maryland during the Seventeenth and Eighteenth Centuries* (South Lancaster, Mass., 1948), p. 211.
[2] *Ibid.* p. 170.
[3] A. P. Stokes and L. Pfeffer, *op. cit.* p. 72.

4-2

ticularly found expression. Its leaders were Isaac Backus, President Manning of Rhode Island College, John Gano and Morgan Edwards. They laid their case before every available forum of opinion; they represented their grievances to the Continental Congress and to the new state legislatures.[1] Other Protestant dissenters joined the effort, especially the Presbyterians. In Connecticut they employed the Republican Party as the vehicle of their ideas, and the result was a political clash: the Federalists choosing to stand by the Congregational establishments—a unique commitment of an American political party to the establishment principle. But in 1817 the Republicans won the state elections and in 1818 a constitutional convention at Hartford disestablished the church. In New Hampshire, where the campaign was rather less lively, disestablishment came more quietly in 1817. It was in Massachussetts, however, that the classic battle was joined in the north.

Massachussetts had adopted a state constitution in 1780 which recognized full religious toleration, but provision of public funds for the support of the Congregational churches had also been recognized.[2] There was a saving clause, similar to the 'General Assessment' scheme uselessly proposed for Virginia, which allowed taxpayers to direct their contributions to denominations of their own choice if they dissented from the established church.[3] But the dissenters were disatisfied with an arrangement which left the Congregationalists in a position of privilege and superior wealth. Under their excited pressure modifications to the exclusive rights of the establishment were made by legislation. The Religious Freedom Act of 1811 enabled those seeking to avoid taxation for religious purposes to opt out with greater facility. At the

[1] W. W. Sweet, *The Story of Religion in America* (New York, 1939 edition), p. 266.
[2] Williston Walker, *A History of the Congregational Churches in the United States* (American Church History Series, New York, 1894), p. 236.
[3] First Part, Article 3; printed in F. N. Thorpe, *The Federal and State Constitutions, Colonial Charters and other Organic Laws of the United States of America* (Washington, 1909), III, 1889.

state Constitutional Convention of 1820-1, the entire method of religious taxation and the principle of establishment were discussed, and although it became apparent that the supporters of the *status quo* were still far stronger than their opponents, some minor concessions were made. Meanwhile religious pluralism was beginning to increase. Catholics were just beginning to arrive from Ireland. Pressures became irresistible, and, at last, in 1831, the Massachussetts legislature approved disestablishment in principle. It came into effect in 1833 when the Standing Orders were suspended by a constitutional amendment. Even this victory would not have been so easily accomplished had not many of the Congregational meeting-houses passed into the hands of Unitarian pastors[1] and so offended orthodox Trinitarians that they would rather have the churches disestablished than countenance the propagation of error out of public funds. The last religious establishment was thus brought to an end in the United States. With the westward expansion of the nation during the nineteenth century, new states were added. In each case the separation of church and state, with guarantees of religious liberty, were written into their constitutions. Even states which had once known established religion were admitted without it: in California the secularization of the missions had fortuitously occurred before the cession of the province to the United States.[2] The new government, indeed, compensated the Franciscans for their lost properties.

The federal separation of church and state was no less ambiguous than the procedures in some of the states. The Continental Congress clearly regarded religion as something to be retained within the competence of individual member states, and at no time was separation contemplated as a national provision.[3] In the Northwest Ordinance of 1787, furthermore, religious belief was ex-

---

[1] Henry Caswall, *America and the American Church* (London, 1839), p. 126.

[2] See G. J. Geary, *The Secularization of the California Missions, 1810-40* (Washington, 1934).

[3] E. F. Humphrey, *Nationalism and Religion in America, 1774-89* (Boston, 1924), p. 439.

plicitly given national approval as 'necessary to good government and the happiness of mankind'.[1] The Philadelphia Convention of 1787, which drafted the new federal constitution, also intended to leave things more or less as they were. A large number of Episcopalians sat as delegates, but like so many of the politically sophisticated of the period, they inclined to supposing little need for federal dealing with religion, and the general temper was certainly at first to leave things alone.[2] The federal instrument which they drew up, unlike the Declaration of Independence and the new state constitutions, made no reference to God or Providence, except in the formal dating of the document by the years of Christ. To safeguard the position of denominational interests in national affairs, and to prevent discrimination against individuals on account of their religious opinions, the Constitution prohibited the imposition of religious tests for federal office. It was during the ratification debates in the various states that this general solution was upset. In widely scattered places there were demands for a Bill of Rights which would make an actual federal provision for religious liberty and religious equality: those dissenting groups most active in the various state campaigns for disestablishment were now employing the ratification debates to secure a national separation of church and state. In Virginia, for example, the Baptist Association voted against ratification because there were no safeguards for religious liberty in the Constitution.[3] Those still holding establishment principles, on the other hand, tended to oppose the clause prohibiting religious tests for office. In South Carolina, Presbyterian frontiersmen opposed ratifica-

[1] Quoted in E. B. Greene, *Religion and the State. The Making and Testing of an American Tradition* (Ithaca, New York, 1959 edition), p. 83.
[2] At the convention, of those members whose religious affiliation is known, there were 19 Episcopalians, 8 Congregationalists, 7 Presbyterians, 2 Roman Catholics, 2 Quakers, 1 Methodist, 1 Dutch Reformed, and a declared Deist. This gave the adherents of the two former established denominations an absolute majority, but then these delegates, especially the Episcopalians, were scarcely representative of feelings within their own churches.
[3] Forrest McDonald, *We The People, The Economic Origins of the Constitution* (Chicago, 1963 edition), p. 268 n.

tion simply because it was favoured by the Episcopalians on the east coast.[1] But these tendencies are to be noted as indications of religious division at work: nowhere did the question of ratification seriously depend on religious issues standing alone. The heated arguments were enough, however, to secure a Constitutional amendment, accepted by Congress in 1789 and ratified two years later. Yet the history of the adoption of the First Amendment and the Bill of Rights well illustrates the absence of any general intention by the founding fathers to hasten the disconnexion of church and state in the various states. Madison first introduced a fairly radical provision in the House of Representatives. This was to prohibit the establishment of any 'national religion'. The House itself diluted the proposal into a prohibition of 'laws establishing religion'. And after consultations with the Senate the final, and even more diluted formula was arrived at—the words which stand in the First Amendment: 'Congress shall make no law respecting an establishment of religion, or prohibiting the free exercise thereof.' This clearly prevented any federal interference with surviving state churches, and left any other official dealings with religious belief in the hands of the state governments; and it seems equally clear that the pressure for alterations to Madison's unilateral proposal came from those out to protect the principle of local competence in the religious sphere.[2] It was not until years later, when he was President, that Jefferson spoke of the First Amendment as having built 'a wall of separation between church and state'. The redefinition of church and state was, in the United States, an achievement of religious opinion.[3] This quality it shared with Canada and Britain, but the difference from Europe is marked: there separation was largely the result of state hostility to the influence of religious organization.

It was not until the passage of the Fourteenth Amendment in

[1] *Ibid.* p. 216.
[2] Wilbur G. Katz, *Religion and American Constitutions* (Northwestern University Press, 1964), p. 8.
[3] Winthrop S. Hudson, *The Great Tradition of the American Churches* (New York, 1963 edition), p. 42.

1868 that the states were formally bound by the 'no establishment' clause of the First. Until that time there was no federal provision which prevented any state from creating religious establishments after their admission to the Union.[1] Even this is a technicality of hindsight, for it was not until 1934 that the 'due process' clause of the Fourteenth Amendment actually applied 'no establishment' restrictions to state laws.

2. SEPARATION IN BRITISH NORTH AMERICA

In Upper Canada the separation of church and state resulted largely from the successful agitations inspired by dissenting opposition to the clergy reserves. The issue was debated, that is to say, as it was in Britain, around the question of state *endowment* of religion. The upshot therefore turned upon the resolution of a series of concrete grievances, rather than upon legislative acceptance of abstract principles. When public financial support of religion was withdrawn, Canadians were on the whole satisfied that the battle had been won. The constitutional significance of the clergy reserves question—the realization that an attack on the reserves was an attack on the confessional office of the state—was as fully appreciated in the Imperial Parliament as it was in the Canadian assembly. In March 1840, Sir Robert Inglis, who for half a century scarcely conceived a thought which was not in some way related to the need to preserve the establishment principle, recognized the scope of the question when he argued against a Bill for the redistribution of the reserves. 'The common bond of religion', he said on that occasion, 'is the best security on which the Crown could rely for the permanency of its possessions, and this bond the bill proposed to weaken'.[2] And five years after the successful passage of this legislation, Charles Greville, Clerk to the Privy Council, in an anonymous work on the Irish question, underlined the precedent which Canada had created for Britain:

[1] Leo Pfeffer, *Church, State and Freedom* (Boston, 1953), p. 126.
[2] Hansard, Third Series, LII, 1347.

'the history of these clergy reserves is curious, because it exhibits more distinctly, perhaps, than any other act, the abandonment of the principle of exclusive religious appropriation and the adoption of that of concurrent endowment'.[1]

In the Maritime Provinces too, it was the dissenters' awareness of the inferiority of their position relative to the privilege and legal protection of the Church of England which prepared the ground for the separation of church and state. The local politics of the region were rather different from those of the Canadas, and solutions to religious problems were largely arrived at independently. They will therefore have to be examined separately. The westward expansion of British North America mostly occurred after the establishment question had already received at least partial solution in the older areas of settlement. State churches were unknown to the Canadian west. Only in Quebec did anything like a close association of church and state survive the first half of the nineteenth century, and this was on a provincial basis.

The Church of England was implicitly established in Upper Canada from the first settlement of the province under English direction, simply on the basis that as part of the King's realm overseas it participated in the Royal Supremacy. With the shock administered to the colonial administrators by the revolt of the thirteen American colonies, with the subsequent flood of settlement by loyalist exiles, and with increasing awareness of the need to counterbalance the influence of the Catholic Church of Quebec (which enjoyed rights and incomes guaranteed by statute in 1774), the establishment principle was accorded new utility. Loyalty to the throne could readily be estimated as co-extensive with respect to the altar, as necessary conditions for the survival of British sovereignty in the Canadas. Thus in the Constitutional Act of 1791, which defined the government of the Upper and Lower provinces,[2] provision was made for the established church—or rather, as the Act stated, for 'a Protestant clergy', a phrase which at the time

[1] *Past and Present Policy of England Towards Ireland* (London, 1845), p. 262.
[2] 31. Geo. III. c. 31.

could only legally mean the Church of England. The Act provided for the collection of tithes and the endowment of rectories from the public funds. In fact the former were never actually levied and the latter were only created in 1836. But most significant of all was clause 36: this required the reservation of one-seventh of all Crown lands for the support of the clergy.[1] Reservations were begun immediately, and by the middle of the nineteenth century the lands concerned amounted to some two-and-a-half-million acres, scattered freely among other holdings. Colonel Simcoe, the first Governor under the Constitutional Act, was personally committed to the successful planting of the establishment principle. He hoped to place education in the hands of the Church of England, and also—for this too he regarded as a necessary element in the reproduction of British conditions—to foster a Canadian aristocracy. 'In regard to the colony of Upper Canada which is peculiarly situated among a variety of republics', he wrote in 1791, 'every establishment of Church and State which upholds a distinction of ranks and lessens the undue weight of the democratic influence must be indispensably introduced.'[2] These endeavours were undertaken in the face of a religious pluralism which already existed: the Catholics of Lower Canada, and the swelling number of Protestant dissenters in the Upper Province. Many of the exiled loyalists were Nonconformists in religion. It was unfortunate for the establishment that, from the beginning, the Church of England became popularly associated with aristocracy and the governing party. 'To attempt to give that Church the same exclusive political advantages that it possessed in Great Britain, and which are even there the cause of so much clamour', remarked Richard Cartwright in 1793, 'appears to me to be as impolitic as it is unjust.'[3]

The clergy reserves, whilst by far the most important subject of the church and state controversy, was not the only one. The

[1] For a brief summary of this part of the Act, see Aileen Dunham, *Political Unrest in Upper Canada, 1815–1836* (new edition, Toronto, 1963), p. 83.
[2] *Ibid.* p. 84.
[3] Quoted in S. D. Clark, *Church and Sect in Canada* (Toronto, 1948), p. 130.

question of denominational education will be discussed in a later chapter, but its place in the dissenters' struggle, as in Britain itself, was central. Lesser marks of the ascendancy of the Church of England were washed away as the tide of religious equality lapped into the more notorious grievances. Thus the exclusive rights of the Church over marriages were diminished by a cumulative series of adjustments. In 1793 civil marriage by justices was permitted in Upper Canada if there was no clergyman of the state church within 18 miles; and in 1797 the ministers of the Church of Scotland, the Lutheran and the 'Calvinist' clergy were given the statutory right of performing marriages if licensed by a justice at Quarter Sessions. Baptists and Congregationalists, claiming the Calvinist title, benefited from this measure. But it had been conceded only after painful ill-feeling provoked by the imprisonment of several ministers for conducting illegal weddings. As had been the case of the Church of England in the American colonies, the quality of the clergy was often questionable. Most of the abuses of contemporary Britain—non-residence, pluralism, and disregard for discipline—easily crossed the seas to Canada and the Maritime Provinces, with the added disadvantage that many of those who perpetuated them had only emigrated because of their ineligibility for satisfactory preferment at home. The feeling among colonial dissenters that the establishment was merely an extension of the corrupt ways of Britain was nurtured on these abuses. There were, at least, no religious tests preventing the election of Christians of any denomination to the provincial assemblies of Upper and Lower Canada under the Constitutional Act of 1791, and dissenters readily took advantage of the opportunity to bring their grievances to the legislatures in person. This produced the pattern of dissenting-radical pressures which shortly, though rather less extensively, was to characterize the Imperial Parliament as well. Roman Catholics had been admitted to the Canadian legislatures and to public office by subscribing to a special oath specified by the Quebec Act of 1774. This oath, omitting the condemnations of their religion which were still a part of the British Parliamentary oath until 1829, was widely disapproved in England on the grounds that it removed one of the essential safeguards to the Protestant Constitution.[1] Catholics were admitted to the Nova Scotian legislature in 1781.

It was, however, the contentious spirit set alight by the clergy reserves issue which destroyed any hope of ultimate survival which the establishment might have cherished. The reserves were leased on the assumption that the parsons would be able to live off the incomes. But until the end of the first quarter of the nineteenth century the lands remained largely uncultivated because of a superabundance of other holdings readily available to settlers. As a result the annual income to the church was only around £150, and support had to come from other sources. There were occasional grants from the Society for the Propagation of the Gospel, and, after 1825, from the Canada Company. Both of these were indirect forms of state subvention. Individual direct payments were made by the government to bishops and a few senior clergymen, and similar hand-outs went to the ministers of other denominations: an early essay in concurrent endowment. But the sort of incomes to which religious establishments were usually entitled were absent. 'It must be borne in mind that the Canadian Church is, with the exception of a very inconsiderable revenue derivable from the reserved lands, entirely unendowed', wrote Ernest Hawkins in his report for S.P.G. in 1849; 'she has no tithes, no Easter offerings, and but few glebes of any real value.'[2] The Church of England therefore existed from the start to quite a large extent on the voluntary system. It was true, on the other hand, that the number of clergy to be supported was small. In his controversial 'Ecclesiastical Chart' of 1826 Archdeacon Strachan[3]

---

[1] W. R. Riddell, *The Constitution of Canada in its History and Practical Working* (Yale, 1912), p. 45.

[2] *Annals of the Diocese of Quebec* (published for S.P.G.) (London, 1849), p. 300.

[3] John Strachan, born in 1778, the son of an Aberdeen quarry foreman, emigrated to Upper Canada in 1799 and became a private tutor. Ordained in the Church of England in 1803, he later became archdeacon of York (Toronto) and, in 1839, the first bishop of the new see of Toronto. He was a leading High Churchman

estimated the total at thirty-one, and this was a slight exaggeration. In 1815 Clergy Corporations were created by the Governor and his Executive Council, charged with the administration of the reserved lands. After the creation of the Canada Company by the Imperial Parliament in 1825—an agency to administer the Crown lands—large areas of the clergy reserves were sold to it, and the proceeds from these and other sales were invested with the intention that the revenues should supply a permanent fund for the maintenance of the clergy.

Meanwhile, however, opposition to the reserves, and to the entire policy of exclusive endowment of the Church of England, was becoming articulate. This was to some extent a reflexion of the increasing value of the clergy reserves themselves. As available land for settlement diminished, all land values rose, and complaints about the state of the reserved lands, which were scattered among private holdings, were heard with a disturbing frequency.[1] But much more, opposition indicated the rise to militancy of a vigorous religious pluralism. The comparative sizes of the different churches was a controversial question at the time, but it is clear that the Methodists, Presbyterians, Baptists and Catholics of Upper Canada hugely outnumbered the Church of England, even though the Church was the largest and most influential single body. Dissent was becoming conscious of its latent power, and was allying itself with radical reform politics. 'We remark, far and wide', wrote Strachan simply, during a visitation of the diocese of Toronto in 1842, 'the prevalence of religious division, and its attendant is too frequently in this diocese a feeling of hostility to the Church of England.'[2] In striving to protect its legal rights against the dissenters, the establishment became even more closely identified

and contender for the rights of the establishment, and a prominent figure in the Tory politics of the Upper Province. He died in 1867.

[1] Ernest Hawkins, *Annals of the Diocese of Toronto* (published for S.P.G.) (London, 1848), p.170.

[2] *A Journal of Visitation to the Western Portion of his Diocese by the Lord Bishop of Toronto. The Church in Canada, No. 1* (published for S.P.G.) (third edition, London, 1846), p. 41.

with conservative provincial politics, and this in turn helped to place the clergy reserves, and the general question of state religious endowments, at the centre of the political disagreements between the Reformers and the Tories.[1]

Radical politicians were quick to scoop up the support of the dissenters. William Lyon Mackenzie made his own radical paper, the *Colonial Advocate*, a leading exponent of the doctrine of religious equality, and filled it with attacks on the Church of England, demanding an end to the clergy reserves, to exclusive legal rights for any church, and campaigning for non-sectarian education. Not all dissenters, however, were opposed to state endowments as such: some were opposed only to inequality in the distribution of public funds for religion. There was a good deal of shifting of attitudes on this point between 1825 and 1854, especially by the Wesleyan Methodists, and the question of state support for religion sometimes contributed substantially to schisms inside the leading denominations. The Baptists, like their brethren in the United States and Britain, were the most consistently opposed to any form of connexion between church and state. The Presbyterians, on the other hand, at least until the disruption of the 1840s were largely in favour of state support. From 1819 the Church of Scotland pursued claims as a co-establishment with the Church of England in the Empire, in the belief that the Act of Union between England and Scotland in 1707 had recognized *two* imperial establishments. The Church of Scotland expected, and eventually got, a share in the clergy reserves fund.

So closely had political affiliation begun to correspond to attitudes adopted over the question of state religious endowments, that a change in allegiance resulted necessarily from a change of attitude on that question and *vice versa*. The Methodists, under the inspiration of Egerton Ryerson,[2] had broken the alliance of radicalism and dissent by 1836, and moved over to support the con-

---

[1] S. D. Clark, *op. cit.* p. 131.

[2] Born in 1803, the son of an American Loyalist exile. Converted to Methodism, he was one of five brothers who entered the Wesleyan ministry. He became a leading educational reformer; and died in 1882.

servatives. Ryerson himself had been shocked by the secularism of the English radical leaders whom he had met during a visit to Britain in 1833.[1] These men, who acted as agents and advisors to the Canadian reformers, were assuredly far from supporting the dissenters' grievances from any distinctly spiritual conviction. Ryerson especially singled out Hume and Attwood as the worst examples of the infidelity of English radicalism. 'The notorious infidel character of the majority of the political leaders and periodical publications of this party deter the virtuous part of the nation from associating with them,' he wrote of the radicals.[2] Many colonial Methodists were beginning to suspect the same expediency in the Canadian radical leaders, fearing concealed republicanism too. By 1836 the Wesleyan Methodists were in the Tory camp. Despite this qualification, the union between radicalism and militant dissent was real enough. A series of issues floated the churches along this channel. The advocacy of temperance, for example, added to the growing sense of common political experience, and strengthened the position of the churches as effective pressure groups.[3] In sympathetic response, the radical politicians gave high priority to the dissenters' grievances. Thus after the reformers' success in the 1834 elections, the radical 'Canadian Alliance' managed to get a committee of the assembly to look into some outstanding causes of discontent. Chaired by Mackenzie, it spent a lot of its time examining the use of provincial revenues for religious purposes. But it was the clergy reserves issue, above all others, which excited the dissenters to political organization, which reached to the heart of provincial politics before the rebellions of 1837, and which stayed there until the settlement of 1854. It had, indeed, a strong connexion with the discontent which gave birth to the rebellions.[4] 'There could be no doubt a strong feeling existed on this subject in Canada', Lord

[1] Goldwin French, *Parsons and Politics. The role of the Wesleyan Methodists in Upper Canada and the Maritimes from 1780 to 1855* (Toronto, 1962), p. 143.
[2] C. B. Sissons, *Egerton Ryerson, His Life and Letters* (Toronto, 1937), I, 197.
[3] S. D. Clark, *op. cit.* p. 256.
[4] See Aileen Dunham, *op. cit.* chapter VI.

The separation of church and state

John Russell told Parliament in 1840: 'so much so, that the partial insurrection which took place in 1837 had been ascribed by many persons far more to the excitement prevailing on this question than to any wish to throw off allegiance to the Crown.'[1]

The agitations of the Upper Canadian dissenters, first against the apportionment of the clergy reserves incomes, and then, later, for the complete secularization of the funds, had close affinities with those of the exponents of religious equality in the American commonwealth and in Great Britain. The tyranny of state religious interference was much voiced; the voluntary system of endowments and 'free-trade in religion' were elevated to the level of high principle. But at first there were divisions to be overcome among the dissenters themselves. Some were already in receipt of state aid. The Canada Company made small annual grants to Bishop Macdonnell and his Catholic clergy.[2] The Church of Scotland and the independent Presbyterians received state grants; the Wesleyan Methodists accepted state aid for their missionary and educational institutions. This concurrent endowment had become quite usual throughout the Empire by the early nineteenth century. Receipt of these funds made the churches concerned slightly less critical of the establishment principle: but it did nothing to blunt the edge of their demands for *equal* dealing among the churches, nor to diminish the outraged contempt of those denominations, like the Baptists and the Upper Canadian Congregationalists, whose ideological objection to the connexion of church and state in any form released scorn upon any who touched government gold. The belief that the peculiar religious conditions of the province rendered the establishment principle inappropriate became increasingly a popular commonplace. In 1841 the Presbyterian *Christian Examiner* put it thus:

Year after year, at least during the last decade, the general sentiment of this colony has been uttered in no unequivocal form that no church

[1] *Annual Register*, 1840, p. 148.
[2] Macdonnell even became a member of the Upper Canada Legislative Council, at the invitation of Governor Colborne—a striking illustration of the anomalous acceptance of religious pluralism by authority.

invested with exclusive privileges derived from the State, is adapted to
the condition of society among us. It cannot be doubted that this is
the conviction of nine-tenths of the colonists. Except among a few
ambitious magnates of the Church of England, we never hear a contrary sentiment breathed. Equal rights upon equal conditions is the
general cry.¹

In reply to the various charges laid against the establishment
principle the Church of England ventured most of the classic
arguments in its favour: the cultivation of a national spirituality
and loyalty to the throne; Chalmer's doctrine that those most in
need of religious instruction were also those least aware of the
fact; and that in a poor country of new settlement there was no
inheritance from massive private endowments of the past. In 1837
The Church remarked that 'if there existed the slightest possibility
or even chance that the Voluntary System would prove adequate
to the religious instruction of a whole people we would freely
yield'.² The establishment under the guidance of Bishop Strachan
therefore stood by its legal title, in the Act of 1791, to the exclusive
use of the reserves created for the maintenance of 'a Protestant
clergy'.

The history of the dissenters' campaign against the clergy
reserves of Upper Canada, and their eventual secularization, is
reasonably familiar, and need only be sketched in outline here.³ It
was the claims of the Presbyterians to the rights of co-establishment
which first projected the reserves as the leading test-question for the
connexion of church and state. From 1819 the Church of Scotland
in Canada argued for their inclusion among the 'Protestant clergy'.
A petition for a share in the reserves from a. congregation at

---

¹ E. R. Stimson, *History of the Separation of Church and State in Canada* (second
edition, Toronto, 1887), p. 58.
² Quoted in W. H. Elgee, *The Social Teachings of the Canadian Churches* (Toronto,
1964), p. 14.
³ For the best recent treatment, see J. S. Moir, *Church and State in Canada West,
Three Studies in the Relation of Denominationalism and Nationalism, 1841–67*
(Toronto, 1959), chapters 2 and 3. For official documentation, see Parliamentary Papers: 1840 XXXII 37. (Correspondence on the Reserves, 1819–40);
1851, XXXVI, 227; 1852, XXXIII, 29; and 1852–3, L, 325.

Niagara, sent on to London for the opinion of the Crown Law Officers, established the right of Presbyterians to *some* income from the funds—but not to any endowment of rectories. The Officers also expressed the view that Canadian dissenters were *not* a part of the 'Protestant clergy' mentioned in the Act of 1791. This opinion was not published in Upper Canada. In 1822 the Church of Scotland sent a petition to England seeking clarification of their relationship with the state, and in the following year the radical politician, William Morris, introduced several successful resolutions to the provincial legislature which underlined the Church of Scotland's claim to a share in the reserves, and which attacked the exclusive apportionment of funds by the Clergy Corporations. These moves were supported by the home church through the agency of the Glasgow Colonial Society. There was, however, some difficulty in establishing claims because of the divisions among the Canadian Presbyterians themselves. In 1828 Sir George Murray, Secretary of State for the Colonies, suggested to the United Presbytery that a more favourable consideration of their demands could be made if there was a more substantial degree of unity among the Presbyterian churches—a view already expressed by Sir John Colborne, the Governor of Upper Canada. The truth of this was evidently apparent to the petitioners, and, in the hope of government aid, rationalizations of church structure followed. The Church of Scotland formed a Synod at Kingston in 1831, and the United Presbytery followed in 1832. Both began to receive state funds. The United Associate Synod of the Secession Church of Scotland declined offers of aid, remaining ideologically opposed to state support and steadfast in the voluntary principle. In 1840 the Church of Scotland and the United Synod finally amalgamated.

The Methodists, meanwhile, had entered the struggle. The occasion was Strachan's funeral panygeric for Bishop Mountain of Quebec, who had died in 1825. Strachan, then still Archdeacon of York (Toronto), attacked 'uneducated itinerant preachers'— implying the Methodists—and pointed to the need for maintaining the integrity of the Canadian religious establishment.

'When it is considered', he declared with characteristic over-emphasis, 'that the religious teachers of the other denominations of Christians, a very few respectable ministers of the Church of Scotland excepted, come almost universally from the Republican states of America, where they gather their knowledge and form their sentiments, it is quite evident that if the Imperial Gover-ment does not immediately step forward with efficient help, the mass of the population will be nurtured and instructed in hostility to our parent Church, nor will it be long till they imbibe opinions anything but favourable to the political institutions of England.'[1] The dissenters, and particularly the Methodists,[2] exploded with anger, and it was their clamours which provided the background for a renewed and lengthy debate on the whole question of the clergy reserves in the provincial assembly during January, 1826. The assembly addressed the King, stating an opinion from which they were never to depart. It was based on the principle of religious equality:

The lands set apart in this Province for the maintenance and support of a Protestant clergy ought not to be enjoyed by any one denomina-tion of Protestants, to the exclusion of their Christian brethren of other denominations equally conscientious in their respective modes of wor-shipping God, and equally entitled, as dutiful and loyal subjects, to the protection of your Majesty's benign and liberal Government; we therefore hope it will, in your Majesty's wisdom, be deemed expedient and just that not only the present Reserves, but that any fund arising from the sales thereof, should be devoted to the advancement of the Christian religion generally and the happiness of all your Majesty's subjects, of whatever denomination; or, if such application should be deemed inexpedient, that the profits arising from such appropriation should be applied to the purposes of education and the general im-provement of the province.[3]

This statement allowed two solutions: concurrent endowment, by the equal redistribution of the reserves; and secularization, by the removal of the funds to purposes of general public utility.

[1] E. R. Stimson, *op. cit.* p. 109.
[2] For Ryerson's criticism of the sermon, see C. B. Sissons, *op. cit.* 1, 23.
[3] Parliamentary Papers, 1826–7, xv, 499.

Both had appeared among the proposals for the disendowment of the American establishments, and both were to be debated at great length in the cases of Ireland and Wales. Everywhere secularization was eventually adopted. But this address of the Upper Canadian assembly brought no advance in 1826. In June the reply from London referred to the reserves as 'specially allotted by the Imperial Parliament to the Established Church'.

At this point Strachan, in his determination to protect the rights of the state church, successfully procured an act from the home Parliament which allowed the Clergy Corporation to sell off portions of the reserved lands and to apply the proceeds exclusively to the Church. In support of his position, Strachan also published an 'Ecclesiastical Chart' which purported to reveal the exact numbers of clergymen in the province: 30 of the Church of England, 2 Church of Scotland, 6 other Presbyterians, some 20 or 30 Methodists, and a very small number of other religious teachers, mostly 'very ignorant'.[1] The chart was intended to discredit the claims of the Church of Scotland to the benefits of co-establishment, but the associated vilification of the Methodists drew strong retaliation from that quarter instead.[2] In May, 1826, Egerton Ryerson, by then a leading preacher in the York circuit, reviewed Strachan's opinions and statistics in the radical *Colonial Advocate*. The ensuing controversy, which was popular and heated, resulted in the appointment of a select committee of the House of Commons in London, which examined the whole state of religion in Canada.[3]

These events left the Methodists as the leading champions of religious equality. In 1829 the Wesleyan Conference established the *Christian Guardian*, a paper which was not slow in advocating the total disestablishment of the Church of England. The Methodists were beginning to prefer the secularization of the clergy reserves to some scheme for the redistribution of the funds. They

[1] A. Dunham, *op. cit.* p. 91.
[2] A. N. Bethune, *Memoir of the Right Reverend John Strachan* (Toronto, 1870), p. 123.
[3] Parliamentary Papers, 1828 (569) VII, 375.

cooperated with 'The Friends of Religious Liberty', an inter-denominational pressure-group of dissenters and radicals,[1] which favoured the application of the state religious endowments for general educational purposes. Unhappily for the union of reform and dissent, the Wesleyans defected to the Tory side between 1833 and 1837, but the machinery created by the Methodist leaders to influence political contests was not lost. It, too, was used in the conservative interest. Under the leadership of Ryerson, the Wesleyans gradually discharged their enthusiasm for the voluntary system, and although—as at the Conference of 1837—they were still formally loyal to voluntaryism, in practice they were quite prepared to accept state aid.[2] Co-religionists who were less happy about this outcome, like the Methodist Episcopal Church, organized themselves into independent bodies.

The controversy was stimulated yet again in 1836 by the endowment of rectories for the Church of England by Governor Colborne on the eve of his retirement. The provision in the Act of 1791 for the endowment of rectories out of public funds had never been put into effect. In 1818 and 1825 suggestions that the clergy reserves incomes be used for that purpose had not matured into action. In 1826 the government had authorized the creation of rectories, but in the heated atmosphere attendant upon the dissenters' campaign against the reserves, then especially intense, nothing was done. In the middle of 1831, however, S.P.G. decided to terminate its grants to the Upper Canadian Church, and this made some new source of endowment crucially necessary. So it was that in 1836 Colborne issued patents for the creation of 57 rectories, each to receive four hundred acres of reserved lands: 44 of these were actually set up. The provincial assembly was deluged with petitions of protest from a dissenting public opinion inflamed as never before.[3] After some confusion, the Law Officers of the Crown in London declared the rectories legal, citing the

[1] H. H. Walsh, *The Christian Church in Canada* (Toronto, 1956), p. 176.
[2] Goldwin French, *op. cit.* p. 160.
[3] A. N. Bethune, *op. cit.* p. 156.

original royal warrant issued by Bathurst.[1] It was at this point that the rebellion in Upper Canada intervened—the affair of the rectories considerably adding to the general unrest.

In his Report on the condition of the two Canadian provinces, Lord Durham recognized the clergy reserves as 'the great practical question', whose solution was 'essential to the pacification of Canada'.[2] One of the last acts of the Upper Canadian assembly, before Durham's recommended union of the two provinces was carried into effect, was legislation for the redistribution of the reserves among the denominations. Strachan and the Church party pulled at every available string to prevent the act becoming law. The Imperial Parliament did indeed disallow it, but only because it was constitutionally incompetent. For accepting the new practice of responsible government, Britain had conceded that the reserves, being an internal one, should be determined by the Canadians themselves. In 1840, therefore, the Imperial Parliament passed an act which, though still friendly to the prior claims of the Church of England, *was* based on essentially the same principle as the abortive colonial bill.[3] The Act of 1840 prohibited any future reservations of lands for religious purposes, and authorized the division of incomes from land already sold between the Churches of England and Scotland in a proportion of two to one. Income from all new sales of land was to be halved: one portion to be allowed to the Churches of England and Scotland as stipulated for the older revenues; the other to be distributed among any churches which might apply for state aid. Through the operation of the Act, the Churches of England, Scotland and Rome, the United Synod and the Wesleyan Methodists, all benefited; the established church continuing to draw by far the most substantial sums when, eight years later, the Act finally began to produce effects in cash. Thus statute law had come to recognize the principle of concurrent endowment—the indiscriminate application of

[1] Parliamentary Papers, 1839 (141) XXXIV, 33.
[2] Parliamentary Papers, 1839, XVII, 62.
[3] 3 & 4 Vict, c, 78.

the national religious funds to all expressions of Christian belief.
But the Act was not well-received in Canada. The establishment
regarded it as 'spoliation'; as an act of national apostasy. The
Church of Scotland resented the inequality represented by its share
of the spoils, and the Methodists were dissatisfied at the size of their
cut too. The leading voluntaryist denominations—the Baptists,
Congregationalists and Episcopal Methodists—could only see the
new arrangement as a derisory reply to their demands for effective
religious equality. The Act, intended as a final settlement, was
successful in buying a period of religious peace, on the reserves
question at any rate, only because during the following decade
the Churches were themselves absorbed in reorganization or, as
in the case of the Church of Scotland, disruption, and because
the radical politicians were diverted to a complicated scrutiny
of the workings of the new United Legislature under responsible
government.

This period of relative quiescence ended abruptly in 1849.
Public opinion, which had endured the settlement of 1840 as
something foisted upon them by the Imperial Parliament, was in
that year again roused by religious passions over the reserves
question. The Act was beginning to work. 'The conditions were
ready, even conducive, for a union of the forces of political radicalism and militant voluntaryism.'[1] From early in 1850 meetings
of the Grit reform party declared the urgent priority which should
be set upon the separation of church and state, and an Anti-
Clergy Reserves Association was established to organize petitions.
This body later changed its name to the Anti-State-Church
Association, and opened communication with the powerful British
society of that name. The British counterpart, which itself became
the Liberation Society, worked for the cause of the Canadian
voluntaryists and acted as their agent.

Opposition to the settlement of 1840 continued to issue from
the Churches of England and Scotland in Canada. In 1851 the
Wesleyan Methodist Conference abandoned its acquiescence in

[1] J. S. Moir, *Church and State in Canada West* (Toronto, 1959), p. 52.

concurrent endowment and declared for pure voluntaryism. The ranks of those agitating for the secularization of the clergy reserves were accordingly strengthened, and with the Russell administration back in office in London a new initiative from the Imperial Parliament was expected. The Act of 1853 authorized the Canadian legislature to settle the reserves question as it thought fit, with the exception that existing vested interests should be protected. The result was the Canadian Act of 1854, passed by the Conservative MacNab-Morin ministry, and largely drafted by John A. Macdonald, then Attorney-General.[1] Secularization and the preservation of vested life interests were the leading principles of the Act. Some 664,400 acres of reserved lands still unsold in 1854 were to be realized, and the residual income to be paid into a municipalities fund, to be used for general purposes of public utility. The Churches in receipt of funds at the time of the passing of the Act were granted a final payment totaling £381,982, of which the Church of England got 64 per cent, the Church of Scotland 28 per cent, the Methodists 2·6 per cent and the Catholics 5·4 per cent.[2] Provision was made, as it was later to be in the comparable British statutes which disestablished the Churches of Ireland and Wales, for these denominations to allow their clergy to commute their life-interests and pay the sums over to church bodies for investment, and so provide permanent endowments. The Church of England, and seventy-six of the ministers of the Church of Scotland, took advantage of the commutation clause. This arrangement, like its later Irish counterpart, caused much disappointment to the militant voluntaryists, who complained that the generosity of compensation and the virtual creation of endowments was scarcely an adequate separation of church and state. Some churches were to be left with an unfair advantage over others; an advantage which had now been given renewed statutory sanction. As the Anti-State-Church Association declared

[1] Donald Creighton, *John A. Macdonald, The Young Politician* (Toronto, 1956), p. 185.
[2] J. S. Moir, *op. cit.* p. 79.

in its protest to the Governor, this provision subverted 'the great object sought by the enactment, *viz.*, the ultimate practical recognition of the civil equality of all religious denominations'.[1] For its part, the Synod of the Church of England, meeting under Strachan in 1854, protested against an Act which 'dispossessed the said Church and other religious bodies in this province, of all the right and title to the benefit and proceeds arising out of the lands formerly set apart by the Crown for the support of the Protestant clergy'.[2]

The settlement of the clergy reserves question was in itself a large redefinition of the relations of church and state in Upper Canada: religious equality had more or less received official recognition as the principle which should govern public policy in religious questions. It was also a measure of disestablishment. The Church of England lapsed as a state church in men's minds. There was no need for any formal statutory separation. Canadians assumed that with the end of state support the establishment principle was defeated—a characteristically anomalous solution. The point was seen by diehard secularizers and extreme voluntaryists at the time, and as late as the 1880s a Baptist minister, the Reverend E. R. Stimson, reflecting on the protracted controversies which had led to the separation of church and state, correctly described the curious result:

We speak of the *Separation* in its popular acceptation. For a *complete* separation has not occurred, otherwise we would not witness the wrangling of lawyers over denominational and religious differences of opinion, nor find courts adjudicating over some millions of dollars held in trust for the promotion of the tenets of a particular Church, established, so far as this very money [the commuted interests funds] is concerned, upon this peninsular part of the Dominion.[3]

But in 'popular acceptation' the deed was done. With the Canadian Confederation in 1867 there was no mention of established churches

[1] *Ibid.* p. 78.   [2] E. R. Stimson, *op. cit.* p. 160.
[3] E. R. Stimson, *History of the Separation of Church and State in Canada* p. 198.

—the question had quietly laid itself to rest. Theoretically, therefore, the Church of England is still established. It still draws, as does the disestablished Church of Ireland, on the commuted invested funds which are the last remnants of the old national religious endowments. The patents for the endowed rectories created by Colborne in 1836 are still valid in Ontario, and their incumbents still profit from the slight incomes they afford: a strange survival of state confessionalism.[1]

Despite the shared experience with Upper Canada during the period when the provinces were united, Lower Canada's history in the relations of church and state enjoyed some peculiarities. In Lower Canada, the Protestant denominations found themselves in a small minority everywhere except the Eastern Townships. Like their co-religionists in Ireland, that is to say, they were set amidst a numerous Catholic population which embraced national and cultural aspirations rather alien to their own. The clergy reserves controversy never reached anything like the significance it attained in Upper Canada. Lands were reserved for 'a Protestant clergy' in Lower Canada too, under the Act of 1791, but the Quebec Act of 1774 had already guaranteed the tithes and seigniorial rights of the Catholic clergy and, by allowing a simple oath of allegiance to the Crown without subscription to the Royal Supremacy in religion, the Catholic population had already acquired political emancipation. The relative privilege of their position was recognized by the Catholic hierarchy. There was, with legally protected incomes and rights of their own, no pressing sense of injustice or inferiority which led to any significant Catholic assault upon the Lower Canadian reserves. In the Upper province the Catholics actually benefited from the reserves funds after 1840.

By the end of the eighteenth century, Quebec Catholicism was peculiarly 'ultramontane'. The conquest, and separation from France, had protected the Church from the revolutionary upheaval, and under British sovereignty the clergy even extended their control over the laity. At the same time the tradition of

[1] J. S. Moir, *op. cit.* p. 191, Appendix VI.

intimate church and state connexion was weakened by the imposition of a Protestant state power.[1] As an addition to their other
advantages the Catholics also got some direct state aid. During
the War of 1812 Bishop Plessis had secured a grant of £1,000 a
year from a government anxious to retain French-Canadian loyalty
during the struggle with the southern republicans. He also acquired
the right to sit in the legislative council, and to use his title of
Bishop *of* Quebec without fear of prosecution.

As a counterbalance to Lower Canadian Catholicism, on the
other hand, the British administrators sought to strengthen Protestantism. In 1763, and again 1775, the Governors were directed
to establish the Church of England by law. No legislative enactment ever confirmed establishment, but official correspondence
always referred to the Church of England as 'the established
church' in Quebec. The clergy reserves formed an endowment
after 1791, and there were also direct payments from the state for
the maintenance of the Church. As in Upper Canada, funds came
additionally from S.P.G. To head this rather ill-defined state
church, Jacob Mountain was named by the Crown as Bishop of
Quebec in 1793, and provided with a stipend and a cathedral
church at the expense of the public. But the supremacy of Catholicism made the prospects bleak for a Protestant establishment
from the start: by the 1830s it was clear that the Church of
England, which was by then itself largely existing on the voluntary
system, was merely one among the minority of Protestant denominations competing without much prospect of enlargement in a
predominantly Catholic inheritance.[2] The Church of Scotland, as in
Upper Canada, claimed its rights as an imperial co-establishment.[3]
From 1793 state grants were given towards the maintenance of its
ministers in Quebec and Montreal cities, and, though small compared with the size of allowances to the Church of England, they
were at least an official recognition that exclusive support for only

[1] Mack Eastman, *Church and State in Early Canada* (Edinburgh, 1915), p. 265.
[2] H. H. Walsh, *The Christian Church in Canada* (Toronto, 1956), p. 148.
[3] See N. S. Reid, *The Church of Scotland in Lower Canada; its struggle for Establishment* (Toronto, 1936), which contains an account of these endeavours.

one Protestant Church was impossible in the face of existing conditions. Concurrent endowment, as in Upper Canada, was an easy solution to the facts of religious pluralism. After the concessions to the Catholics, it was difficult to see how the conscience of the state could be more gravely violated by endowing Presbyterianism too. In Britain the Imperial Parliament was supporting Irish Catholicism (the Maynooth grant), Scottish Presbyterian and the Church of England at the same time. In Lower Canada a Bill declaring the Church of Scotland an established church, actually passed by the assembly in 1804, was thrown out by the executive council.[1]

The Quebec clergy reserves were incorporated in 1816. Though not a striking cause of dispute, they were still evident enough to provide material for disestablishmentarianism excited by the voluntaryist denominations. In 1838 the Baptists tried to get them secularized by legislation. Rancorous feelings were lamented at the time and correctly attributed to the effects of religious pluralism, 'marked often', as Bishop George Mountain noticed in 1843, 'by a mutual jealousy, heightened, where the Church is the object of it, to an acrimonious and unscrupulous hostility'.[2] There were, at that time, some sixty Church of England clergymen in the diocese.[3] If the main agitation against the reserves was left to the Upper Canadians, the campaign for equal marriage rights with the Churches of England and Rome was strongly engaged in Quebec. This was accomplished for all dissenting groups by the end of the 1830s.

Although the hesitant attempts to establish the Church of England in Lower Canada were abandoned according to a scale determined by the defeats of the Church in the upper province, the privileged position of the Catholics survived. A careful educational compromise—the reservation of policy to the provincial governments—was worked out before the Confederation of 1867

---

[1] W. H. Elgee, *op. cit.* p. 17.
[2] *A Journal of Visitation to a part of the Diocese of Quebec by the Lord Bishop of Montreal in the spring of 1843. The Church in Canada, no. II* (published for S.P.G.) (third edition, London, 1846), p. 18.
[3] *Ibid.* p. iv.

in order to satisfy the demands for state support of Catholic schools in Quebec. As Pfeffer has remarked of the present position, 'the political authority of the Catholic hierarchy, the entrenched position of their schools in the public educational system, the subsidies that church welfare enterprises receive from the provincial treasury, amount to many aspects of a state church, though establishment in the literal sense is absent'.[1] In most districts it is still necessary for government permits to be issued before public religious worship may be conducted.[2] This in a sense results from a cultural situation comparable to the 'Protestantism' of the United States. As Marcel de Grandpré has noticed: 'Quebec governments have gladly proclaimed themselves to be Catholic in spite of the wording of the Constitution that assigns to them a more impartial rôle.'[3]

Conflict between church and dissent in the Maritime Provinces, and claims to religious equality, centred much more in controversy over public educational policy. Here there were clergy reserves which ante-dated those of the Canadas, and therefore a burning reminder of the supremacy of the state church; but it was over other issues that the great clashes occurred. Religious pluralism in the Maritimes had been reinforced at the end of the eighteenth century by the arrival of the loyalist exiles (many of whom, from the Congregationalist New England colonies immediately to the south, were not Episcopalians), and by the preaching of Henry Alline and the Newlight Revival. The latter stimulated new sectarianism and added to the religious diversity. Newlightism itself avoided the question of establishments, but it wrecked one body which had stood by the union of church and state. The Nova Scotian Congregationalists were of New England parentage and had remained loyal to the concept of state confessionalism. During the revival the Congregationalist churches were sharply divided, and a majority were finally absorbed into the Baptist Church.

[1] Leo Pfeffer, *Church, State and Freedom* (Boston, 1953), p. 42.
[2] *Ibid.* p. 43.
[3] 'Traditions of the Catholic Church in French Canada', in *The Churches and the Canadian Experience*, edited by J. W. Grant (Toronto, 1963), p. 12.

The separation of church and state

Voluntaryism spread among the new adherents, and they rapidly assimilated all the traditional hostility of the Baptists to the establishment principle. The Church of England was itself weakened in public esteem by its clear detestation of the revival. In 1799 Charles Inglis—who had twelve years previously been appointed by the Crown as Bishop of Nova Scotia, and so became the first colonial prelate in the empire—attacked the Newlight movement and condemned its leaders for being 'engaged in a general plan of total revolution in religion and civil government'.[1] There was, it is true, a certain affinity with American social ideals in the movement, but the accusation, like that later made against the Methodists of Upper Canada by Strachan, was largely inspired by incomprehension: the Newlight movement was really a-political. But increased definition between the denominations was certainly a result of its influence.

The Church of England had been established in Nova Scotia by an Act of its first provincial assembly in 1758. This declared 'that the sacred rites and ceremonies of divine worship according to the liturgy of the Church established by the laws of England shall be deemed the fixed form of worship among us'.[2] Religious freedom was granted to all other Protestant groups, but Catholic priests were expelled. In 1783 the priests were tolerated by statutory provision—a necessary removal of an anomaly, for the government was already paying a stipend to the Abbé Maillard for his missions among the Micmac Indians and the surviving Acadians. New Brunswick recognized the Church of England as the legal establishment in 1786, and Prince Edward Island followed in 1803. State support of the Church was generous. Land was granted for the building of places of worship. In some places the vestries were empowered to levy church rates, as at Halifax, N.S., where a stipend for the bishop was also furnished from the public funds. Glebes were granted to clergymen in each parish, though members

[1] H. H. Walsh, *op. cit.* p. 122.
[2] T. R. Milman, 'Tradition of the Anglican Church in Canada', in *The Churches and the Canadian Experience*, edited by J. W. Grant (Toronto, 1963), p. 16.

of the Church were themselves reluctant to sanction the attempt to introduce tithes.[1] In Prince Edward Island, 130 acres of land were reserved in each township for the state church, and church rates were collected. The Church of Scotland tried, as in the Canadas, to secure a position of co-establishment, and in Prince Edward Island a double-establishment actually existed early in the nineteenth century. Between 1810 and 1835 St Paul's Church at Charlottetown, established and maintained out of the public revenues, was used by both the Presbyterians and the Church of England.[2] The Church in the Maritimes enjoyed a high degree of government protection. In the 1790s the Methodists were subjected to rigorous interference, amounting at times in New Brunswick almost to persecution.

Yet it was not, as in Upper Canada, the Methodists who led the dissenters in the agitation of grievances against the establishment. Like the Baptists they were weak and divided, split between American and British affiliations. Many of the Wesleyans, loyal to current British practice, stood by the maintenance of the state church. In 1825 they refused to join with other dissenters in the formation of a Nova Scotian committee for the protection of religious rights—'as we entertain', they declared, 'a sincere esteem for the venerable Establishment of our country and believe that we are called to promote real religion and not mere political views'.[3] Opposition to the claims of the church establishment was led by a majority of the Presbyterians. Historically associated with Congregationalism in the Maritimes, large numbers of Presbyterians were quick to abandon their Scottish inheritance of state confessionalism when the Congregational churches disintegrated under the pressure of the Newlight revival, and adopt voluntaryist positions similar to those of the Congregationalists in Upper Canada. The adjustment was not without its pains. There were divisions in the Presbyterian body; some remained loyal to the

[1] W. H. Elgee, *op. cit.* p. 117.
[2] A. W. Warburton, *A History of Prince Edward Island* (St John, 1923), p. 390.
[3] Quoted in Goldwin French, *Parsons and Politics* (Toronto, 1962), p. 62.

formal teachings of the Church of Scotland and the Westminster Confession on the duties of the civil magistrate in religion. These men worked for the attainment of equality with the established church, and a share in the national religious endowments: they were opposed to any reform which presupposed its overthrow.

From the earliest days of the establishments in the Maritimes there were dissenting objections, even though in Nova Scotia, where the government was prepared to concede a practical concurrent endowment, the Presbyterians, Congregationalists and Lutherans had accepted state aid for the payment of their clergy. In the 1750s, however, when an attempt was made in the Nova Scotian assembly to introduce the full English parochial system, with church vestries collecting taxes and administering poor relief, opposition came from those dissenters in the legislature who would rather have had the New England system, based on the town-meeting, than submit to a tacit acceptance of the establishment's social rôle.[1] This early opposition was partially successful. By the end of the century dissenting militancy had moved to still greater confidence—now stirred to enhanced conviction and sharpened in evangelical zeal by the Newlight revival. The leading grievance was the Church's monopoly of the right to perform marriages, and the privileged civil status given to the state clergy by keeping the registers. In 1761 civil registers were authorized in Nova Scotia in those places where no parish machinery had been provided. This, however, was a reflexion of the small numbers of Church of England ministers in the province, rather than a victory for dissenting pressures. Representatives of the Nova Scotian Presbyterian, Methodist and Baptist Churches decided in 1789 to organize a campaign for religious equality: for the right to perform marriages, for legal securities for their property-holdings, and for a share in the state educational funds—then exclusively in the hands of the establishment. They enjoyed some success in 1795, when the executive was authorized to allow dissenting ministers to conduct marriages in those places where there was no Church of

[1] H. H. Walsh, *The Christian Church in Canada* (Toronto, 1956), p. 94.

England clergyman. In 1830 they were given this right without qualification.[1] The same right was achieved in the other two provinces through a similar series of stages, as the bulwarks of the establishment were penetrated by piecemeal reform. In 1849, when the Free Baptists of New Brunswick were allowed to perform marriages, the process was complete. Other reforms which broke down the legal protection of the establishment also came in series. During the first quarter of the nineteenth century, religious tests for office were removed from the various statute books, and it was only in the educational field that the conflict of church and dissent, occurring around the principles of establishment and concurrent endowment, remained fiercely engaged.[2] The campaign against the test acts in Nova Scotia was led by Haliburton and Uniacke, both of whom were members of the established church. Their attitude compares with that of the Virginian churchmen who had carried through disestablishment forty years before, convinced that religious belief was best served by accepting the facts of religious pluralism in society.

It was in these various ways that the provinces of British North America laid aside the establishment principle. A process of redefinition in the relations of church and state had achieved practical separation before the birth of modern Canada in the confederation of 1867. The rise of religious pluralism had frustrated the government's endeavour to duplicate British religious institutions overseas. It had been frustrated, too, by the rise of religious pluralism at home, for in Britain itself dissenters and radicals had allied to scrutinize the state support of colonial churches, and had demanded the end of overseas establishments. By 1867 a satisfactory solution had worked itself out in the North American provinces, and there was no need for any definition of the relations of church and state in the British North America Act. This had been achieved without any real borrowing from the experience of the United States. It was, on the contrary, an expression of dissenting and radical forces similar, but more advanced and more numerous, to

---

[1] W. H. Elgee, *op. cit.* p. 41.   [2] See chapter 4.

those arising in British politics during the first half of the nineteenth century. With westward expansion into the prairies and along the Pacific coast, the voluntary system prevailed from the beginning. Apart from government aid for Indian missions, and the (rather haphazard) provision of chaplains by the Hudson's Bay Company, the Church of England's expansion to the west was paid for entirely by the eastern dioceses and by missionary societies like the Church Missionary Society. There were one or two minor exceptions: in 1859 a church and rectory were built near Fort Langley with public funds, in an attempt to bring religion to the lawless followers of the Cariboo gold rush.[1] The Crown continued for a time to retain control of appointments—nominating the first Bishop of Vancouver Island and British Columbia when the territory became a Crown colony in 1858. But as the Canadian Church, disestablished in fact if not in theory, evolved an autonomous organization and discipline of its own, this vestige of state confessionalism lapsed as well.

[1] Philip Carrington, *The Anglican Church in Canada* (Toronto, 1963), p. 122.

3

THE EFFECTS OF SEPARATION ON STATE AND CHURCH

I. SURVIVALS OF STATE CONFESSIONALISM

When Gladstone realized that the old theoretical justifications for the union of church and state were being removed in Britain—during the Maynooth grant crisis in 1845—he had the perspicacity to recognize the implications. 'The State cannot be said now to have a conscience', he wrote to Newman; 'but the State still continues to act in many ways *as if* it had a conscience.'[1] This assessment equally applies as a description of the American republic after the separation of church and state. Many survivals of state religious confessionalism endured throughout the nineteenth century and some have remained to the present day. In his remarks to the United States Supreme Court on the Regents' prayer case[2] in 1962, Mr Justice Douglas referred to American government, at both federal and state levels, as 'presently honeycombed' with public aids to religion.[3] The remains relate a great deal about Americans' views on the nature of their society. For in the nineteenth century, and at the present time, most citizens identified the nation as corporately religious. In the last century the identification was distinctly Christian—indeed, nativism and allied anti-Catholicism did nothing but stimulate the popular notion, of which they were both an effect and a cause, that the American nation was inherently Protestant. The strength of this popular belief, which also characterized Canadian and English society, ex-

---

[1] *Correspondence on Church and Religion of William Ewart Gladstone*, edited by D. C. Lathbury (London, 1910), I, 72.
[2] See chapter 4, section 1.
[3] John J. McGrath, *Church and State in American Law, Cases and Materials* (Milwaukee, 1962), p. 403.

plains the rather anomalous survivals of state confessionalism despite the formal separations of church and state in America. Robert Baird noticed this continuing association of church and state, in 1844, though it was, he wrote, 'wholly of a moral nature'.[1] And with equal truth he observed that 'among our American population the sentiment is well-nigh universal, that Christian institutions—the Church, the Sabbath, the School—are indispensable for our temporal and material, as well as our spiritual and eternal well-being'.[2]

Early nineteenth-century evangelicalism, accepting the separation of church and state in America, popularized a dualistic interpretation of the political order. 'God's government', expressed in the divine laws and revealed through Scripture, provided the conditions within which secular politics held their court.[3] Since the laws of God were readily vouchsafed to the inquiring conscience, it followed that the secular area of politics must be clearly circumscribed, and in reality only concerned the adjustment of overlapping claims in society. This view coincided with the natural harmony of interests preached by political economy, and with the popular libertarian argument that the best government is that which has least to do. As Christian men knew all about the religious moralism which alone could establish a proper adjudication over questions affecting society, Christian precepts must apply to political issues, to retain them within the overruling bounds of 'God's government'. Popular evangelicalism was therefore a force making for a close identification between American political experience and religious conviction.

In 1864 a Presbyterian minister, the Reverend B. F. Morris, published a monumental, if now forgotten work, entitled *Christian Life and Character of the Civil Institutions of the United States*. There were some wild exaggerations of the real implications of the instances of state support for religion which he described. But he had

[1] Robert Baird, *Religion in America* (revised edition, New York, 1856), p. 662.
[2] *Ibid.* p. 658.
[3] C. I. Foster, *An Errand of Mercy, The Evangelical United Front, 1790–1837* (University of North Carolina Press, 1960), pp. 55–6, 185.

hit on one great truth: that surviving legal safeguards for beliefs and practices had imparted to national non-sectarian Christianity a quasi-establishment. In 1854, for example, federal appointment of Christian chaplains in the army and navy was upheld by a Congressional Committee against the protests of strict separationists—but *not* with the argument that the practice protected the constitutional right of the enlisted men to freedom of worship. 'Any attempt to level and discard all religion would have been viewed with universal indignation', was how Meacham explained the committee's interpretation of the separation of church and state: 'The object was not to substitute Judaism, or Mohammedanism, or infidelity, but to prevent rivalry among sects to the exclusion of others.'[1] State appointment of chaplains was therefore to be supported because it corresponded to the real desire which existed for official links between the state and non-sectarian Christianity. Christianity, Morris remarked, was 'the religion of the people—the national religion'.[2] This belief was popularly echoed. In upholding a Sunday observance law in 1861, Judge Allen of the New York Supreme Court ruled that 'Christianity is part of the common law of this State, in the qualified sense that it is entitled to respect and protection as the acknowledged religion of the people.'[3] It is not, therefore, surprising that in 1851 John Hinton should have reported that 'politically speaking the United States count themselves a Christian nation; and the courts maintain that Christianity is part and parcel of the law of the land';[4] or that in 1839 Henry Caswall, an English immigrant, should have declared the paradox that 'the great mass of the Americans themselves are not aware of the extent to which Christianity, at least in theory is acknowledged by their own government'.[5] It

---

[1] B. F. Morris, *Christian Life and Character of the Civil Institutions of the United States, Developed in the Official and Historical Annals of the Republic* (Philadelphia, 1864), p. 321.
[2] *Ibid.* p. 25.
[3] *Ibid.* p. 659.
[4] J. H. Hinton, *The Test of Experience; or the Voluntary Principle in the United States* (London, 1851), p. 37.
[5] Henry Caswall, *America and the American Church* (London, 1839), p. 63.

is also hardly surprising, in view of the truth of this observation, that historical interpretation should have tended to exaggerate the degree of uniqueness and completeness in the American experience of the separation of church and state.

A substantial majority of nineteenth-century opinion, indeed, went considerably beyond Baird's belief that the relations between Christianity and public life were 'wholly of a moral nature'. In 1872 a convention of evangelicals meeting in Cincinnati launched the National Reform Movement. It had clearly defined aims:

The object of this Society shall be to maintain existing Christian features in the American government, and to secure such an amendment to the Constitution of the United States as will indicate that this is a Christian nation, and will place all the Christian laws, institutions and usages of our government on an undeniable legal basis in the fundamental law of the land.[1]

The Movement, and its journal, suggestively called *The Christian Statesman*, attracted a wide following before it merged eventually into the general Sunday observance agitation. The idea of constitutional amendment to secure the clear legality of state diffusion of broadly-established religious precepts was proposed as recently as 1962—in this instance over the question of religion in the public schools, and by those opposed to the Supreme Court's ruling in the Regents' prayer case.[2]

The widespread religiosity of contemporary America, whatever its quality otherwise, certainly assumes a national acknowledgment of God as essentially relevant to national identity. Its most extreme expression, though this is somewhat ludicrous, is surely realized in the 'Liberal Church'—a sect which has actually incorporated the American Constitution as its creed.[3] More typical, and en-

[1] A. H. Lewis, *A Critical History of the Sabbath and the Sunday in the Christian Church* (The American Sabbath Tract Society) (New York, 1886), p. 459.
[2] See Philip B. Kurland, 'The School Prayer Cases', in *The Wall between Church and State*, edited by D. H. Oaks (Chicago, 1963), pp. 143 ff., where there is a discussion of the reactions to the case.
[3] Elmer T. Clark, *The Small Sects in America* (revised edition, New York, 1959), p 16.

joying greater currency, was the recent declaration of the Florida Supreme Court that 'the concept of God has been and is so interwoven into every aspect of American institutions that to attack this concept is to threaten the very fibre of our existence as a nation'.[1] Anti-Communist and other loyalty oaths used in contemporary America assume the validity of this sort of national ideology. It is, on the other hand, likely that the present series of legal test cases will shortly clear the vestigial remnants of state confessionalism, whatever their popular acceptance, from the statute books. In 1854, when Philip Schaff noticed how incomplete the separation of church and state had actually been in America—'on account of the influence of Christianity on the popular mind'— he went on to add that it was 'even quite possible that the two powers may still come into collision'.[2] Court rulings in recent years have fully sustained the reliability of his vision.[3]

The surviving materials of state confessionalism were of many textures. Although there was no religious reference in the federal instrument,[4] the new state constitutions, and all those which came to be written with the nineteenth- and twentieth-century expansion of the Union, contained references to the providence or blessing of God or Christ. Only Michigan and West Virginia did not.[5] These pieties have remained to the present time. And although every constitution guaranteed religious liberty, only Virginia and Rhode Island, out of the founding States, omitted to provide confessional tests for office-holders. These were varied: New Hampshire, Connecticut, New Jersey, and the Carolinas required Protestantism. Pennsylvania insisted on assent to the Divine inspiration of the Scriptures, to belief in heaven and hell, and to monotheism. Delaware required Divine inspiration and

---

[1] W. L. Miller, 'Religion and Americanism', in *A Journal of Church and State* v, no. 1 (1963), p. 25.
[2] Philip Schaff, *America, A Sketch of the Political, Social and Religious Character of the United States of America* (New York, 1855), p. 92.
[3] See chapter 4, section 1.
[4] Except the words of dating, 'Done in the year of Our Lord'.
[5] S. H. Cobb, *The Rise of Religious Liberty in America* (New York, 1902), p. 518.

the Trinity. South Carolina expected its responsible citizens to subscribe to Divine inspiration, heaven and hell and monotheism. Maryland asked only a declaration of Christianity.[1] These restrictions were gradually removed during the nineteenth century, though in some cases imperfectly. Catholic emancipation came slowly. Disqualification from office was removed for Catholics in New York during 1806, in Connecticut and Massachussetts when disestablishment was accomplished—in 1818 and 1833 respectively—in North Carolina in 1835 and New Jersey in 1844.[2] In New Hampshire there were still restrictions against Catholics until 1852. The admission of Jews to office, and later of freethinkers, was more delayed but followed a similar course. In some cases it is still only a matter of practice, not of law: the New Hampshire constitution still technically restricts legal protection to 'every denomination of *Christian*'.[3] And by 1864 Morris could write that 'an examination of the present Constitutions of the various States, now existing, will show that the Christian religion and its institutions are recognized as the religion of the Government and the nation'.[4] Non-sectarian, but Christian, confessionalism, that is to say, had replaced the old exclusive tests, but it was not until the present century in many cases that anomalous restrictions on non-Christians and atheists were tackled. Some still remain. Not until 1961 was a Maryland law requiring belief in God as a condition for certain offices struck down after being ruled unconstitutional by the Supreme Court.[5]

Tax exemption for church property and some of the expenses

---

[1] E. F. Humphrey, *Nationalism and Religion in America, 1774–89* (Boston, 1924), p. 499. See also, B. F. Morris, *op. cit.* p. 229.

[2] P. J. Dignan, *A History of the Legal Incorporation of Catholic Church Property in the United States* (1784–1932) (New York, 1935), p. 44.

[3] Amended Constitution of 1902, First Part, Article 6; printed in F. N. Thorpe, *The Federal and State Constitutions of the United States* (Washington, 1909), IV, 2495.

[4] B. F. Morris, *op. cit.* p. 237.

[5] *Torcaso* v. *Watkins;* see J. J. McGrath, *op. cit.* p. 351. The case arose out of an action brought against the state officials of Maryland by a Notary Public who had been refused a commission because he declined to declare his belief in God.

incurred in the exercise of religion is provided both federally and by the states It is one of the most obvious modern connexions of religion and government. Begun originally in the colonial era, state exemptions from taxation for property in religious use were incorporated into the new legal codes after independence, and have been 'most often cited to support the position that the Constitution does not require the absolute separation of church and state, nor bar preferential aid to religion'.[1] There is a good deal of variation in the degrees of exemption among the practices of the states. Nowhere are taxes levied on land which actually has a place of worship built on it, and in many states the exemption extends to the house of the minister, other property in religious use, and to church schools and colleges. In some states a maximum valuation is prescribed for exemption; in some also there are stipulations requiring tax-free property to be entirely devoted to religious uses. At the federal level, religion is indirectly aided by regulations which allow income-tax payers to claim deductions for religious contributions they have made, as well as for other forms of charitable donation and gift. These exemptions were sanctioned in the Revenue Act of 1916.

Tax exemptions have been defended on the ground that they are not a direct aid to religious belief, but to welfare—that the churches provide social benefits which represent a saving to the general tax-payer where otherwise the state would be forced to provide services of its own. This argument had applied especially to church-related schools, hospitals and refuges for the destitute. In test cases, the courts have upheld this view,[2] and there is at present no popular objection to the practice or any significant attempt to repeal the laws protecting it.[3] There seems, however, to be a growing feeling among religious leaders that the churches ought to surrender the privilege of tax exemption voluntarily. Perhaps a middle course may be followed, for there is clearly a

[1] Leo Pfeffer, *Church, State and Freedom* (Boston, 1953), p. 184.
[2] Paul G. Kauper, 'Tax Exemptions for Religious Activities', in *The Wall between Church and State*, edited by D. H. Oaks (Chicago, 1963), p. 108.
[3] *Ibid.* Introduction (by Dallin H. Oaks), p. 10.

distinction between the welfare agencies of the churches, which could retain exemption, and the actual places of worship, which could surrender it.[1] This would considerably lessen the existing implied connexion of church and state, if such a connexion is to be thought either undesirable or unconstitutional.

Survivals of confessionalism are also clearly evident in state laws against blasphemy and in support of Sabbath observance. The former are really anachronistic, and are almost entirely in abeyance. They too, like tax exemptions, are a legacy from the colonial codes, and were quite unexceptionably carried into the statute books of the new states. Early test cases established their validity. In 1811, for example, in the case of *People* v. *Ruggles*, the New York Supreme Court ruled that blasphemy was a civil offence. On that occasion Judge Kent declared that 'blasphemy against God, and contumelious reproaches and profane ridicule of Christ or the Holy Scriptures, which are equally treated as blasphemy, are offences punishable at common law, whether uttered by words or writings'.[2] Since the state constitution also made reference to God, this position was doubly fortified. In every state, indeed, colonial statutes against blasphemy were upheld in the courts. Thus in 1824 the Pennsylvania Supreme Court accepted the validity of an Act of 1700.[3] The celebrated prosecution of Abner Kneeland, a Massachussetts freethinker, kept the laws current during the 1830s. There have been prosecutions even in the present century. In 1928 an atheist propagandist was convicted for 'ridiculing the Christian religion' in Arkansas.[4] At the present time there are fourteen states which have retained anti-blasphemy laws on their statute-books, although it is likely that as test-cases are brought against them they will be progressively repealed. British laws against blasphemy also remained unchanged during the nineteenth century, but they are scarcely evidence of any

[1] P. G. Kauper, *op. cit.* p. 113.
[2] B. F. Morris, *Christian Life and Character of the Civil Institutions of the United States* (Philadelphia, 1864), p. 655.
[3] *Ibid.* p. 647.
[4] Leo Pfeffer, *op. cit.* p. 543.

stronger survival of confessionalism. In the case of the *Crown* v. *Ramsey and Foot*, (1882), the Court of Queen's Bench ruled that the laws were not a protection of the Christian religion: they were to prevent a breach of the peace. Even the most fundamental tenets of Christianity could be attacked, provided that no public disturbance resulted. There have been no prosecutions during the present century in Britain, though blasphemy continues to be a common law crime.

Similarly a survival, but more relevant in practice, are the American state codes enforcing Sunday observance—popularly referred to as the 'blue laws'. They have been maintained with arguments comparable to the welfare criteria applied in support of school-bus transportation for parochial schoolchildren, or tax-exemption for religious property. There have been, in this sense, recent defences of existing laws on the secular ground that a day of rest is healthy and therefore beneficial to the people. But it is, of course, the selection of the Christian Sabbath for that day which must add conviction to the view that Sunday observance laws form a connexion of church and state. This was certainly their original purpose. In the 1840s Robert Baird, remarking on the universal practice of the American states in enforcing Sunday observance, both upheld the separation of church and state and also explained that the laws were maintained 'on the avowed principle that we are a Christian nation'.[1] In the mid-century, in fact, the churches were considerably disturbed by a prevailing shortage of respect for Sunday observance, especially evident on the frontier. Evangelical groups formed numerous Sabbatarian committees and societies in an attempt to persuade back-sliding citizens. Their enthusiasm usually resorted to coercion, and demands were freely made that the states should enforce their existing laws and even frame new ones. Railway and steamship companies were closed on Sundays, and in many places, especially in New England, the mails were not handled on that day. Theatrical pro-

[1] Robert Baird, *The Progress and Prospects of Christianity in the United States of America* (London, 1851 edition), p. 28.

83

ductions were also prohibited: in 1861 there was something of a test-case when the New York Supreme Court, in *Lindenmuller* v. *the People*, upheld a law against dramatic representations on Sundays passed in the previous year.[1] The zeal of the evangelical societies, with their reliance on the coercive jurisdiction of the state, provoked reactions from those small and unpopular minorities who urged a strict separation of church and state. In 1848, when an anti-Sabbath convention was held in Boston, a resolution was passed which summarized their position. It is the position which has in recent years been given general application by the decisions of the Supreme Court.

Resolved, That the penal enactments of the State legislature, compelling the observance of the first day of the week as the Sabbath, are despotic, unconstitutional and ought to be immediately abrogated, and that the interference of the State, in matters of religious faith and ceremonies, is a usurpation which cannot be justified.[2]

English Sunday observance laws remained substantially unaltered during the nineteenth century, and were, as in America, usually enforced. During the present century there have been a series of modifications which have allowed a greater degree of Sunday trading and a larger volume of public entertainment. This also parallels the twentieth-century experience of most American states —those with a more conservative attitude to change have their counterpart in Scotland.

National and official symbols and observances have also continued to recognize religious beliefs. Feasts and fast days proclaimed by Congress during the nineteenth century mentioned the sanction of 'Divine Providence', and numerous 'days of thanksgiving' proclaimed by the individual states had religious justifications appended. At the present time coins and currency notes bear the legend 'In God we Trust'. Public buildings are closed on Sundays and the greater Christian festivals: at Christmas

[1] B. F. Morris, *op. cit.* p. 659.
[2] A. H. Lewis, *A Critical History of the Sabbath and the Sunday in the Christian Church* (New York, 1886), p. 497.

time a crèche is a familiar sight on public property. Federal franchise permits have come to require the allotment of religious space on the broadcasting networks.[1] The pledge of allegiance mentions the name of God. Chaplains for the leading religious denominations, Christian and Jewish, are provided by state governments for pastoral work in prisons. Congress also pays military chaplains, and originally even stipulated the number of services they were to hold for their charges.[2] Oaths prescribed by Congress include the invocation 'So Help me God', and Congress appoints chaplains, representative of the larger denominations, to say daily prayers. The Supreme Court, whose deliberations have in recent years done so much to define the strict neutrality of the state, itself opens each session with the prayer, 'God save the United States and this Honorable Court'.

There are also many examples of indirect state aid to religious belief. Federal financing of Indian missions conducted by denominational agencies was a clear instance during the nineteenth century.[3] In contemporary America it is in the field of public education that most interest is centred: on state provision of bus transportation, meals, and textbooks for the denominational schoolchildren of many states, and on the allowance of time for Bible-reading and non-sectarian prayers in public schools. Since these all form an important series of aids, provided by state governments, and since they are being so steadfastly and on the whole successfully resisted by exponents of complete separation of church and state, they are treated in a separate chapter.[4] The provision of public education in a populous nation required the creation of state machinery. In America this occurred during the middle and later years of the nineteenth century, when people were satisfied that non-sectarian Christian instruction in the schools fulfilled the re-

[1] Philip Wogaman, 'The Changing Role of Government and the Myth of Separation', in *A Journal of Church and State*, v, no. 1 (1963), p. 72.
[2] Henry Caswall, *America and the American Church* (London, 1839), p. 60.
[3] See chapter 4, section 1; and also R. Pierce Beaver, 'Church, State and the Indians: Indian missions in the New Nation', in *A Journal of Church and State* (May, 1962), p. 11.　　　　[4] See chapter 4, section 1.

quirements imposed by the formal separation of church and state. But this did mean that the real problems of secularism in the schools—faced and solved in Britain by compromise during the same period—were postponed in the United States until the present century.

Some instances of indirect aid to religion are the results of other aspects of state collectivism. Thus welfare institutions conducted by the churches not only receive tax-exemption but actual grants of public funds on the principle that they perform a service which the state would otherwise have to duplicate. As early as 1899, in *Bradfield* v. *Roberts*, the United States Supreme Court upheld such grants when applied to hospitals run by religious bodies.[1] Federal loans have been provided to assist in religious projects conducted by private universities, and scholarships and fellowships, with public money, have been given for study in theological seminaries.[2] Most of the states have passed statutes to protect the religion of children in adoptions: these 'religious protection' laws constitute a connexion between the state and the personal choice of religious affiliation.[3] A similar protection of religious opinion is involved in the right of conscientious exemption from military service: it is only granted on religious grounds.[4] This, of course, has been a considerable relief to Quakers and Mennonites. The principle was first embodied in the federal Militia Act of 1792, and maintained in amendments of 1903 and 1916. There are comparable British protections to religious belief in both military exemption and child adoption procedures.

Not all continuing state connexion with religious opinion has been in the form of aid, however. The 'free exercise' of religion guaranteed in the First Amendment of the Constitution has not inhibited the courts from intervening in those instances where

[1] J. J. McGrath, *op. cit.* p. 93.
[2] Robert M. Hutchins, 'The Future of the Wall', in *The Wall between Church and State*, edited by D. H. Oaks (Chicago, 1963), p. 21.
[3] See Monrad G. Paulsen, 'Constitutional Problems of Utilizing a Religious Factor in Adoptions and Placements of Children', *ibid.* p. 117.
[4] See E. B. Greene, *Religion and the State* (New York, 1959 edition), p. 137 ff.

Survivals of state confessionalism

what Mill would have called the other-regarding acts of religious communities were believed to be in conflict with the general good. The famous Mormon cases of the later nineteenth century are the most obvious examples. The Church of the Latter-Day Saints was scarcely popular anyway. Robert Baird described it as 'one of the silliest and basest of all delusions that arch-villainy ever attempted to propagate'.[1] Congress had made bigamy a federal offence in an attempt to deter the Mormons from the practice of plural marriage which, they asserted, was part of their religious observance. In the leading cases before the Supreme Court— *Reynolds* v. *United States* (1878), and *Davis* v. *Beason*, (1890)— polygamy was declared unconstitutional. The Court ruled that the Mormons might believe whatever they pleased: that was a constitutional freedom. But it also restricted their right to practice their beliefs in the United States.[2] In 1890 the Court upheld a Congressional Act of 1887 which provided for the seizure of Mormon property should the practice of polygamy continue.[3] Subsequent to this, the Mormons in fact gave up the offending practice, and the only surviving traces of the conflict are embodied in the state constitutions of Utah, Idaho and Oklahoma, which explicitly outlaw polygamy. More recently, some states have legislated against the ritual handling of poisonous snakes—a practice reminiscent of medieval trial by ordeal which is found among several small religious cults in the south. In a Tennessee test-case of 1948, *Harden* v. *State*, the court, in a sort of appeal to the real will of the defendants, declared that the state must protect its citizens' life and health in disregard of their religious beliefs.[4] Christian Scientists and Jehova's Witnesses will increasingly encounter similar difficulties.

[1] *The Progress and Prospects of Christianity in the United States of America* (London, 1851 edition), p.29.
[2] Joseph Tussman, *The Supreme Court on Church and State* (New York, 1962), p. 20 ff.
[3] *The Late Corporation of the Church of Jesus Christ of the Latter-Day Saints* v. *United States*; J. Tussman, *op. cit.* p. 33.
[4] J. J. McGrath, *op. cit.* p. 323.

Effects of separation on state and church

Since the Canadian separation of church and state occurred simply by the piecemeal removal of the exclusive rights and endowments of the establishment, and not by a general legislative enactment or constitutional amendment, the sort of crucial tests for state religious neutrality typical of the United States have been lacking there. Canadian vestiges of state confessionalism are more closely allied to the British ones: both have been the result of compromises which stopped at a rather greater distance from full neutrality than the United States. There are more traces of confessionalism in the educational field, and these will be considered separately.[1] As in the United States and Britain, legislation against blasphemy and in support of Sunday observance are still on the provincial statute-books of Canada. It is true that during the 1850s, popular petitions for legislative closure of railways, canals and postal services on Sundays were rejected by the assembly of the united provinces of Upper and Lower Canada on the principle that concession of the demands would violate the separation of church and state.[2] But other restrictions on labour and entertainment on the Christian Sabbath were maintained and enforced, closely protected by strong Sabbatarian organizations which were themselves inspired by contemporaneous British and American movements.[3] In Ontario particularly, this vigilance has continued, and the province's modern Sunday Observance laws, whose liquor licensing clauses amount to a limited prohibition, are staunchly upheld by rural voters. The French-Canadians, on the other hand, have never shown much concern with either Sabbatarianism or heavily restrictive liquor licensing.

The Canadian government, like the British and American, continues to pay the stipends of military chaplains. In Canada the government, in appointing chaplains, actually accepts the recommendations of a religious agency—the Committee on Chaplains' Services of the Canadian Council of Churches. This inter-

[1] See chapter 4, section 2.
[2] J. S. Moir, *Church and State in Canada West* (Toronto, 1959), p. 25.
[3] W. H. Elgee, *The Social Teachings of the Canadian Churches* (Toronto, 1963), pp. 209–11.

denominational body nominates the Protestant chaplains.[1] There are also Catholic and Jewish chaplains. Tax-exemption for church property is provided by the provincial governments, and there is income-tax relief on expenses incurred through religious activity. Even the costs of spiritual healing for Christian Scientists are accepted as legitimate tax relief claims. Indian missions conducted by denominational bodies receive public financial aid; so do hospitals and welfare services under church control. The Canadian Broadcasting Corporation—a Crown corporation—provides space for religious programmes, although no actual statutory provision is made for this, as it is in the British Independent Television Act and the charter of the B.B.C. Even the fate of the Mormons has shown that the Canadian government too, in certain circumstances, imposes restrictions on religious liberty. In 1887 a company of Mormons left Salt Lake City to settle in the northern wilderness which was soon to become the Canadian province of Alberta. The issue of plural marriage was at once agitated in the press, with the result that in 1891 Canadian legislation against polygamy was passed.[2] Canadian official life today continues to be redolent of Christianity, with public buildings closed on the major church festivals, and with many national symbols of allegiance to divine providence. The Queen of Canada is required by law to be a member of the Church of England, for she is also head of the religious establishment in England itself. And there is, indeed, an eloquent memorial to state confessionalism in the national hymn, 'O Canada'. It contains an intercession for 'altar and throne'.

2. ANTI-CATHOLIC TRADITION

During the nineteenth century Roman Catholicism, as it had done since the Reformation, provoked distaste and fear on a scale which it is now difficult to imagine. In North America—and especially in the United States—hatred of Catholicism increased the popular

[1] D. J. Wilson, *The Church Grows in Canada* (Toronto, 1966), p. 153.
[2] *Ibid.* p. 178.

identification of national spirituality with Protestantism. It was also a striking illustration of the religio-cultural unity of the British Isles and North America during the nineteenth century. 'Much of the religious life of the country', observed Gladstone of England in 1845, 'is very nearly associated with the word *Protestantism*, and it is the form under which the public at large hold in great part their idea of state religion.'[1] Despite the constitutional separation of church and state, the same could also have been written of the American republic. For anti-Catholicism, particularly in the excesses of Know-Nothingism and the American Protective Association, at times came close to providing a sort of popular national confessionalism. In the British North American provinces, the issues which stirred the Protestants to militancy usually had their sources in Britain itself. All the great anti-Catholic agitations were reproduced across the Atlantic, especially in the mid-century, so that even the humblest Canadian working man was convinced of the iniquity of the Maynooth grant in 1845, and of the insolence of the English Catholic hierarchy created by the Vatican in 1851. The essentials of the Italian question, and disgust at the temporal sovereignty of the Popes, united British and American anti-Catholicism in a peculiarly English and mildly anti-clerical association between national Protestantism and civil liberty.

There follows a brief sketch of the character of this shared religious tradition, and a summary of the incidence of anti-Catholicism in North American society and political experience. The tradition itself existed at two levels, and this must always be kept in mind: one, a set of intellectual assumptions common to most articulate and educated Protestants; the other residing as a latent force for social disturbance among groups of Protestant working men, whose muddy religiosity was easily stirred to acts of violence. But what is most striking in the present context is the continuation of the tradition itself, as virile in the townships of the American frontier as in the industrial cities of Victorian England.

[1] Quoted in W. R. W. Stephens, *The Life and Letters of Walter Farquhar Hook* (London, third edition, 1879), II, 237.

The same vocabulary of vituperation, the same historical interpretations, and usually even the same examples were employed in the vilification of Rome by men of British origin everywhere. Nineteenth-century Britain and North America were littered with pamphlets and journals on the evils of 'Popery'. There were also replies to the wide range of imputations, and perhaps the most useful of these—because it attempted to penetrate the ideological basis of the anti-Catholic tradition rather than counter only on specific points raised in the controversy—was Newman's *Present Position of Catholics in England*, a series of lectures delivered in 1851. Newman saw that the shared intellectual assumptions necessary for men to meet in fruitful controversy were absent in the disputations of Catholics and Protestants. The Church of Rome was regarded quite simply as outside civilized reference: 'she is considered too absurd to be inquired into, and too corrupt to be defended, and too dangerous to be treated with equity and fair dealing'.[1] This prejudice was represented under several distinguishable heads of argument, and these cumulatively provided the rational causes for outbreaks of anti-Catholic agitation, not only in Britain, but in the United States and Canada too.

It was not merely the institution but its doctrines which gave most offence to Protestants. A large measure of ignorance about the actual nature of both did not deter their critics. Even intelligent men, who had examined Catholicism closely, still felt able to sweep it away unilaterally. 'The greater part of the errors of Romanism', declared Archbishop Whately of Dublin, 'may be considered as so many branches of superstition.'[2] This belief, which was a nineteenth-century commonplace, was increased—indeed it seemed to be confirmed beyond disbelief—by the *Syllabus of Errors* in 1864 and the definition of Papal Infallibility in 1870. In contrast to the modern liberalism of nineteenth-century Britain and America, the Catholic Church seemed as monolithically sunk

---

[1] J. H. Newman, *Lectures on the Present Position of Catholics in England* (London, 1892 edition), p. 11.
[2] Richard Whately, *Essays* [*Third Series*] *on the Errors of Romanism* (fifth edition, London, 1856), p. xvi.

in 'medieval' intransigence as ever. Superstitious doctrines and idolatrous worship were bad enough, but Protestantism also had its reasons for supposing that Rome was capable of some fairly nasty practices too. These were held to be inseparable from Catholic beliefs, whose fruits they were. The Catholic Church was as a whole felt to be 'replete with things almost inconceivably mean and contemptible—things unworthy of men to utter, to believe, or to do'.[1] There was a popular belief in the personal vice and indecencies of the Popes, not just in the middle ages, but in the nineteenth century as well. Even Pius IX was apparently credited with discreditable morals.[2] The rule of clerical celibacy seemed to ask for trouble, and Protestants were not reluctant to suggest examples, both real and fictional, of its corrupting tendencies. According to the Archdeacon of London, writing in 1875, it was 'a command contrary to the plain sense of Scripture, and to the practise of the first Christians, and producing many effects which it is not decent to mention'.[3] The religious orders were supposed to be still worse. 'Protestants take it for granted that the history of the monks is a sore point with us', Newman explained; 'they fancy that Catholics can do nothing when monks are mentioned but evade, explain away, excuse, deny, urge difference of times.'[4] He was right. The Protestant tradition certainly suspected frightful goings-on in the seclusion of the monastic cells.

To the accusations of superstition and moral depravity, Protestants added a third and much more immediate reason for opposition to the claims of Rome. In this argument, Catholics were believed, as the subjects of a foreign sovereign whose dominion was temporal as well as spiritual, and who could depose heretical princes, to entertain both theoretically and by force of circum-

[1] John Montgomery, *Popery as it exists in Great Britain and Ireland, Its Doctrines, Practices, and Arguments* (Edinburgh, 1854), p. 666.
[2] Herbert Thurston, *No Popery, Chapters on Anti-Papal Prejudice* (London, 1930), p. 15 ff.
[3] John Martin, *A Brief Survey of Popery* (London, 1875), p. 11.
[4] J. H. Newman, *op. cit.* p. 20.

stances, the doctrine of 'double allegiance'. Doubts about the reliability of Catholic loyalty to the throne and 'Protestant Constitution' of Great Britain were easily conceived and readily formulated into arguments against concessions. They took a leading part in delaying Catholic emancipation until 1829, and even in the Act as passed, careful safeguards were incorporated to contain Catholic political influence. In the 1870s Gladstone joined his authority to this aspect of the tradition by campaigning in print against the tendency, as he saw it, of the Vatican Decrees to divide the loyalties of English Catholics.[1] Pastor Charles Chiniquy, a French-Canadian Catholic priest for twenty-five years, before his conversion to militant Protestantism, become a leading American exponent of the view that Catholicism and national allegiance were incompatible. He freely told the public, in the dedication of his sensational and unreliable *Fifty Years in the Church of Rome* (1885), not only that 'Abraham Lincoln was mudered by Rome', but that 'Romanism, under the mask of religion, is nothing but a permanent political conspiracy against all the most sacred rights of man'. In 1856 Robert Baird noticed that 'the assertion has often been made by the opponents of the Roman Catholics in the United States, that they can never be safe citizens of a republic, and that the predominance of their Church would involve the overthrow of our political constitution'.[2] Protestants saw the agency of the Vatican in every international intrigue. Samuel Wilberforce, when Archdeacon of Surrey in 1844, expressed his credence in the most popular American myth of the first half of the nineteenth century—that Popish subversives were working to establish a Catholic state in the vast Mississippi valley. 'The Romanists', he explained, 'have always known how to modify their doctrines and disciplines, so as to turn to the best advantage the political circumstances of the country and the

---

[1] W. E. Gladstone, *The Vatican Decrees in their Bearing on Civil Allegiance; A Political Expostulation* (London, 1874).

[2] *Religion in America* (revised edition, New York, 1856), p. 543. For a contemporary statement of this viewpoint, see Paul Blanshard, *American Freedom and Catholic Power* (second edition, Boston, 1960).

times'.[1] Catholics, and especially, of course, the Jesuits, were widely accepted as uncontrollably steeped in intolerance. Could not Catholics always argue round an oath of allegiance with the aid of Jesuit scholarship? Several official inquiries in nineteenth-century Britain actually examined the possibility that they could.[2]

This, then, in the barest outline, was the ideological nature of the tradition of anti-Catholicism latent in British and North American society during the nineteenth century. It was drawn from a heritage extending to the Reformation and even further backwards. Causes of actual outbreaks of agitation are rather more difficult to define. The inclination to 'No Popery' existed among all social groups everywhere: humble working-men were as susceptible as legislators or clergymen. But it is clear that apart from highly localized petty rioting and industrial disturbance, working-class men were only stirred to 'No Popery' clamour on a significant scale when excited by particular exercises of anti-Catholicism coming down to them from agitation among men of better social standing and education. Typically, this meant from the clergy, for this seepage downwards was usually through the pulpit—especially the more popular dissenting pulpit—and in the cheap religious press. But there was one important indigenous cause of anti-Catholic feeling among all non-skilled workers which was almost wholly independent of influence from above. This was the impact of Irish immigration on the cities of Britain, the United States, and Canada. The outpouring of these unskilled labourers was rising steadily during the first half of the century; it increased dramatically during the Famine years of the later 1840s, and fell off again towards the end of the century. The arrival of the Irish led to competition in the labour market and the reduction of wages. Engels noticed that the Irish immigrants added 'an ex-

---

[1] Samuel Wilberforce, *A History of the Protestant Episcopal Church in America* (London, 1844), p. 443.

[2] See, for example, the proceedings of the Harrowby Commission on Maynooth College, appointed in 1853. Most of the witnesses were asked the circumstances under which ecclesiastical authorities would grant release from oaths of allegiance. Parliamentary Papers, 1855, XXII, 1, 129, is an instance.

plosive force' to society.[1] One manifestation of that was the 'No Popery' cry. Hatred of those who threatened employment and wages easily flowed into hatred of the Irishmen's religion— Catholicism—especially as British and American working-men were already soaked in the anti-Catholic ideology, and at a crude level of it too, The Stockport riots of 1852, in the north of England, when a Catholic chapel in a district of heavy Irish settlement was sacked and desecrated by a mob of working-men, the rioting between Irishmen and native Americans during election campaigns in Philadelphia and New York City after 1834,[2] and the Orange and Green clashes of Montreal and Toronto in the 1840s and 1850s, expressed this aspect of the popular causes of religious disharmony at work. In Ireland itself, on the other hand, disputes among working-men, especially in Belfast and Dublin, where they were most heavily concentrated, were rarely characterized by embittered religious feeling between Protestants and Catholics until late in the century. On the exceptional occasions when a religious issue was evident in a dispute, the chances were strong that it had been deliberately fostered by employers' agents to prevent the organization of labour.[3] Anti-Catholic and anti-Irish feeling among British and American working-men, as in the hatred of cheap eastern and southern European immigrant labour in later nineteenth-century American cities, is familiar enough.

One important if small group of men provided a connexion between the working population and the articulate promoters of the anti-Catholic tradition in the skilled artisan and middle-classes. These were the itinerant preachers—familiar figures in Victorian religious life. Meetings which the anti-Catholic preachers addressed in the towns where they stopped often turned into violent mobs. The most celebrated of the itinerants was unquestionably

---

[1] Frederick Engels, *The Condition of the Working Class in England in 1844* (Blackwell edition, Oxford, 1958), p. 309.

[2] R. A. Billington, *The Protestant Crusade, 1800–60. A Study of the origins of American Nativism* (New York, 1938), p. 196.

[3] J. Dunsmore Clarkson, *Labour and Nationalism in Ireland* (New York, 1925), p. 90.

Alessandro Gavazzi, a Barnabite monk from Naples who had quit his order, and the entire Catholic Church, in order to join the campaign of the Italian Liberals against the Papal States. His disclosures of the inner-workings of the Catholic religion, which he made in direct and sensational language, prompted literally hundreds of 'No Popery' disturbances during his preaching tours of Britain and North America in the mid-century. In 1853, for example, Gavazzi's appearance in Canada coincided with religious strife inspired by the 'Papal Aggression' episode of 1850 in Britain. The result of his speeches was the 'Montreal Massacre', when several men were killed by troops trying to break up rioting between inflamed Protestants and Catholics.

The Orange Order, founded in Ireland during 1795, was the only really significant permanent organization against Catholic claims. The British govenment dissolved the Order in 1836 as an attempt to bring peace to Irish politics, and there were then 1,600 separate lodges in the country—a striking sign that some sort of public need was being satisfied.[1] During the mid-1840s the Order began to re-establish itself,[2] and it has taken a leading part in opposition to Catholicism ever since, with lodges in British and Canadian towns, in New York, and throughout the Britsh empire, as well as in Ireland itself. The Order has enjoyed a multi-class appeal.

Above the labouring population expressions of anti-Catholicism were usually caused by ideological objection to the political claims made by Catholics. It was, of course, the several aspects of the 'Irish Question' which kept the tradition near the centre of British political life during the nineteenth century. In the United States and Canada, anti-Catholicism in politics was largely precipitated by Catholic educational demands—for state support for their schools and colleges. Ignorance and suspicion hedged everything. It did not help matters that when Catholic practices first became

---

[1] For a recent, and full study of the early period, see Hereward Senior, *Orangeism in Ireland and Britain, 1795–1836* (London, 1966).

[2] *Orangeism in Ireland and Throughout the Empire*, by a Member of the Order (London, 1942), II, 317.

better-known, it was through the theology of Oxford and the later excesses of the Ritualists in the Church of England and the Episcopal Church in America. The imitators were hated with a special bitterness. The 1850s saw the highest level of 'No Popery' feeling everywhere, and this was because that decade saw not only the heaviest Irish immigration, but also the first real advances of pseudo-Catholic practices among groups of Protestant clergymen themselves. Most Protestants found any leniency to Catholicism almost intolerable. Newman put it thus: 'As English is the natural tongue, so Protestantism is the intellectual and moral language of the body politic.'[1] Indeed, the Papacy shared this view too. In 1899, when Leo XIII chose to condemn certain liberal attitudes on social questions adopted by priests and bishops of the Church in the United States, which Fr Felix Klein had identified as borrowed from their Protestant fellow-countrymen, he did so by defining their error as 'Americanism'. And except for Quebec province, British North America was also regarded as fixedly Protestant, whatever the diversity of the denominations: 'Protestantism may be said to be the genius of Upper Canada', as a Toronto journal put it in 1856.[2] The 'Protestant Constitution', that is to say, continued to be a meaningful concept in public life long after the reality had been made anomalous or obsolete in both Britain and North America.

By the end of the nineteenth century, Roman Catholicism received slightly more respect from the upper levels of society everywhere, but old prejudices continued to preserve the transcendence of the anti-Catholic tradition among the working-classes.[3] The distinction should not be made too sharply, however, for if toleration was beginning to seep downwards, just as previously anti-Catholic arguments had entered working-mens' awareness by downward seepage, its progress was as slow as its predecessor's had been rapid.

[1] J. H. Newman, *op. cit.* p. 366.
[2] *News of the Week*, 18 July, 1856.
[3] K. S. Inglis, *Churches and the Working Classes in Victorian England* (London, 1963), pp. 141–2.

Effects of separation on state and church

The 'No Popery' tradition was not, of course, exclusive to Great Britain and North America. Most European countries had their own histories of anti-Catholicism, although many of these were characterized by anti-clericalism rather than by positive revulsion to Catholic doctrine. Their class and regional appeals also differed greatly. But in those parts of the world where British institutions were duplicated, as in Canada or Australia, or where British people created institutions of their own, as in the United States, the ideology of the old anti-Catholic tradition, with its peculiarly English context of common law notions of liberty, survived and developed through a common inheritance of literature and example. *Foxe's Book of Martyrs* has united English Protestants everywhere.

Thus to the thirteen American colonies the Anglo-Saxon emigrants took with them 'that same spirit of hatred of Popery which characterized the England of that day'.[1] Roman Catholics had to fight for toleration in America, before the Revolution and after it. Although during the Revolutionary War period itself anti-Catholic prejudice rather receded, there was still enough around to inspire local opposition to the ratification of the new federal constitution. This resulted from the belief of a few men that the prohibition of religious tests for federal office might allow Catholics to infiltrate government. Some, apparently, even feared that the Pope might be elected President.[2] And after 1830 particularly, the nation was as redolent of anti-Catholicism as under the Crown. Most of the states had retained vestiges of penal enactments against Catholics on their statute-books. These soon vanished, but there were occasions in the nineteenth century when law was still employed as an expression of popular anti-Catholic feeling. In 1855, for example, the Putnam Act in New York State compelled lay ownership of ecclesiastical property.[3] This intervention by the

[1] R. A. Billington, *op. cit.* p. 4.
[2] Cecilia M. Kenyon, 'Men of Little Faith: The Anti-Federalists on the Nature of Representative Government', in *The William and Mary Quarterley*, Third Series, XII, no. (1958), 17.
[3] J. Tracy Ellis, *American Catholicism* (Chicago, 1955), p. 45.

state in religious organization was inspired by the nativist Know-Nothing party's suspicion of Catholic sacerdotalism. In the same year the Know-Nothings won control of the Massachusetts State legislature, passed a number of laws specifically intended to discriminate against Catholic immigrants, and appointed a 'Nunnery Committee' to investigate the alleged evil practices in convents, schools and seminaries of the Church.[1] This last exhibited all the characteristics of the English Parliamentary inquiries into Maynooth College (1853) and into conventual institutions (1870). Similar causes were producing similar effects.

There was a marked increase of anti-Catholic agitation during the later 1820s in the United States. In 1830 a group of clergymen founded *The Protestant*, a weekly anti-Catholic paper. This inaugurated a revival of 'No Popery' journalism and organization. In 1842 the American Protestant Association was established, with the declared belief that the 'principles of Popery' were 'subversive of civil and religious liberty'.[2] The growth of agitation was associated, as it was in England and Canada, with the concentration of Irish immigrants in the urban centres.[3] There were anti-Catholic classics too. In 1834 S. F. B. Morse, inventor of the telegraph, published his *Foreign Conspiracy Against the Liberties of the United States*, where he argued that European Catholics in league with American priests were out to wreck the Constitution.[4] In 1836 there appeared one of the most notorious works in the entire library of anti-Catholicism as well-read in Britain as in America—the *Awful Disclosures* of Maria Monk. The authoress related in excruciating detail the criminal and superstitious practices she had witnessed during the five years she claimed to have endured as a Black Nun at the Hôtel Dieu in Montreal. No indelicacies were withheld, and the frightful murders and sexual indulgences of the

[1] Leo Pfeffer, *Church, State and Freedom* (Boston, 1953), p. 375.
[2] Tracy Ellis, *op. cit.* p. 63.
[3] Bob Considine, *It's the Irish* (New York, 1961), p. 132.
[4] R. A. Billington, *op. cit.* p. 123. Particular reference was made to the Leopoldine Foundation in Vienna, which provided financial assistance for Catholic missions in America.

convent were so shocking to public conscience that three-hundred thousand copies were sold in the first printing of the book alone.[1] Maria Monk was suspected by some of having invented the whole thing, and when in 1838 she gave birth to a second illegitimate child, and her supporters announced that this had been 'arranged' by the Jesuits to discredit her,[2] these suspicions took on more solid shape. A group of Protestant ministers toured the convent and declared the book a lie. Maria Monk, as it eventually transpired, had certainly been enclosed at Montreal but it had been in the Magdalen, a house for ladies of easy virtue.[3] Yet her book was never really discredited with the public, who were unprepared to forfeit their vicarious horror because of contrary evidence, and it appeared in numerous later reprints.[4] It was used, for example, against Al Smith in the presidential election campaign of 1928.

Actual violence against Catholics was employed on a scale somewhat greater in America than in Britain during the nineteenth century. In 1831 a Catholic Church was burned in New York City. In 1834 an Ursuline convent was sacked at Charlestown, Massachusetts, by a frenzied mob of Protestants who suspected dark practices among the nuns, and the incarceration of little girls.[5] There were three days of bloodshed at Philadelphia in 1844, when forty persons were killed in clashes between Protestants and Catholics. In 1854, ten were killed at St Louis in 'No Popery' rioting, and in 1855 there was a toll of one hundred in Louisville's 'Bloody Sunday'.[6] This aspect of anti-Catholic feeling, with all its violence, has remained a significant force in the United States until very recent times.[7]

---

[1] R. A. Billington, *op. cit.* p. 99 ff.
[2] Theodore Maynard, *The Story of American Catholicism* (Image Books edition, New York, 1960), I, 267. [3] B. Considine, *op. cit.* p. 133.
[4] The latest edition was published in 1965 in England (Consul books) 'Even today after countless reprints' the editor writes, 'it still survives as a shocking indictment against an institution that was, to the outside world, a pillar of purity'.
[5] C. E. Olmstead, *Religion in America, Past and Present* (Englewood Cliffs, N.J., 1961), p. 82. [6] B. Considine, *op. cit.* p. 136.
[7] W. W. Sweet, *The American Churches. An Interpretation* (The Social Service Lecture, 1946) (London, 1947), p. 52.

Anti-Catholic tradition

In 1877 the American Protective Association was founded in Iowa: a resurgence of nativistic anti-Catholicism, inspired by Henry F. Bowers and others who believed that Catholicism implied a threat to civil liberty.[1] The background to the new movement was provided by the Protestant fears of an increasing and huge immigrant Catholic population in the eastern and midwestern cities, and by alarm at Catholic social organization—in 1882 the Knights of Columbus, a society of Catholic laymen, had been chartered in Connecticut. The A.P.A. lacked the political acumen and relative respectability of the old Know-Nothing parties of the mid-century, however, and although its output of propaganda was formidable, and although it offered support to the Republican Party, it was a spent force by the first years of the present century. The mantle of anti-Catholicism fell readily upon the revived Ku Klux Klan.

In British North America the duplication of English civil and religious institutions in Upper Canada, and the legal privileges secured to the French Catholic institutions of Lower Canada, produced a situation somewhat comparable to the relationship of England and Ireland. All the old animosities were successfully exported to the Canadian settlements, and the clash of Protestant and Catholic, especially in Ontario, where they met through greater social mobility, was the direct result of large-scale immigration in the mid-century.[2] Disputes were translated into extreme religious-party terms: 'Orangeism has been made the pretext of Fenianism, and Fenianism is doing its best to justify and magnify Orangeism', as one observer put it.[3] It was in Upper Canada, with its more faithful reproduction of the religious pluralism of Britain, that 'No Popery' feeling was most easily roused. 'The growth of Puseyism...in the 1840s...the 'Papal Aggres-

---

[1] See Michael Williams, *The Shadow of the Pope* (New York, 1932), which is a history of the movement.
[2] J. A. Raftis, 'Changing characteristics of the Catholic Church', in *The Churches and the Canadian Experience*, edited by J. W. Grant (Toronto, 1963), p. 84.
[3] *The Irish position in British and Republican North America* (anonymous) (Montreal, 1866), p. 13.

sion' controversy which raged in the early 'fifties, and the renewed vigour of the Church of Rome under Pius IX...each of these developments in turn was reflected in the religious and political life of Canada West.'[1] Indeed, all the ingredients for strife were present.

The Upper Canadian Catholic Church expanded as a result of Irish immigration, and by the 1860s it was, numerically, only second to the Church of England. It became progressively less subject to French-Canadian influence. Conservatives suspected any liberal reform which might place the Catholics in a position of real religious equality—especially in education—for there were popular fears of Catholic domination. As Bishop Strachan said: 'with the help of our liberal and infidel Government, the Roman Church is likely to raise its head again'.[2] Copious reference to the horrors of the Inquisition appeared to settle the point. During the 1840s the Orange lodges provided a noisy, and sometimes even violent ally. Popular Catholicism and radical reformism, as in Ireland under O'Connell, usually went together. Dissenting Protestants sometimes sided with the Catholics, upholding their right to benefit from the general advance of religious equality. This tolerance largely came to an end in the 1850s and the endemic anti-Catholicism of Protestant dissent, in a return to normality, was poured out. The reasons for this change were to be found in England. The reaction of the Canadian Protestants to the creation of an English Catholic hierarchy by the Pope, in 1850, was as abusive as in the scene of the intrusion itself, and the question actually affected the elections for the Upper Canadian legislative assembly in 1851.[3] There were also public clamours against Catholic religious orders. In 1855 the Toronto press was full of the story of Sarah Bolster, a Protestant girl allegedly enticed into a nunnery for immoral purposes by priests. The murder by a group of Catholics of one Robert Corrigan, who had been converted to to Protestantism, inspired a religious frenzy in 1855 which brought

[1] J. S. Moir, *Church and State in Canada West* (Toronto, 1959), p. xi.
[2] *Ibid.* p. 14.   [3] *Ibid.* p. 17.

down the Conservative government. Several deaths occurred in serious religious rioting during 1857 and 1858. By that time, there were some hundred thousand Orangemen in Canada, and their sturdy determination to stand by the 'Protestant Constitution' and the principles of the Reformation, met the Irish immigrants and French Catholics of Montreal in head-on collision.[1] The Fenian raids across the border from the United States, in the 1860s, did nothing to lessen the popular and political appeal of 'No Popery' among the Protestants of Canada.

Actual penal laws against the Catholics existed in the Maritime Provinces during the second half of the eighteenth century, but then the official treatment of Protestant dissenters, especially Methodists, revealed a comparable intolerance.[2] The Methodists were thought to be over-sympathetic towards the republican institutions of the United States. Like the Catholics, that is to say, they were regarded as committed to a foreign ideology and government. In 1758, Nova Scotia had passed an Act banishing Catholic clergy from the province, and although its enforcement was scarcely vigorous, it was not repealed until 1783. Something of the 'No Popery' excitement of Upper Canada was released in the Maritimes during the nineteenth century, but the absence of a large Catholic Irish immigrant group, and the corresponding lack of militant Orangeism, prevented the appearance of anti-Catholic rioting and the associated political upheavals.

3. REORGANIZATION OF THE CHURCHES

After the withdrawal of state support and protection, the disestablished churches needed to formulate constitutions for themselves. And so did those churches which, though they had not been established by the state in the American colonies and the British North American provinces, had been dependent for their

---

[1] See Leslie Saunders, *The Story of Orangeism, Its Origin and History for more than a century and a quarter in Canada* (Toronto, 1960), p. 30 ff.

[2] W. M. Elgee, *The Social Teachings of the Canadian Churches* (Toronto, 1964), p. 118.

discipline and regularity on parent bodies overseas. The most striking result of their endeavours was an increasing tendency to sectarian emphasis within the newly autonomous churches. Forced to rely upon authority other than the seal of state approval, each body re-stated its *raison d'être* in increasingly exclusive terms. The effects were most noticeable in the Church of England for the obvious reason that it was, with the sole exception of New England, the victim of the disestablishments. The Catholic Church, too, as it emerged from the penal enactments of the eighteenth century, made bold to emphasize its exclusive mission—later in the nineteenth century this merged into ultramontanism. Other churches, in free competition, stimulated by revivals, and threatened by frontier conditions, over-developed their own sectarianism and were also periodically bled by the formation of external sects.

The primary loser by the advent of religious equality—the Church of England—was as prone to identify itself in sectarian terms at home as it was in North America. In Canada, an emphasis on the church as a spiritual community with a mission and discipline quite independent of the state, had in fact occurred *before* the ending of its connexion with the state. It had evolved as the Church, especially under the High Church inspiration of Bishop Strachan, had turned to sectarian arguments to defend its authenticity, on theological grounds, to act as the national establishment. The increasing emphasis on sacerdotalism, implied in the High Church movement of the nineteenth century, led to straight demands for ecclesiastical autonomy in England itself. There, in contrast to Canada, a greater degree of autonomy was proposed in order to secure a measure of independence *from* the state—or at least from the more galling aspects of erastianism. Most men in England, of course, still expected the Church to receive the support of the state, despite the growing volume of appeals for disestablishment from Irish Catholics, English, Scottish and Welsh militant dissenters, philosophical and other radicals, and even a small wing of the High Church party in the

Church of England itself. The movements for the revival of Convocation, and for clergy discipline, were in reality appeals to the
idea of a church whose identity and authenticity were quite
separable from the state. There was nothing new in the claim:
the establishment had always hoped that it was a part of the universal church. But the climate of opinion which enveloped the
claim *was* new, for the openly sectarian arguments of the dissenters, formulated for use against the exclusive position of the
state church, had suggested a view of Christian societies which was
itself rather exclusive. The dissenters' monopoly of the practice of
autonomy had therefore produced a widely accepted ideal of what
an independent church body should be like: when the Church of
England came to stake a claim to some measure of self-government,
it was these concepts of religious identification which came most
readily to mind, however unaware churchmen may themselves
have been of the fact. This subtle emphasis underlay all the discussion about synods and convocations and the rediscovery of
primitive practice. Clergymen, when excluded from public life,
tend to find a release for their sense of unique authority in pre-
siding over a narrower realm. In England, of course, the establishment's claims to autonomy were modest, limited, and only
imperfectly realized. There was, indeed, never a very wide area
of agreement among churchmen themselves as to what they were
trying to secure from the control of the Crown. Members of the
Scottish Church were more coherent, and actually split into schism
during the 1840s over the question of autonomy from the state.
English statesmen were reluctant to give much independent
authority to the clergy anyway. 'Let me first say', Lord John
Russell had once announced, 'that I conceive it is the nature of all
ecclesiastical bodies to attempt to trench on temporal matters.'[1]
This view enjoyed considerable support. It is interesting that on
the other hand, the claims of many English churchmen to a
greater measure of autonomy reflected a distrust of the liberalism
of nineteenth-century government. This was especially true of the

---

[1] Hansard, CXIV, 194, (7 February, 1851).

Oxford movement's revulsion to the Whigs' reforms, and to public control by a legislature which had come to include both Catholics and Protestant dissenters. Similarly, the Papacy revolted against a political liberalism which undermined its right to arbitrate among the consciences of men. Now in England, the liberalism of the governments was in large part a response to the demands of the dissenters for religious equality. And there was the complicated dialectical relationship between sectarianism and the withering away of the establishment principle. It underlay church reorganization quite as much as the arguments for efficiency urged by ecclesiastical law-givers.

Thus in being obliged to surrender their official functions as the conscience of the state, and released from its control, the disestablished churches everywhere turned in upon themselves, and in doing so revised their own views of Christian society. The result was decidedly more sectarian. This withdrawal, though it is much less easily described, was just as significant as the cessation of public support for the establishment principle, in accounting for the growth of the 'neutral' modern state. The disengagement when it came, that is to say, was on both sides.

The period of constitution-making in the American churches occurred with the political separation from Britain. The disruption of connexions with churches in Britain forced the issue, and to some extent the experience of national and state political reorganization suggested both the means and the occasion for new church constitutions—'so we find', as Humphrey remarked, 'American ecclesiasticism, like the American political estate, stamped with the contract theory of government, with the doctrine of the separation of powers, and with the ideal of the consent of the governed'.[1] There was a correlation between those who had helped to draw up the new constitution for the Episcopal Church and those who drew up the federal instrument. But there was also a sense in which the political disruption was merely

[1] E. F. Humphrey, *Nationalism and Religion in America, 1774–89* (Boston, 1924), p. 14.

coincidental to the reorganization of the churches. The colonial churches had suffered poor organization because of distance from parent authorities in Britain, as the long controversy over the colonial bishopric had demonstrated. The time had anyway arrived for the churches to put their houses in order, and this was apparent before the separation from Britain. Church leaders were immensely disturbed by the increasing moral laxity of American life, and were coming to see the reorganization of their own resources as an aid to solution. In 1798 the Presbyterian General Assembly was frank about the condition of society as they viewed it: 'profaness, pride, luxury, injustice, intemperance, lewdness, and every species of debauchery and loose indulgence greatly abound'.[1] The Presbyterian churches clearly indicated the needs for new organization. Despite their complaints about the evil ways of society, they in fact considerably increased their numbers after the Great Awakening of the mid-century. The obligation upon each minister to attend the annual synod in person became progressively difficult to fulfill, and forms of representative government for the church were being suggested, to remedy this situation, long before the revolutionary upheaval and the new forms of political structure had consecrated the representative principle as the one most suited to American conditions.

To this sort of situation, which was common, the separation from Britain added just the right amount of stimulus to bring new church organization into existence. Only the Baptists, Lutherans, Congregationalists, and Quakers were unaffected by the change. It was the Methodist Church which first undertook adjustment in the revolutionary period. Still closely linked with the Church of England at the time of the Revolution, most members were still communicants, and they suffered the stigma of loyalism by their association with the parent body. The Methodists reorganized themselves independently of both the Church and the English Wesleyans in 1784, the year of the Peace of Paris. The need was urgent. Of the ten preachers who had formed the first

---

[1] L. W. Bacon, *A History of American Christianity* (London, 1899), p. 231.

8-2

Methodist Conference in 1773, only Francis Asbury elected to remain in America after independence. Asbury himself, indeed, was—as Humphrey put it—'very blue over the outlook'.[1] Declining to take the new state oath of Maryland, he removed himself to Delaware for two years of exile. Between 1779 and 1780 the Methodists parted in schism; the northern, more conservative wing, led by Asbury, stood by episcopalian disciplines, while the southern Methodists, under the leadership of William Watters adopted a governmental autonomy very similar to Presbyterianism. Reconciliation was achieved by 1783, and it was Asbury who was recognized by Wesley as the head of the American Church with the title of 'General Assistant'. Wesley himself only imperfectly understood the implications of the Americans' new position, and continued to attempt some sort of control over his followers. Hence his ordination of Thomas Coke, who was to cooperate with Asbury as Superintendent, and his composition of a plan of govenment for the American Church, with a three-fold ministry and a doctrinal formula based on the Thirty-nine Articles of the Church of England. Coke and Asbury had other plans. They established their own independence, and that of the American Methodists, by calling a conference at Baltimore in December 1784 to discuss and ratify Wesley's plan of government. Wesley had not foreseen the need for ratification. 'Superintendents' were now called 'bishops'. In 1808 the plan was finally adopted as the regular constitution of the Church.

The reorganization of the Church of England was complicated by the bishopric problem, and this itself depended on the state of the law in England. Popular prejudice against episcopal government had survived in the colonies. Regular discipline also encountered threats from the friends of the Church. In Maryland, for example, the new state legislature, in a bill of 1783 to reorganize the disestablished Church, also made provision for the ordination of clergy. This erastianism was opposed by the clergy

---

[1] E. F. Humphrey, *op. cit.* p. 174. Asbury was born in 1745, converted by Wesley, and went to America to become the apostle of Methodism there. He died in 1816.

themselves, and episcopal ordination was insisted upon.[1] The acquisition of a bishop for America was recognized as the most urgent of all requirements after independence. In 1783 some Connecticut clergymen had dispatched Samuel Seabury to England to get himself consecrated to episcopal orders. Two difficulties frustrated this endeavour: the doubtful legality of appointments of bishops to territories outside the dominion of the Crown, and Seabury's own refusal to take the oath of allegiance to the Sovereign. Both were avoided, as is well-known, when in the following year he was consecrated in Scotland, where the Episcopal Church existed in as anomalous a legal position as it now did in the former colonies. While Seabury was regularizing his position, his co-religionists at home, at both national and state level, were redefining their position.

Recommendations for a national Church constitution were put by a *vorparlament* of Episcopal leaders which met in New York City during October, 1784. Lacking any tradition or experience of this sort of autonomous action, and finding no precedent for it in the canon law, this conference merely staked out claims to future independent action. It was meanwhile left to the churches of the individual states to arrive at some sort of internal organization. There were dangers to national uniformity in this. Pennsylvania's clerical convention, of May 1785, selected a bishop with lay help and defined their independence from other Epicsopal churches. In Maryland, during August 1783, the clergy had approved a 'Declaration of Certain Fundamental Rights and Libties', and in claiming 'ecclesiastical and spiritual independence' held that the Maryland Church, organized as a synod, was 'competent to revise her Liturgy, Forms of Prayer, and Public Worship in order to adopt the same to the late revolution and other local circumstances of America'.[2] This attempt to keep the churches as distinct and separate as they had been as colonial establishments

---

[1] A. W. Werline, *Problems of Church and State in Maryland during the Seventeenth and Eighteenth Centuries* (South Lancaster, Mass., 1948), p. 171.
[2] *Ibid.* p. 207.

was a considerable threat to the integrity of the Church of England in America. If in each new state the Episcopalians altered their formularies and disciplines to please themselves only, the creation of a national church was plainly impossible. This was apparent to the Episcopalians of New York and the middle colonies, and to their leading spokesman, Dr William White, rector of Christ Church, Philadelphia. Their preliminary conference was therefore followed up with a Constitutional Convention of the Church which met at Philadelphia in December 1785. A small number of clergy and laymen from seven states were present. The threat of division was underlined by the nature of this assembly: the New England Churches, who had their own bishop in Seabury, were unsympathetic to the proposals for a national organization and did not attend. But under the chairmanship of White, the Convention produced an ecclesiastical constitution and sent an address to the Archbishop of Canterbury. Negotiations then opened with the Primate for the consecration of American bishops, with John Adams, the American ambassador in London, offering his services as a private citizen to secure liaison. In return for assurances from the Convention that no alterations would be made to the formularies or historical discipline of the Church of England, the Primate ushered a Bill through Parliament which enabled the consecration of foreign bishops without requiring oaths or subscriptions from them. In accordance with this understanding, the Convention dropped several contemplated alterations to the Prayer Book, and in 1787 White and Samuel Provoost were raised to the episcopacy in Lambeth Palace Chapel. There were now three bishops in America: the number required by canon law for the consecration of bishops. An independent episcopate could now begin.

Under the new constitution, as passed by the Convention, the first triennial convention of the Church assembled in 1789. Seabury and the New England clergy were represented at this, and something of the former rancour and risk of schism passed away. It was this gathering which drew up the canons for the American Episcopal Church, revised the constitution, and established a separate House of Bishops. At the General Convention of 1792 Bishop James Madison of Virginia proposed a reunion with the Methodists. But this attempt to widen the basis of the Church was frustrated by its rejection in the House of Deputies.[1]

Independence from English control had also to be secured by the Roman Catholics, but in their case the matter was more easily accomplished. They already had a centre of jurisdiction to which they were subject—Rome. Threats to discipline and regularity were becoming apparent in America, however, and the rising problem of lay trusteeism[2] was already suggesting the need for a domestic episcopate. The appointment of a Catholic bishop for America was now conceivable: the climate of crude 'No Popery' which the colonists had elevated to new heights at the time of the Quebec Act in 1774 was temporarily in abeyance. The sympathy of the small numbers of Catholics for the revolutionary cause had enabled the Church to benefit from the general sense of religious toleration which their Protestant fellow-countrymen had acquired, to, it is true, a still rather limited degree, during the struggle. Before the renewed anti-Catholic agitations of the new century, the Church was able to reorganize its resources. In June, 1783, a small group of priests meeting at Whitemarsh in Maryland discussed the possibilities. In November of the same year another clerical gathering, of priests from the middle states, petitioned Propaganda to remove them from the jurisdiction of the vicar-apostolic of the London District. This was especially necessary since the authority concerned, Bishop James Talbot, had virtually ceased communication with the American clergy, whom he regarded as implicated in civil rebellion and guilty of having broken their canonical obligation of loyalty to the Crown of Great Britain.[3] The Sacred Congregation of Propaganda in Rome responded favourably to the American requests, and in 1790 Dr John

---

[1] W. W. Sweet, *Religion in the Development of American Culture, 1765–1840* (New York, 1952), p. 105.
[2] See below, section 4.
[3] Theodore Maynard, *The Story of American Catholicism* (Image Books edition, New York, 1960), I, 155.

Carroll, a Jesuit, and a member of an 'Old Catholic' Maryland family, was consecrated in London as the first Bishop of Baltimore. In 1808 his diocese was raised to a metropolitan see and four new dioceses were created.

The other American churches either required no independence from external control, for none had ever existed among them, or else had already achieved autonomy before the revolutionary period. The Congregationalists had worked out a pattern of church government in New England which, though shaken by Unitarian divisions and generally rather lethargic compared with the energy of other religious bodies, survived the revolutionary years without disruption. There was no disestablishment: no need to alter the Standing Orders. The Baptists and the Quakers had also agreed upon governmental rules for themselves which required no change. Both were internally democratic, and both recognized the sovereignty of each individual congregation—though the Baptists did establish a large number of voluntary organizations, during the later years of the eighteenth century, to assist cooperation between their churches.

The Lutheran Church had established its independence from the German parent bodies. Since the Ministerium of Pennsylvania had been founded in 1761, largely under the dircetion of Henry Muhlenberg, it had created an ecclesiastical organization suited to American conditions. In 1781 a formal synodical constitution was set up, and in 1820, to complete the process, the General Synod was established. The Dutch Reformed Church, which was divided over proposed adoptions of the English language for its services, had separated itself from Dutch control long before the revolution, although it was not until 1867 that it established effective internal unity and discipline. It was then known as the 'Reformed Church in America'.[1] The Presbyterians had enjoyed independence from external control since the creation of the first presbytery in 1706. But the Church took advantage of the prevailing

[1] Gustave Weigel, *Churches in North America* (Baltimore and Montreal, 1961), p. 38.

ferment of reorganization to reconstitute itself. At the Synod of 1788 a new constitution was adopted which embodied the principles of representative government. It also revised the teachings of the Westminster Confession on the rights of civil magistrates over religious faith and discipline. This recognized the separation of church and state. It was now declared, significantly, that the magistrate's sole concern in such questions was 'to protect the Church of our Common Lord without giving the preference to any denomination of Christians above the rest'.[1]

In British North America the need for church reorganization resulted, as in the United States, from growth and sophistication on the one hand, and from the withdrawal of external jurisdiction on the other. The ending of state support for the Church of England implied the end of state control too, although there was a delay before the latter occurred. During the first half of the nineteenth century those dissenting churches which were dependent upon parent bodies in other lands—especially in Britain and and the United States—began, rather painfully, to create distinctively Canadian organizations of their own.

It was, of course, the Church of England which most urgently needed to replace the relative erastianism of its position as an establishment by an autonomous constitution. During the 1830s there were frequent discussions of possible church self-government, with the American Episcopal Church as the obvious—indeed the only—example to turn to.[2] The position was becoming intolerable. Although the state was withdrawing financial and moral support from the establishment, the Church itself continued to be intimately subject to the Crown. Bishops and deans could not be appointed without royal letters-patent; only the Archbishop of Canterbury, as metropolitan of the colonies, could perform consecrations; and the Canadian Church was unable to frame legal canons for its own discipline. A first step towards autonomy came with the founding of the 'Church Societies', promoted by the

[1] Quoted in E. F. Humphrey, *op. cit.* p. 276.
[2] Philip Carrington, *The Anglican Church in Canada* (Toronto, 1963), p. 82.

113

bishops and clergy of each diocese to collect funds, discuss policies, needs, and missions, and to supervise church properties, clergy stipends and the income from the clergy reserves. The societies had the advantage of not requiring permission from the Crown for their creation. New Brunswick began the movement in 1836. Others followed: Nova Scotia in 1837, Prince Edward Island in 1840, Toronto and Quebec in 1842, and Newfoundland in 1843. Each society was incorporated by legislation in the provincial assemblies.

By the early 1840s, however, the concession of Responsible Government to the Canadas following the Durham proposals had suggested bolder moves to leading churchmen. At a Quebec episcopal conference in 1851 autonomous government for the Church was discussed in concrete terms. Diocesan synods with lay representation, on the American model, were approved in principle,[1] yet the bishops had no power to act as the law then stood. The question was raised at the London conference of the colonial bishops in 1853, but attempts to secure the necessary legislation from the Imperial Parliament proved fruitless.[2] In the same year Bishop Strachan tried to precipitate government action by allowing a conference of clergy and lay representatives from the diocese of Toronto to declare itself a synod. This body then petitioned the Queen for an act of Parliament to declare their legality. Low Churchmen, especially those of Irish Protestant origin, were profoundly suspicious of all attempts at ecclesiastical independence, seeing in them the further advance of 'Puseyism' and episcopal aggrandizement. Opposition to Strachan's tactics in Toronto came fiercely from these men[3]—whose diagnosis was not, after all, that far wide of the mark. In 1856 Bishop Binney followed the Toronto example by declaring a synod in Nova Scotia. Under the pressure of these events, the provincial assemblies, acting according to the new practice of Responsible Government, then took steps to re-

[1] T. R. Millman, 'Tradition in the Anglican Church of Canada', in *The Churches and the Canadian Experience*, edited by J. W. Grant (Toronto, 1963), p. 21.
[2] P. Carrington, *op. cit.* p. 115.   [3] *Ibid.* p. 116.

lieve the Church. In 1857 the Canadian legislature declared the Anglican synods legal: an act which was upheld from London with a royal proclamation. The Nova Scotian synod received incorporation from the local legislature in 1864. Synods had by then been created in Quebec (1859), Fredericton (1861), and in the new diocese of Ontario (1861) which Strachan had separated from Toronto.

Final steps to full ecclesiastical autonomy were begun in 1860 when the Crown issued letters-patent creating a Canadian Church province, comprising the dioceses of Quebec, Toronto, Montreal, Huron and Ontario. Bishop Francis Fulford of Montreal was named as the first metropolitan. The government in Britain was explicit about the principle on which the independence of the Church had been conceded: 'where there is a responsible local government the Crown should not interfere in ecclesiastical matters'.[1] This was not, it must be noticed, a declaration of the separation of church and state, but simply a statement that any governmental action over religion must initiate in the provinces themselves. Now independent, the Church of England in Canada carefully maintained the ceremonies and doctrinal statements of the mother church, as the American Episcopal Church had done. The Church Societies, their functions transferred to proper synods, withered away. Only in Quebec and Prince Edward Island have they survived to the present time, still administering funds and endowments. Despite the near proximity of their co-religionists in the United States, the Church of England in Canada—which changed its title in 1955 to 'The Anglican Church of Canada'— has continued to fall decisively under English rather than American influence.[2]

For the Catholic Church of Quebec there was no problem of reorganization. Legally protected in its rights by the Act of 1774, the Church's development was uninterrupted. In other parts of British North America, the problem of Catholic church extension

[1] H. H. Walsh, *The Christian Church in Canada* (Toronto, 1956), p. 208.
[2] T. R. Millman, *op. cit.* p. 23.

presented itself not in terms of new types of organization or the adaptation of structure, but in the creation of new sees.[1] These were directed through the authority of Rome. Quebec had been elevated to metropolitan jurisdiction in 1844, with Montreal, Toronto and Kingston as dependent sees, and to which Ottawa, Newfoundland, and the diocese of the North West were added three years later. Provincial councils, at which representatives from the Maritime Provinces (which were still governed by vicars-apostolic) presented themselves, assured uniformity of action. The first was convoked in 1851. British North America was still under the administrative jurisdiction of Propaganda, and full independence for the hierarchy was not conceded by Rome until 1908.

Methodism, which enjoyed massive growth in the Maritimes and Upper Canada during the first years of the nineteenth century, suffered divided allegiances. It was drawn between the Methodist Episcopal Church of the United States and the British Wesleyans. In Upper Canada the Methodist Episcopalians were at first subject to American control. Hostility to southern republicanism during and after the War of 1812 proved a heavy liability to the Canadian members, however, and after considerable disputation the Americans tardily conceded independence to their Upper Canadian membership in 1828.[2] British Wesleyan Methodists had by then arrived in some numbers, encouraged by government officials grateful for their loyalty to existing institutions. A union between the two branches of Methodism was arranged in 1833, and this also allowed independence from the control of the English Wesleyan conference. It was never a happy union. Although the Episcopal Methodists had dropped episcopacy, there were grave differences of emphasis over questions relating to state support and the establishment principle—the Wesleyans, who were clearly in the ascendancy, tending to espouse the more conservative positions.[3] After

[1] See G. T. Daly, *Catholic problems in western Canada* (Toronto, 1921).
[2] Goldwin French, 'The People called Methodists in Canada', in *The Churches and the Canadian Experience*, edited by J. W. Grant (Toronto, 1963), pp. 74-5.
[3] See Goldwin French, *op. cit.* chapter 7.

1840, the Union was in dissolution for seven years. Dispute and division were endemic in Canadian Methodism, and broke out over questions of discipline and organization as well as politics. In Nova Scotia too, the American Methodist Episcopal Church had at first taken control. But in 1800 the local Methodists put themselves under the English Wesleyan conference. They did not secure their autonomy until 1855, when an independent conference was set up for all the Wesleyan churches of the Maritime Provinces. The rise of new Methodist sects after 1820, in both the Canadas and the Maritimes, reflected a reaction to growing independence and formalism of organization.[1] Yet after a series of preparatory steps and lesser amalgamations, a United Canadian Methodist Church was ushered into fully independent existence in 1884.

Presbyterianism was at first also pulled from two directions. Exiled Loyalists brought the American versions to the Maritime Provinces and to Upper Canada, and Scottish settlers introduced the more conservative and establishmentarian Church of Scotland. But since the Loyalists, on arrival, turned to the British mother church for inspiration and financial assistance, Presbyterianism in British North America fell under Scottish influence. Overseas supervision was slight, however, and not at all comparable with the close strings tied to Canadian Methodism by the British Wesleyan connexion.[2] Synods enjoyed full independence. But movements in the parent body, both theological and institutional, were duplicated in the colonies, and the most dramatic of these came in 1843 when the Church in the British North American provinces divided along the lines of the Scottish Disruption—a dispute essentially concerned with the relations of church and state. This, and numerous other fragmentations, were brought to an end in 1875 when a united Presbyterian Church for the whole of Canada was created. The Baptist churches, which again first came

[1] S. D. Clark, *Church and Sect in Canada* (Toronto, 1948), pp. 273 and 292.
[2] N. G. Smith, 'The Presbyterian Tradition in Canada', in *The Churches and the Canadian Experience*, p. 39.

from the United States, and then with later immigration from Britain, were even more divided than the Presbyterians, and looked to the leadership of the English Baptists. But the democratic tradition and structural localism of the Baptist churches allowed them full autonomy from the beginning. Like the Methodists, they suffered considerably from sectarian splintering during the mid-nineteenth century. The Free Baptist Movement withdrew the allegiance of many congregations from the Baptist Association both in the Maritimes and in the Canadas. Tolerable measures of unity were not achieved in the Maritimes until 1905 and in the rest of Canada until 1944. The Congregational churches—for the same reason as the Baptists—also lacked the need to establish new patterns of independent organization. They had suffered desiccation in the Maritimes during the Newlight Revival, and grave unpopularity in Upper Canada due to their supposed association with American republicanism. During the 1840s the Congregationalists were aided by grants from the London Missionary Society and its subsidiary agencies, and successfully established themselves in the Canadas. Following the example of the English Congregational union, loose federal associations between congregations occurred in the Maritimes during 1846, and in Canada during 1853. A Congregational Union for the whole country was created in 1906. The small groups of Lutherans increased dramatically in size in the middle and later nineteenth century,[1] largely under the direction of the Pittsburgh Synod from 1853 and the Missouri Synod from 1879. In 1905 churches affiliated to the Ohio Synod were set up in the Canadian west. These relations with the American branches of Lutheranism have survived. Finally, it should be noticed that in 1925 the Methodists, Congregationalists, and a majority of the Presbyterians combined to establish the United Church of Canada—a symbol, perhaps, as much of Canadian religious autonomy as of ecumenicalism.[2]

[1] D. J. Wilson, *The Church Grows in Canada* (Toronto, 1966) p. 72.
[2] See E. Lloyd Morrow, *Church union in Canada: Its history, motives, doctrine and government* (Toronto, 1923).

4. CHURCH PROPERTY AND LAY INFLUENCE

At certain times and in certain conditions the active participation of laymen in the conduct of the Catholic and Episcopal Churches resulted in ecclesiastical irregularities or innovations in church government. Claims of the laity to a voice in the organization of these churches have often been seen as a characteristically American expression of the representative and democratic principles at work upon institutions originally more suited to highly stratified societies of aristocratic inflexion. William Warren Sweet has described this belief with precise point:

The history of religion in America holds a peculiarly close relationship to the general history of the American spirit due to the fact that more than elsewhere the American Churches have been managed by laymen. In other words, the ecclesiastical history of American has not been principally the history of ecclesiastics. Instead of reflecting merely the thoughts and sentiments of a priestly caste, American Church history deals with a great mass of active and influential laymen.[1]

The non-Episcopal Protestant churches, with their more traditionally representative basis (like the Congregationalists and Baptists), or with their lay control of ministerial appointments (like the Presbyterians), were not, of course, effected by any *increase* of lay influence comparable to the early nineteenth-century experience of the Episcopal and Catholic bodies. Yet the American example of lay participation, in the two hierarchical institutions, is certainly not unique. The conditions which prompted the appearance of lay claims were present in the British North American provinces, and in Britain itself.

Everywhere the tendencies of the voluntary system of endowments were similar. It was the Catholic Church which endured the greatest dangers. The problem of 'Trusteeism' in the United States during the first half of the nineteenth century was the direct result of the operation of voluntaryism in a society also steeped

[1] *Religion in the Development of American Culture, 1765–1840* (New York, 1952), p. viii.

Effects of separation on state and church

in the doctrines of liberty and property associated with British constitutionalism, and especially with the rights of patronage. To show that this phenomenon in American Catholicism was not unique—was not the result of a democratic πολίτευμα exclusive to America—something can be said of the appearance of lay insistence on 'patronage' rights in the Catholic Church of Ireland. Nothing on the scale of American Catholic Trusteeism occurred in Ireland. In taking Irish examples, in fact, tendencies are being examined which were produced by the same causes—but held in check by a more rapid diffusion of ecclesiastical discipline. For it was the ecclesiastical disorganization of the penal years of the eighteenth century which had allowed voluntaryism to plant a legacy of lay irregularities. The people, providing the incomes and materials for their priest, in some places began also to demand a voice in his appointment and dismissal. Thus in Galway at the end of the eighteenth century 'the ecclesiastical government partook in some manner of a Presbyterian or rather popular character'.[1] Parish priests, known improperly as 'vicars'—a title borrowed loosely from their Protestant neighbours—were elected by their congregations. So also was the 'warden', a priest who exercised a sort of episcopal jurisdiction.[2] Early in the nineteenth century this arrangement came to an end, stamped out by the imposition of properly constituted authority. It survived only in occasional manifestations of independence by particular priests. In 1830 Galway was erected into a diocese and so brought finally within regular episcopal control. Galway was a special case, but then every instance of lay intrusion into the ecclesiastical discipline of the Catholic Church must be a special case. Each reveals the incidence of voluntaryism coinciding with administrative disorganization. In the second half of the eighteenth century large numbers of Catholic parishes in Ireland suffered disturbances when distant episcopal authorities appointed or removed priests without

[1] W. Maziere Brady, *The Episcopal Succession in England, Scotland and Ireland, 1400 to 1875* (Rome, 1876), II 234.
[2] See *Analecta Hibernica*, 14 (Irish Manuscripts Commission, 1944), on the Galway Wardenship system.

confiding in the parishioners. Local Catholic gentry sometimes nominated priests to churches on their estates—just like the Protestant lay patrons. The parish priest of Killarny was appointed by Lord Kenmare until the mid-nineteenth century. Although irregularity of appointment was sometines described as 'Presbyterian', there was generally no actual emulation of Protestant practice: it was the factual breakdown of episcopal control which allowed the *vox populi* to declare itself. Only a few Catholics in the North of Ireland seem to have been openly influenced by their Presbyterian neighbours—in north-east Ulster there were more Presbyterians to learn from. In the same area, during the later eighteenth century, there were numerous attempts by the laity to nominate their own priests. Bishop MacMullan of Down and Connor was among those troubled. 'In two or three parishes the hearers not long since were claiming a right of choosing their own parish priests', he informed Rome in 1814: 'they were wanting that I should send them none other than the priest or priests they called for'.[1] Being an old and tired man, he gave in to the demands. But by the mid-century, even in his diocese, the practice had died out—due to the imposition of ecclesiastical discipline from above, and as a result of the division of many of the parishes.

The American states shared the same background: penal laws which restricted the proper exercise of Catholic ecclesiastical organization, and which were removed (apart from anomalous survivals) at the end of the eighteenth century. The American counterpart of Ireland's temporarily disrupted ecclesiastical machinery was a rudimentary one struggling to find its feet after the severance of relations with England. Like the British Catholics, those in the United States were wholly dependent upon the voluntary system of endowments: in this both were unlike most other branches of Catholicism in the world, which still leaned on the financial assistance of the state. In America it was the continuation of English Common law notions of property contract which furnished the immediate threat to ecclesiastical regularity. And,

[1] James O'Laverty, *The Bishops of Down and Connor* (Dublin, 1895), p. 587.

much more than in Ireland, lay Catholics were there inspired to independent action by direct emulation of their Protestant fellow-countrymen, especially since the latter, in the late eighteenth-century burst of reorganization, were incorporating lay representatives as part of the formal constitution of church government. Some American Catholics found the example offered irresistible.

Without a legacy of state endowment, Catholic churches and cathedrals in the United States were typically financed by boards of lay trustees.[1] It was they, and not the congregation as a whole, who in most of the states received legal incorporation. The trustees were the almost inevitable result of the obtaining laws concerning ecclesiastical property—laws formulated by predominently Protestant legislatures which were familiar only with the requirements of their own denominations. All non-Episcopalian Protestants more or less expected the benefactors and financial managers of their churches to appoint and dismiss their ministers. Even in the disestablished Episcopal churches the old erastianism of the vestries survived, so did the rights of lay patronage; both fortified by the introduction of a lay element into the new representative structure of the Church. It was hardly surprising that lay Catholics should attempt to enjoy the same rights. And it is interesting that the increasing number of Irish Catholics in America should have exploited the trusteeship system. Herberg, indeed, saw the whole problem of trusteeism as merely an incident in the rise of the Irish element to supremacy in American Catholicism,[2] taking over from the English and the French, and later warding off the Germans and the Italians. In fact the competition between Catholics of different national origin inflated the trusteeship question to serious proportions, leading to petty schism in large numbers of parishes, especially where there were language difficulties, and where different ethnic groups demanded priests who spoke their own

[1] Theodore Maynard, *The Story of American Catholicism* (Image Books edition, New York, 1960), I, 177.
[2] Will Herberg, *Protestant-Catholic-Jew. An Essay in American Religious Sociology* (New York, 1960 edition), p. 138.

tongue. But this was in a sense accidental: it was the trusteeship system itself, suggesting the idea of Catholic lay patronage, which afforded proof of the disintegrating influence of voluntaryism. It echoed Irish experience. It was a minor recurrence of the proprietary church system of early medieval Europe.

Catholic ecclesiastical authorities simply had to accept trusteeism in America, as the only legal safeguard to church property. For most of the time, after all, it operated without any threat to regular discipline.[1] It was not contrary to the canon law,[2] provided the boards of trustees did not try to transfer their managerial interests from the temporalities to the spiritualities of the Church. With some slight exceptions, the disturbances of the east were not reproduced in the expanding Catholic Church of the mid-west, where trusteeism was scarcely a problem.[3] This was probably because the frontier sectarianism of the Protestant churches was hardly evident in Catholicism: the mid-west was already, in outline, Catholic. When the Americans poured across the Alleghenies, they found an existing thread of Catholic missions originally established for the French fur-trading settlements. This was soon submerged by the extension of Protestantism into the region, but in the period when trusteeism was causing most disruption in the east, early in the nineteenth century, the elementary structure of the Catholic Church in the mid-west stood waiting to be regularized and redirected—from Baltimore, and not from Quebec. The degree of ecclesiastical discipline was always high, and a careful control was exercised over the mid-western missions from the Propaganda in Rome. There was no breakdown of regular discipline which allowed the ecclesiastical authorities to be set aside, as in Ireland and eastern America.

[1] 'The Church has no aversion to admitting laymen to a share in the administration of Church property, if they are subordinated to ecclesiastical jurisdiction and discipline'—P. J. Dignan, *A History of the Legal Incorporation of Catholic Church Property in the United States 1784–1932* (New York, 1935), p. 266.
[2] John Tracy Ellis, *American Catholicism* (Chicago, 1955), p. 44.
[3] R. F. Trisco, *The Holy See and the Nascent Church in the Middle Western United States, 1826–50* (Analecta Gregoriana, Rome, 1962), p. 15.

Effects of separation on state and church

The first serious conflict over the trusteeship question occurred during 1787 in New York City. A board of trustees, who had been incorporated two years previously, had built a church in Barclay Street and appointed their own priest. Dr John Carroll, as Prefect-Apostolic, intervened to lay aside this patronage as irregular. As it happened, the trustees accepted his authority, but a schism resulted among the members of the congregation, abetted by two Irish Franciscans. Carroll spelled out the dangers for the future: 'If ever such principles should become predominant, the unity and catholicity of our Church would be at an end; and it would be formed into distinct and independent societies, nearly in the same manner as the Congregational Presbyterians'.[1] Early in the new century local conflicts between Catholics of different national origin led to more serious disturbance. The increase of Irish immigration also swept a rather large number of irresponsible priests into the country, some of whom readily sided with trust-eeism and against episcopal authority. Not infrequently, resort had to be made to the civil courts. A schism in Philadelphia was ended during 1802 by legal action: so was one at Baltimore in 1805. In both cases, the courts upheld episcopal jurisdiction against the trustees.[2] In both, too, the trustees had appointed German priests without reference to the bishop. In some places, the priests joined the lay trustees in asserting independence. The long schism at St Mary's Church in Philadelphia, for example, which lasted from 1820 to 1830, was engineered by Fr William Hogan, an Irish priest. The lay trustees, in supporting him, were advised by Fr Rico, a Fransiscan who kept a cigar store, and by Fr Mier, who had been a pupil of Blanco White.

Attempts were also made in some places to coerce episcopal authority into accepting lay demands. Threats to withhold the bishop's stipend were sometimes made by the trustees of cathedral churches. In 1829, when Bishop Conwell of Philadelphia had been deprived of his income in this way, he actually gave in to the

[1] Quoted in E. F. Humphrey, *Nationalism and Religion in America, 1774–89* (Boston, 1924), p. 253. [2] T. Maynard, *op. cit.* I, 180.

trustees' demands—and was deprived of his see by the Vatican for doing so. In 1837 Bishop Dubois was refused his stipend by the trustees of New York Cathedral, and a long period of ill-feeling ensued. This ended, happily for the future of episcopal authority in the city, with the victory of his coadjutor, Dr John Hughes, over the trustees. In 1847 the militant lay trustees of the pro-cathedral in Buffalo shut Bishop Timon out of the building. And it was in the same city that an appeal to the civil courts over the appointment of a clergyman to St Louis Church led to a decision in favour of the rights of the trustees. They had called on the Know-Nothing nativists to support their case against their own bishop.[1] The issue had another importance: it provided the occasion for the Know-Nothings, who had just won control of the New York State legislature, to pass the Putnam Act of 1855, compelling the lay ownership of all ecclesiastical property and prohibiting clergymen from securing the legal title to property in their own names.[2] This virtually established the trusteeship system in the state, and although the law was not strictly enforced—reflecting, after all, the temporary success of a nativist, anti-Catholic outburst—it remained unrepealed until 1863.

So devastating, in fact, could the disrupting effects of the trusteeship system become, that at times it even seemed as though a large-scale and permanent national Catholic schism might grow out of the numerous local ones. In 1817 the Catholic trustees of Norfolk, Virginia, petitioned the Holy See to assert their rights of patronage over a church they had built. They also dismissed the parish priest appointed by Bishop Maréchal, whom they disliked because he was a French Sulpician, and 'presented' a Fr Thomas Carby to the living, resolving to elect him as their bishop.[3] This incident galvanized Rome into action. Two new bishops, both Irishmen, were appointed: Patrick Kelly for Richmond, Virginia, and John England for Charleston, South Carolina. Kelly arrived to find his diocese split between two factions—the

---

[1] P. J. Dignan, *op. cit.* p. 193.   [2] J. Tracy Ellis, *op. cit.* p. 45.
[3] T. Maynard, *op. cit.* I, 210–12.

bishop's and the trustees'. In Charleston, meanwhile, schism over the question of episcopal control of appointments had suggested one logical solution: a committee of priests were planning, in 1819, to set up an independent American Catholic Church, headed by a bishop to be consecrated by a Jansenist in Holland.[1] This illustrated the threat of trusteeism in an extreme form. The new bishop, in attempting to regularize the administration of the diocese worked out a plan of government in 1833. The 'Charleston Constitution' was based upon that of the Episcopal Church.[2] It gave some slight advisory capacity to the laity, in a house of representatives. A convocation of clergy was also to enjoy the right of being consulted by the bishop. Pew-rents, originally copied from the Protestant churches, and one of the most useful financial weapons available to recalcitrant lay trustees, were abolished. Instead, a system of taxation was instituted on a diocesan basis. The 'Charleston Constitution' was, like voluntaryism, an innovation in Catholic experience. It was never adopted in any other diocese, but it did offer an example of firm action, and removed the chance for independent lay action. The First Provincial Council of Baltimore, in 1829, had passed decrees emphasizing the authority of the episcopate and condemning lay patronage. The First Plenary Council of the Catholic Church in the United States, which met at Baltimore in 1853, confirmed and added to these decrees. Rome continued to watch carefully. In 1854 Archbishop Bedini, on a mission to President Pierce connected with the question of diplomatic relations with the Holy See, was also asked to report back on the trusteeship problem. The Third Plenary Council, of 1884, continued to declare on the subject. But by then the irregularities of trusteeism were at an end,[3] and the effects of voluntaryism, in that respect, were being felt rather less in an established society.

The Episcopal Church, too, experienced some departure from its customary discipline. Being, as in England, already filled with lay and Crown patronage, the revolutionary period merely saw

[1] T. Maynard, *op. cit.* I, 215   [2] *Ibid.* p. I, 219.   [3] P. J. Dignan, *op. cit.* p. 180.

the transfer of some patronage rights from one hand to another, with rather a substantial amount remaining intact. The new church constitutions, adopted with some variations of detail in all the dioceses, accepted the principle of lay participation in church government. It was, however, only the representative element, not the fact of lay participation, which was a new departure. The typical Episcopal parish of the early nineteenth century was incorporated by the state legislature and so could hold property. There was an annual vestry elected by ballot from among the male pew-holders, and there were two wardens, one a nominee of the incumbent, the other elected by the vestry. The wardens and vestry together enjoyed the right of patronage—the right of engaging the services of a clergymen for the parish. Often they chose a candidate recommended by the bishop, but there was no obligation for them to do so.[1] Some parishes, like Trinity Church in New York City, which had considerable endowments—though this was rare—also had a considerable degree of independence. Elsewhere, funds were raised by a general assessment on pews: a systematized version of the old pew-rents. The parish vestries also appointed lay delegates to meet, usually once a year, in a Convention with the bishop and clergy of the diocese. The Convention had legislative powers whose only limitation arose from an inability to overrule canons and regulations framed by a General Convention of every diocese in the country. In each diocese the laity participated in the election of bishops. Despite some local variations, it was everywhere the custom for the laity to confirm a nomination to the episcopate made in the diocesan convention. Each diocese also had a Standing Committee, composed of clergy and laity, elected for terms of one year. Its relation to the diocese was like that of the vestry to the parish.[2] The parish had itself, after disestablishment, lost its old existence as a civil administrative unit, containing all men of all faiths. The only tests for the Episcopalian parishes were now congregational ones.

[1] Henry Caswall, *America and the American Church* (London, 1839), p. 66.
[2] *Ibid.* p. 74.

Effects of separation on state and church

The general loyalty of Episcopalians to the episcopal system, and the absence of ethnic tensions among church members like those felt in the Catholic Church, meant that there were no popular attempts at irregular lay control. The careful introduction of the lay element into ecclesiastical constitutionalism proved to be a sufficient concession—enough, even, to withstand the bitter mid-century conflicts between high and low church parties. But there had been threats to episcopal government. In 1782 Dr William White had suggested the adoption of a Presbyterian type of ordination in a work entitled *Case of the Episcopal Churches in the United States Considered*. And in 1783 the Maryland state legislature had tried to provide for ordinations and discipline in the newly disestablished Church by mooting legislation which would have set up an ecclesiastical structure independent of episcopal control. This was defeated by opposition from the Episcopalians themselves.[1] The Church constitution eventually adopted in the United States, which has in most essentials survived to the present, with its representative structure and lay participation at both diocesan and national levels, was also roughly the scheme adopted in Canada during the mid-nineteenth century, in Ireland after disestablishment in 1871, and in Wales in 1919. And in a non-legislative sense it was structurally similar, if not with the English revived convocations of 1852 and 1861, at Canterbury and York, than at least with the assembly of Church Congresses after 1861.

The American state legislatures, for their part, assisted the churches by passing laws for the protection of their property. At first they provided individual acts of incorporation in response to an application from any denomination, but by the 1860s all the states except Rhode Island and South Carolina had enacted general incorporation statutes. During the 1870s many states went further, and created different classes of general incorporation, one suitable for each of the leading types of denominational structure.[2]

[1] A. W. Werline, *Problems of Church and State in Maryland During the Seventeenth and Eighteenth Centuries* (South Lancaster, Mass., 1948), p. 171.
[2] P. J. Dignan, *op. cit.* p. 214.

These were especially satisfactory, since they recognized the differences of internal government in the various bodies. And in 1871 the Supreme Court of the United States, in *Watson* v. *Jones*—a case arising out of a Presbyterian dispute in Kentucky—ruled that the obligations incurred by members of churches as a result of their internal rules and disciplines, and the judgments of church tribunals on their own members, should be upheld at law. At the present time there continues to be a wide range of variation in the laws of the different states concerning the incorporation of ecclesiastical property.

The Catholics of Quebec province in British North America had been effectively regularized by the start of the nineteenth century, but during the previous century extraordinary conditions, not dissimilar to those in Ireland and the American colonies, had posed actual threats to the traditional structure of government in the Church. From the middle of the seventeenth century, indeed, the Quebec parishes, which had become both civil and religious corporations, began to elect wardens as part of the local church council, thus introducing a representative element to ecclesiastical government similar to that of Galway. This has remained a peculiarity of Quebec Catholicism to the present day,[1] but the wardenship elections, having passed into the control of the clergy during the eighteenth century, are not now a violation of regular discipline. A French royal edict of 1692 which gave the Quebec clergy a virtual freehold in their incumbencies was a threat to proper episcopal jurisdiction too. Bishop Laval circumvented the law, which lapsed with the British conquest anyway. There were, however, two attempts by British authority to secure Crown control over Catholic episcopal and clerical appointments. At the beginning of the nineteenth century Sir James Craig, when Governor of Quebec, demanded the right to nominate Catholic parish priests and even managed to get Bishop Denault's acquiescence. The claim lapsed during the War of 1812, as part of a programme of conciliation aimed at the retention of Catholic

[1] H. H. Walsh, *The Christian Church in Canada* (Toronto, 1956), p. 4.

loyalty to the Crown. But in 1824 Lord Dalhousie suggested the revival of the claim, and it remained as a recurrent threat until the rebellion of 1837, when the loyalty of the Catholic clergy, expressed in their condemnation of the rebellion as a contravention of the laws of the Church, resulted in the government's surrender of all claims over appointments. The issue has particular interest because of its close similarity to the Irish 'Veto question' of the early nineteenth century: there the British government's claims to a negative voice in the election of Catholic prelates for Ireland was accepted by Rome but never given expression due to a sharp division among the Irish Catholic bishops and politicians themselves. In Upper Canada the Catholic Church was originally represented by a thin line of Indian mission stations, but with the British settlement of the province Catholicism was planted in a systematic and ordered form: the conditions of release from regular supervision, which allowed for lay intervention in ecclesiastical organization, were absent there.

The Church of England in British North America was never subject to undue lay incursions, for the same sort of reasons which kept it innocent of interference in the United States. There was, as elsewhere, a good deal of private lay patronage. There were also, especially in the early nineteenth century, constant complaints about lax clerical discipline; but the complaints themselves indicated an awareness and an acceptance of regular order in the Church. Lay revolts against properly constituted authority were rare—but one, at St Paul's Church in Halifax, Nova Scotia, the pro-cathedral of Bishop Inglis, became a crucial issue. From 1785 the vestry claimed the right to appoint rectors for the church quite independently of episcopal jurisdiction. Despite Inglis's denunciation of this 'Congregationalism' in the Church,[1] the vestry acted on its own initiative until the 1820s, when the secession of many of its leading members to the Baptist Church[2] allowed the imposition of more regular government.

[1] H. H. Walsh, *op. cit.* p. 114.
[2] W. H. Elgee, *The Social Teachings of the Canadian Churches* (Toronto, 1964), p. 63.

Church property and lay influence

At the start of the nineteenth century there was no general statutory provision for the incorporation of church property in any of the British North American provinces, and the question was almost hopelessly complicated, as it was in England, by denominational suspicions and the law of mortmain. Those ecclesiastical bodies requiring incorporation—all, that is, except the Church of England and the Catholic Church in Quebec, the former protected as an establishment, the latter under the clauses of the Act of 1774—had to proceed, as they did in contemporary America, by individual Bills in the legislatures. Sometimes these were contested by local religious factions and rival churches, and Catholic Bills were frequently greeted with popular fears of priestly temporal pretension, especially during the 'No Popery' agitations of the mid-century. This never constituted a serious threat to Catholic property, however; nor did the form of incorporation give control to lay trustees as in the United States. In 1859 a general act for the incorporation of ecclesiastical property was passed in the united provincial assembly of Canada, and this effectively disposed of remaining legal difficulties there.

The history of lay attempts to control some aspects of ecclesiastical organization in the hierarchical churches is an indication of the disrupting effects of social and political disturbance. The removal of these threats by episcopal action, and the incorporation of lay representation in church constitutions, illustrates a reassertion of regular discipline over potential anarchy, and a further shift in emphasis towards a sectarian awareness among the competing elements of a religious pluralism.

4

THE PROBLEM OF EDUCATION

Conflict between the denominations: this has seemed, and rightly, to characterize the history of primary education in the nineteenth century. It was the most obvious result of the incidence of religious pluralism. It is, however, important to notice that although ultimately the solutions arrived at in Britain, Canada and the United States differed somewhat in crucial points, they turned upon a common factor—the decision of the state to enter the field of education—and underwent a series of stages which were recognizably similar. Everywhere education was originally under the direct patronage of the established churches, and in receipt of exclusive state aid. Exceptions were the Catholic schools, dissenting academies and the village dame schools, which were entirely self-supported. In Britain, concurrent state aid for both Church and Nonconformist schools was established in 1833 by Lord John Russell: public subsidies and building grants were by then dispensed to the National Society, as the agency of Church of England education, and to the British and Foreign School Society, the nonconformists' counterpart. Catholic institutions received state grants from 1847. Such general state supervision of education as existed—for the allocation of these grants—was in the hands of a committee of the Privy Council. Similar arrangements existed in Scotland, but in Ireland state collectivism in the field of education underwent an early advance. In 1831 a system of national primary schools was created, supervised by a central board in Dublin.[1] Non-sectarian Christian education was included in the instruction given, although this, after a brief experimental period, failed to

---

[1] This Irish national system, which ante-dates all others, rather devalues Leo Pfeffer's remark that 'the American public school, free, secular and open to all, is the supreme achievement of American democracy'—*Church, State and Freedom* (Boston, 1953), p. 274.

satisfy the Catholic hierarchy. From the mid-century they began a campaign aimed at persuading the government to concede the English system of state-aided denominational schools. In this they remained, despite some slight modifications to the national system, unsuccessful.[1]

English dissenters, meanwhile, were seeking to destroy the establishment's virtual supremacy in education by urging the government to abolish the denominational grants, and institute a system of state schools with non-sectarian religious instruction—the Irish system, in fact. Radicals continued to press for wholly secular education. The resulting jealousies and rivalries between Church and Chapel are well-known. In 1870, Forster's Education Act created the arrangements which still largely exist today, at least in point of principle. Church schools of all denominations continued to receive state grants, but government Board schools were also set up, with non-sectarian religious instruction and Bible reading. Safeguards in the Act protected religious minorities from compulsory religious teaching. This 'dual system' of church and state schools was perpetuated in the Education Act of 1944. At the present time, Church of England schools are usually very intimately integrated with the state system, and are fully maintained by public money. State schools continue to give non-sectarian but Christian religious instruction, and each day must statutorily open with an act of worship. Catholic schools, and those Church of England schools less closely connected with the state system, receive large grants from public funds.[2]

Most of the features of the English compromise were reproduced in Canada. Quebec secured fully state-aided Catholic schools. In nearly all the other Canadian provinces a long nineteenth-century clash between the principles of denominational, non-

---

[1] See E. R. Norman, *The Catholic Church and Ireland in the Age of Rebellion, 1859–73* (London, 1965).
[2] There is no comparative study of British and American schools except for J. B. Conant's *Education and Liberty. The Rôle of the Schools in a Modern Democracy* (Harvard, 1953); but this book avoids discussion of religious education.

sectarian, and secular education resulted in the compromise of public schools with non-sectarian Christian instruction. In some provinces Catholic schools receive state support; in two provinces the contemporary American pattern of nearly secular schools has been established. As part of the accommodation made with Quebec sentiment to secure the confederation of 1867, education was left as a provincial concern, and hence the quasi-official sanction accorded the elements of the 'dual system' in many parts of modern Canada. In the United States, too, education was re-served to the individual states. There also public education, from its beginnings in the 1830s, included non-sectarian Christian in-struction, but everywhere state support for denominational schools was soon ended. This gave rise to those Catholic claims for tax-aided denominational schools which have increased so markedly in the last two decades. In the nineteenth century the American Catho-lic bishops extended arguments which almost exactly paralleled those of the Irish hierarchy. Indeed, with a free-trade in Irishmen across the Atlantic, there was a personal as well as an ideological connexion to account for this. Irish-American prelates frequently cited the English system of state-aided denominational education as a model: in 1890, for example, Archbishop John Ireland of St Paul, Minnesota, suggested the extension of the English system to the United States at a meeting of the National Education Association.[1] The present problem of American education is in reality a fault of premature development. Public schools were instituted at a time when national expressions of non-sectarian Protestant Christianity were uncontroversial. But today, when the Constitutional separation of church and state is being strictly applied to the states, through the 'due process' clause of the Four-teenth Amendment, Americans are realising the implications and difficulties of real secular education. 'It would seem then', Evarts B. Greene has written, 'that more than a century after the formal separation of church and state in the American commonwealth the application of this principle to education still leaves some

[1] John Tracy Ellis, *American Catholicism* (Chicago, 1955), p. 109.

highly practical problems to be solved.'¹ Some of these will be considered later.

The solutions of educational questions certainly differed somewhat in the three nations, but the problems and conflicts which characterized them—and which are even now assuming renewed significance in the United States—had many points in common, and reflected a shared experience. At its most basic statement the common problem was this: how to secure religious equality for all the components of a religious pluralism when only some had chosen to create, or were rich enough to sustain educational institutions of their own; when the state required education as a qualification for sound citizenship; when there existed, as a relic of state confessionalism, church schools already in receipt of public funds; and where the proposed solutions of the interested parties were mutually exclusive. Most of the variations in the educational experiences of Britain, Canada, and the United States, were only ones of degree, The arguments employed by the contending parties were echoed everywhere. The schools question, therefore, provides an important illustration of the general principle that the redefinition of the relations between church and state did not, in itself, produce any striking divergences in the experience of the three countries.

I. RELIGION IN THE SCHOOLS—THE UNITED STATES

During the colonial period there were great regional differences in the provision of education. The New England schools, though usually supervised by Congregational ministers, were state schools. Elsewhere Colonial governments tended to leave education as a responsibility of the churches. Religious instruction was acknowledged as the basis of all education—a condition of things which survived in the states after independence. But in the new nation the competing denominations fell into mutual discord about the

¹ *Religion and the State. The Making and Testing of an American Tradition* (Ithaca, New York, 1954 edition), p. 133.

amount of financial aid they should each receive for their schools from the state governments, just as they did in England. And when the first few public schools were created in the middle and southern states, during the 1820s, the churches quarrelled about the type of religious instruction to be given in them. The same conflicting religious pluralism which had spelled doom to the establishments, now operated to weaken the long-term chances for confessionalism in the schools. The formation of sectarian Education Societies after 1815 emphasized the different claims of the churches. From around 1830, in fact, there was a distinct hardening of sectarian religious interests generally,[1] and this served only to clarify the points of controversy between the denominations, and make the problem of school religious education still more difficult to resolve.

Gradually state provision of public education increased, and the problem of religious instruction became more crucial. Much of the conservative opposition to the expansion of the public schools came, in fact, from those who feared that they would create a threat to the survival of religious instruction.[2] In 1827 denominational textbooks were prohibited in the public schools of Massachusetts and New Hampshire by their legislatures. Other states followed this lead during the mid-nineteenth century.[3] Simultaneously, the state legislatures began to prohibit the allocation of public funds to denominational schools. Increasing immigration, and the westward movement of population along the frontier, accelerated the need for government to provide elementary educational facilities which could be open to all children regardless of their brand of Christianity. In the west the educational task was too much even for the generous voluntaryism of the American churches: only the state had the resources required. Michigan in

[1] W. W. Sweet, *The Story of Religion in America* (New York, enlarged edition, 1939), p. 373.
[2] Rush Welter, *Popular Education and Democratic Thought in America* (New York, 1962), p. 104.
[3] For a general account, see S. W. Brown, *The Secularization of American Education* (New York, 1912).

1835, and Wisconsin in 1848, included in their first state constitutions the clause, 'nor shall any money be drawn from the treasury for the benefit of religious societies, or religious or theological seminaries'.[1] New western states copied the practice. Grants from public resources for denominational education were terminated in the eastern states by constitutional amendments—starting with New Jersey in 1844.[2] It should be noticed, however, that church schools, like other forms of church property, were commonly exempted from taxation, and this continued to allow a concealed form of state aid to denominational education. But the universal application of the separation principle (of the First Amendment of the federal constitution) to education, prevented the development in America of the English 'dual system'. The American alternative did not, however, solve the basic difficulties which the English compromise had to some extent resolved.

The 'secularization' of the American public schools was extremely imperfect. 'The issue of separation as applied to education', as R. Freeman Butts has noticed, 'did not become a matter of controversy until *after* the principle of separation was decided in general, and until *after* the movement for the creation of a public school system was under way.'[3] The American compromise was an experiment in non-sectarian religion. The states all came to make provision for the teaching of what in Britain was called 'common Christianity', and what Horace Mann, implying the same thing, described as the 'common core' of Christianity. This was the residuum of shared doctrines believed to exist among the Christian denominations when sectarian finesses had been creamed off. It was a way of solving denominational rivalries. 'Common Christianity' was taught in the English Board schools after the

---

[1] Michigan Constitution of 1835, article 1, section 5; printed in F. N. Thorpe, *The Federal and State Constitutions of the United States* (Washington, 1909), IV, 1931. Wisconsin Constitution of 1848, article 1, section 18; printed *ibid.* VII, 4079.

[2] New Jersey amended Constitution, article 1, section 3; printed *ibid.* V, 2599. See also, E. P. Cubberley, *Public Education in the United States* (Boston, 1919), p. 180.

[3] *The American Tradition in Religion and Education* (Boston, 1950), p. 116.

1870 Act, but had been applied in the national schools of Ireland since 1831. There the Catholic bishops came to object to it through the same ideological opposition to 'Indifferentism' and latitudinarianism which led to its rejection among their American counterparts. America, on the other hand, was perfectly suited to the distillation of Protestant Christianity into a single short statement. The Reverend Henry Caswall, a Church of England minister who had settled in Indiana, explained the process at a practical level. 'The American people, especially those residing in the country, are in the habit of hearing a great variety of preachers, who agree with each other on certain points, and disagree on others', he wrote in 1839: 'the doctrines on which they agree are believed, while those on which they disagree are disputed or denied.'[1] William Ellery Channing remarked on the same phenomenon as it operated in the more sophisticated urban centres. 'We look at Christianity', he wrote of American experience in 1834, 'very much as if no sect existed, and do not exaggerate the importance of certain doctrines because they distinguish us from others.'[2] The Unitarianism, Universalism, and various types of Christian Transcendentalism fashionable in the New England towns of the 1830s and 1840s especially, produced an intellectual climate easily attuned to the sort of wide expression of belief which the formulation of 'common Christianity' required.

It was in 1837, when Horace Mann, himself a Unitarian, became secretary to the first state education board—in Massachusetts—that the first moves towards a systematized conflation of Christian principles were made. A device was required to overcome the problem of denominational disagreements about the sort of religious instruction to be imparted in the new public schools. Mann succeeded in stamping all subsequent American education with the solution he worked out for Massachusetts. Its essence was a statement of 'common Christianity'. Although Mann has fre-

---

[1] Henry Caswall, *America and the American Church* (London, 1839), p. 64.
[2] *Memoir of William Ellery Channing, with Extracts from his Correspondence and Manuscripts* (London, 1851), II, 115.

quently been described as the father of secular education, he was not. He was deeply opposed to sectarian instruction in the schools, and the actual laws of Massachusetts dictated this view too: a statute of 1827 prohibited denominational teaching.[1] His scheme left the public schools Christian—but non-sectarian. The reading of the Bible became a central feature of American public education (until very recent years) because Mann chose to place the open Bible in the schools. In 1848 he explained the theory of 'common Christianity' and its practical intention.

That our public schools are not theological seminaries is admitted. That they are debarred by law from inculcating the peculiar and distinctive doctrines of any one religious denomination amongst us, is claimed; that they are also prohibited from even teaching that what they do teach is the whole of religion, or all that is essential to religion, is equally certain. But our system earnestly inculcates all Christian morals; it founds its morals on the basis of religion; it welcomes the religion of the Bible; and in receiving the Bible, it allows it to do what it is allowed to do in no other system, to speak for itself.[2]

In 1839 Mann had also described how, in the public schools,

The fundamental principles of Christianity may and should be inculcated. This should be done through the medium of a proper text-book to prevent abuses. After this, each denomination must be left to its own resources, for inculcating its own faith or creed.[3]

This was the educational expression of the unofficial 'establishment' of national Protestantism in the United States during the nineteenth century. How far 'common Christianity' was from real secularism can be detected from the respectable support it got from Protestant divines. Channing, who was an avowed and active follower of Mann in Massachusetts, and who entertained the strongest opinions about the need to improve public education, included 'the duties which we owe to God' as among the essential

[1] R. B. Culver, *Horace Mann and Religion in the Massachusetts Public Schools* (Yale, 1929), p. 235.
[2] Quoted in Leo Pfeffer, *Church, State and Freedom* (Boston, 1953), p. 285.
[3] R. B. Culver, *op. cit.* p. 109.

requirements for instruction in the public schools.[1] Indeed, he went a long way in laying the responsibility for Christian education on the state. In 1835, when he was concerned about the fate of children in the factories, and was determined that they should not suffer the moral degradation apparent in England, he wrote of the American government as one professing 'to respect the obligations of Christianity'.[2] Alexander Mackay, the British barrister who toured the United States in 1846, described the operation of 'common Christianity' in the schools and made the same point:

In a country in which the Church has been wholly divorced from the State, it was to be expected that education would be divested of the pernicious trammels of sectarian influence. The Americans have drawn a proper distinction between secular and religious instruction, confining the Church to its own duties, and leaving the schools free in the execution of theirs. They have not fallen into the ridiculous error of supposing that education is 'Godless' when it does not embrace theology.[3]

The shared elements of 'common Christianity', however, were found to be much commoner to Protestants than to Catholics— the latter discovering that many doctrines which they regarded as essential to faith and morals were excluded from the various public school formulae altogether. School religious instruction was held, and rightly, to be stamped with Protestantism. As recently as 1947, in the Everson case, Justice Jackson of the United States Supreme Court remarked that 'our public school, if not a product of Protestantism, at least is more consistent with it than the Catholic culture and scheme of values'.[4] Despite occasional attempts by Catholic prelates to compromise with this scheme of things, the inevitable result was the separation of Catholic educational endeavour—as had occurred in Ireland—and the creation of a vast network of independent Catholic parochial schools. Catholics dis-

[1] *Memoir*, II, 235.
[2] *Ibid*. p. 220.
[3] *The Western World, or Travels in the United States in 1846–7: Exhibiting them in their latest development, social, political and industrial* (Philadelphia, 1849), II, 233.
[4] J. J. McGrath, *Church and State in American Law. Cases and Materials* (Milwaukee, 1962), p. 127.

agreed with the essential premise of 'common Christianity': that it was possible to separate secular instruction from religious truth. They therefore denied that non-sectarian religious instruction was an exercise of state religious neutrality. To them it was clearly an official preference for Protestantism. They have come to deny the position, as stated by Justice Frankfurter in the McCollum decision of 1948, that 'the non-sectarian or secular public school was the means of reconciling freedom in general with religious freedom'.[1]

The first real crisis came for the Catholics in 1840, with the celebrated confrontation between Bishop John Hughes[2] and the New York Public School Society. Without a school system of its own, the only free primary education available in the city came from this philanthropic agency, which was supported by public funds. Although there were still a few Catholics on its managerial committee, the vast majority were Protestants, and the religious instruction in the schools was distinctly Protestant, including the use of the King James Version of the Bible. The Catholics' objection—now advanced with a growing confidence inspired by the settlement of a large Irish Catholic immigrant population in the city—was that no adequate protection was afforded their childrens' faith and morals in schools conducted in the Protestant interest. Hughes began to establish private parochial schools, and because Catholics paid equal taxes, he also demanded financial aid from the city to support them. He was, perhaps, encouraged by the knowledge that William H. Seward, Governor of New York from 1839, was not opposed to the Catholic claims for relief.[3] For two years, amidst mounting hostility between Catholics and Protestants, the classic contest worked into the heart of local politics. Much crude anti-Catholicism went into the opposition to Hughes' demands. There was widespread speculation about a

[1] *Ibid.* p. 178.
[2] Hughes was born in Co. Tyrone in 1797. His family emigrated to Pennsylvania and he was educated at Mount St Mary, Emmitsburg. In 1837 he was appointed coadjutor to Bishop Dubois of New York. He died as Archbishop in 1864.
[3] G. G. Van Deusen, 'Seward and the School Question Reconsidered', in *The Journal of American History* LII, no. 2, (1965), 314.

The problem of education

Catholic conspiracy to remove the Bible from the schools; constitutional questions were secondary considerations. Finally, in the Maclay Act of 1842, a Board of Education was set up and the city assumed direct responsibility for education. No public funds were to be used for sectarian purposes; church schools would have to provide for themselves.[1] In 1840 Hughes had declared: 'We are unwilling to pay taxes for the purpose of destroying our religion in the minds of our children.'[2] Now he had to increase the efforts of providing alternative institutions. Contemporaneous outbursts of anti-Catholic nativism did not help matters. It was, for example Bishop Kenrick's objection of 1842 to the use of the Protestant Bible and prayers in Philadelphia schools, which aroused the anti-Catholic reaction that issued finally in the frightful 'No Popery' rioting of 1844.[3] The Know-Nothing party supposed that Catholic educational demands were an affront to American ideals.

The extensive creation of Catholic parochial schools was a result of all this. At the time of the New York controversy in 1840 there were only about two hundred in the whole of America, and these were still in the somewhat narrow mould originally cast by Mother Seton, the founder of the first free Catholic school at Emmitsburg. A truly remarkable effort by the least wealthy sections of society—many of whom were poor immigrants—achieved an impressive multiplication of educational institutions. The situation exactly paralleled that in Ireland and Canada. There were, however, still occasional attempts to compromise with the public system in various states. Thus in the 1890s Archbishop John Ireland experimented for a few years in certain Minnesota towns with an arrangement whereby parochial school buildings were leased to the local school boards for use during school hours. Religious education was given outside the times stipulated for secular instruction. Although this device had the advantage of allowing a sort of

[1] See E. B. Greene, op. cit. pp. 124–5; T. Maynard, op. cit. I, 274; J. Tracy Ellis, op. cit. p. 66.
[2] Theodore Maynard, Great Catholics in American History (New York, 1962), p. 106.
[3] J. Tracy Ellis, op. cit. p. 66.

concealed aid to the Catholic schools, there were too many practical objections and the scheme lapsed.[1] The Poughkeepsie plan,
approved by Cardinal McCloskey, which was of a similar type,
met a comparable fate in 1898.[2] But Catholics saw that the future
of their schools must lie with private effort. At the Third Plenary
Council, at Baltimore in 1884, a national educational policy had
been adopted by the hierarchy, and subsequently approved by
Rome. A school was to be established in every parish, and parents
were required to send their children only to these Catholic institutions. By 1900, there were around 4,000 parochial schools. In 1961,
there were 10,132, and 462 fee-paying elementary schools. There
were by then, too, 1,546 Catholic high schools, and 869 fee-paying
secondary schools.[3] Thus over ninety per cent of all non-public
school enrolment in contemporary America is under Catholic
auspices. Of the remainder, it is the Lutherans who have shown
a comparable awareness of the need for separate schools. The
German Lutherans of the Missouri Synod of 1847, who created a
system of parochial schools and seminaries, continue today to
provide by far the largest non-Catholic system of religious education in the United States.[4]

   Although the individual states withdrew public aid to denominational schools during the mid-nineteenth century, federal assistance continued in one significant area: the Indian mission schools.
Most of the leading Protestant churches, as well as the Roman
Catholics, received grants from the federal government for their
missionary institutions along the frontier and in reserved lands.[5]
These allowances began in 1819, when Congress voted $10,000

[1] E. B. Greene, *op. cit.* p. 129.
[2] Theodore Maynard, *The Story of American Catholicism* (Image Books edition, New York, 1960), II, 102.
[3] *Religions in America*, edited by Leo Rosten (New York, 1963), p. 267. Never-theless, only half the Catholic children of America actually attend parochial schools. Most parochial schools are not entirely free: nominal tuition fees some-times have to be charged.
[4] *Ibid.* p. 263, for the comparative tables of enrolment in 1958.
[5] See R. Pierce Beaver, 'Church, State and the Indians: Indian Missions in the New Nation', in *A Journal of Church and State* (May, 1962), p. 11.

The problem of education

to be distributed between the denominations. Government grants also paid two-thirds of the cost of school buildings.[1] Federal aid was increased when John C. Calhoun was Secretary for War under President Monroe, so that in 1825 the government was paying out $13,620 to the mission schools alone.[2] This sum only represented about one-seventh of the total outlay by the missionary societies. The churches were dissatisfied about the apportionment of state funds: in 1836, for example, most of the 52 schools receiving grants were Methodist or Baptist, and only three were Catholic. Despite a change in government policy during the 1830s, when the removal of the Indians to the west was attempted, federal aid to the missionary institutions continued. In 1869 a Board of Indian Commissioners was set up by Congress, and its members appointed by the President on the nomination of the different denominational bodies. From this point, Catholic and Protestant endeavours diverged. The Catholics were convinced that they were unlikely to be assigned many benefits under the new Board, and so broke away to establish their own Bureau of Catholic Indian Missions in 1874. It was this body which secured grants for Catholic 'contract schools' out of Indian tribal funds. These were the schools to which Catholic Indian parents could opt to send their children. The Supreme Court upheld the arrangement in 1906.[3] Generally, however, there was a growing opposition to the use of federal resources to support denominational mission schools, and in 1896 Congress announced that it was 'the settled policy of the government to hereafter make no appropriation whatever for education in any sectarian school'.[4] The grants to the Indian schools therefore ceased—except for those allocations made out of Indian tribal funds. These were still applied to both Catholic and Protestant education. As Anson Phelps Stokes saw, the Indian policy of the federal government was an illustration of the impossibility of a total separation of religion and the state

[1] A. P. Stokes, *Church and State in the United States* (New York, 1950), I, 704.
[2] W. W. Sweet, *Religion in the Development of American Culture, 1765–1840* (New York, 1952), p. 242.   [3] A. P. Stokes, *op. cit.* II, 288.
[4] *Ibid.* p. 289.

144

in America, for it 'shows the great religious bodies assuming important tasks as representatives of the government, and at its request'.[1]

At both federal and state level, very little alteration has been made to the essential principles of educational policy since the last third of the nineteenth century. This was not for want of trying. In 1875 the Blaine Amendment, introduced during Grant's presidency, was an attempt to prevent the application of any federal funds to assist schools under religious patronage or direction. This tentative move towards establishing a federal control of education failed to get a majority in the Senate[2]. State attempts to outlaw private—and therefore denominational—schools have also been made and defeated. In 1820 Michigan proposed a constitutional amendment to suppress parochial schools, but this did not get a majority when put to the voters. Oregon, in 1922, went rather further. There a law was actually passed which made attendance at the state public schools obligatory. A convent school and a military academy led the appeals against this legislation; the State of Oregon claiming that it had the right to ensure that its citizens were adequately educated according to criteria supplied by the State itself. In the famous case of *Pierce* v. *Society of Sisters*, in 1925, the United States Supreme Court ruled the Oregon statute unconstitutional—Justice McReynolds declaring that 'the child is not the mere creature of the state; those who nurture him and direct his destiny have the right, coupled with the high duty, to recognize and prepare him for additional obligations'.[3] This judgment provided a federal safeguard for church schools everywhere.

Although the general principles of educational policy have changed very little, the last thirty years in America have seen an accumulating series of legal tests over particular aspects of the 'common Christianity' permitted in the public schools. Catholic demands for financial aid have also increased. Both deserve careful attention, for they illustrate the crucial difficulties suggested by

[1] *Ibid.* p. 288. [2] W. G. Katz, *op. cit.* p. 64. [3] J. J. McGrath, *op. cit.* p. 80.

any insistence on a real separation of religious opinion and public policy in the educational field.

First, it should be noticed that such religious practices as have survived in the public schools—and some have even been reinforced by state laws in the present century—have been expressed in the form of non-sectarian Protestantism. There are certainly wide variations of practice, but considering the fact that American public schools enjoy an intimate connexion with the state, and are frequently believed to be secular institutions, given over more to flag-saluting than Biblical exegesis, a surprising amount of contact with religious opinion continues to be provided in them. A questionnaire answered by 2,183 public schools in 1961 yielded some interesting statistical evidence: 76 per cent of the schools provided teachers with materials for instruction *about* religion; yet in only 4 per cent were there regular Bible classes. Religion was found to have an important place in non-curricular activities ('programs and practices provided by the school in addition to formal classwork'): 41 per cent conducted Bible reading and 22 per cent had regular acts of worship.[1] Though outside school time, these activities obviously associate education and teaching with religious belief, and provide the facilities of public-school buildings for their expression. The provision of materials for instruction *about* religion is important. Teaching *about* religion is the function of a neutral state; one which is not hostile to the idea of religious belief. It would be a confessedly secular state which, in a religious society, prevented the dissemination of information about the religiosity of its citizens. There can be little doubt that in practice, on the other hand, in most American schoolrooms the distinction between *teaching about religion* and *teaching religion* is scarcely apparent to the children, and for the teachers themselves it suggests a degree of objectivity largely unattainable in a church-related society. But the idea of teaching *about* religion is conducive to the propagation of common elements in received faiths—of 'common Christianity' in fact, as well, per-

---

[1] *Religion in America*, edited by Leo Rosten (New York, 1963), pp. 269–70.

haps, as Herberg's even more broadly-conceived American religiosity. The difficulty of avoiding religion altogether, and the real impossibility of any attempt at a total separation of religious and secular instruction, was pointed out by Justice Jackson in the Supreme Court's ruling on the McCollum case in 1948:

I think it remains to be demonstrated whether it is possible, even if desirable...completely to isolate and cast out of secular education all that some people may reasonably regard as religious instruction...The fact is that, for good or ill, nearly everything in our culture worth transmitting, everything which gives meaning to life, is saturated with religious influences, derived from paganism, Judaism, Christianity—both Catholic and Protestant—and other faith accepted by a large part of the world's peoples. One can hardly respect a system of education that would leave the student wholly ignorant of the currents of religious thought that move the world society for a part in which he is being prepared.[1]

In 1950 the New Jersey Courts underlined the point explicitly in the case of *Doremus* v. *Board of Education*: 'While it is necessary that there be a separation between Church and State, it is not necessary that the State chould be stripped of religious sentiment.'[2]

The Doremus case concerned the reading of the Bible in New Jersey public schools before classes began. This practice was declared legal provided those children seeking to absent themselves on conscientious grounds were freely allowed to do so—an arrangement similar in intention to the Cowper-Temple clause of the British Education Act of 1870, and the 'Stopford Rule' of 1847 in the regulations of the Irish National Board of Education. The question of school Bible reading, and the still widespread practice of reciting the Lord's Prayer, remain issues of the utmost controversy. The upholders of a strict separation of church and state

[1] J. J. McGrath, *op. cit.* p. 188.
[2] *Ibid.* p. 238. Some have pointed to the actual impossibility of keeping religion out of the schools. 'Religion will be in the public schools whenever men... honestly seek total explanations of themselves...Religion will be in the public schools through the concrete personal commitments of teacher, administrators and students'—James E. Loder, *Religion and the Public Schools* (New York, 1965), p. 12.

argue that they are unconstitutional aids to religious belief. Bible reading is still obligatory in a few states, is left to the discretion of local school-boards in others, and has almost everywhere else been explicitly defined as unconstitutional. In some places, the practice has been upheld on the grounds that it is non-sectarian (provided that no commentary on the text is offered by the teacher), and this is a very clear indication of the surviving strength of the old belief that 'common Christianity' was genuinely inter-denominational. But in the present century, in addition to Catholic objections to the King James Version of the Scriptures, Jews, atheists and secularists have begun to contest Bible reading as a practice giving state preference to Christianity.[1] In an Illinois case of 1910, the state Supreme Court ruled that the reading of the Protestant Bible *was* sectarian religious education, and therefore unconstitutional. And that, on the whole, seems clearly enough to be the constitutional interpretation at which all the states seem destined eventually to arrive. Although the Doremus case upheld Bible reading in 1950, an important contrary judgment was given in 1959 over the case of *Schempp* v. *School District of Abington*. This upset a Pennsylvania law requiring daily school Bible reading, followed by recitation of the Lord's Prayer. The Schempp decision turned on an interpretation of state neutrality. Justice Clark declared that 'the daily reading of the Bible buttressed with the authority of the State, and more importantly to children, backed with the authority of their teachers, can hardly do less than inculcate or promote the inculcation of various religious doctrines'.[2] And that was held to be contrary to the First Amendment of the federal instrument.

In a particularly dramatic example, during the present century, the educational authorities of Tennessee, Mississippi and Arkansas have actually employed the law to compel Protestant Biblicism. The issue, of course, was that of biological evolution. In 1925 the state of Tennessee, under pressure from effective and popular Fundamentalist agencies, made it a statutory offence 'to teach any

[1] E. B. Greene, *op. cit.* p. 128.   [2] J. J. McGrath, *op. cit.* p. 247.

theory that denies the story of the Divine creation of man as taught in the Bible'. This was state confessionalism *in excelsis*. The sensational prosecution of a Dayton high-school teacher under the law threw the question open to national debate. Clarence Darrow, the defence attorney for John Scopes, argued for the strict separation of church and state by declaring that the Tennessee law was an unconstitutional establishment of religion. He lost the case.[1] It was, it is true, the state of Tennessee which ultimately inherited the wind, but its legal confessionalism marked a late, and extreme illustration of the accomodation of non-sectarian Christianity within public-school education. It showed a surviving popular belief that a total separation of the law and religious opinion, in crucial particulars, may not be either desirable or necessary.

One other, more recent manifestation of that belief has been decisively overruled, however. In 1951 the New York State Board of Regents, in an attempt to heighten 'moral and spiritual training in the schools', drew up a simple prayer to be used in the city's public schools: 'Almighty God, we acknowledge our dependence upon Thee, and we beg Thy blessings upon us, our parents, our teachers, and our country.'[2] The Regents' prayer, of course, is simply the old formula of 'common Christianity' broadened— or reduced in content—to include Jews, and indeed all who profess belief in a Supreme Being. Any child who objected to reciting it each day was free to absent himself. The parents of ten pupils in the city's ninth school district decided to contest the constitutional validity of the Regents' prayer. They claimed that it was inconsistent with their own beliefs, and those of their children, and was a contravention of the 'no establishment' clause of the First Amendment of the federal Constitution. Their suit, *Engel* v. *Vitale*, arrived finally at the United States Supreme Court in 1962. The Court ruled in their favour, Justice Black announcing what

[1] For details of the Scopes Trial, see A. P. Stokes and Leo Pfeffer, *Church and State in the United States* (New York, 1964), p. 396.
[2] J. J. McGrath, *op. cit.* Appendix, p. 397.

will probably prove to be the death sentence on all comprehensive statements of national religiosity for educational purposes:

The petitioners contend among other things that the state laws requiring or permitting use of the Regents' Prayer must be struck down as a violation of the Establishment Clause because that prayer was composed by governmental officials as part of a governmental program to further religious beliefs. For this reason, petitioners argue, the state's use of the Regents' Prayer in its public school system breaches the constitutional wall of separation between Church and State. We agree with that contention since we think that the constitutional prohibition against laws respecting an establishment of religion must at least mean that in this country it is no part of the business of government to compose official prayers for any group of the American people to recite as part of a religious program carried on by government.[1]

Justice Douglas, in concurring, remarked on the degree to which the governmental structure was still 'honeycombed' with aids to religion, and that, he believed, was 'an unconstitutional undertaking whatever form it takes'.[2] Justice Stewart, in dissenting, upheld the right of schoolchildren to a share in what he called 'the spiritual heritage of our nation'.[3] But the majority decision in this crucial case has in fact established the principle that *any* expression of religious belief violates the official neutrality of the state, since it gives an unfair advantage to the opinions of those who believe, in however generalized a manner, over those who do not. It also gave a strict interpretation to the 'no establishment' clause in the First Amendment, applied to the states through the operation of the 'due process' clause of the Fourteenth. As in other recent cases, it was now held to prohibit *any* connexion between the state and religious belief, not merely the favourable treatment of one church over another in law. The Regents' prayer decision caused something of a rumpus in some of the churches. Bishop James Pike led the protests of the Episcopalians, and Cardinal Spellman those of the Catholics. The latter, in remarking that the Court's ruling 'strikes at the very heart of the Godly tradition

[1] J. J. McGrath *op. cit.* Appendix p. 398.   [2] *Ibid.* p. 403.   [3] *Ibid.* p. 408.

The United States

in which America's children have for so long been raised',[1] paid unconscious tribute to the efficacy of 'common Christianity' in the public schools. To many Protestants, however, as well as to most Catholics, generalized interdenominational formularies have always been suspect for inadequately expressing the exactitude of revealed truth; and there were many who welcomed the Supreme Court's verdict in *Engel* v. *Vitale* for sectarian reasons. Still others, strict separationists yet devout believers, applauded what they took to be its justice. The doctrine of state neutrality, after all, is one formulated by Christians. A 1964 report by a commission on religion in the public schools, set up by the American Association of School Administrators, declared that 'along with government and all its agencies, the school must be neutral in respect to the religious beliefs of individual citizens'. The reporters added: 'but this does not mean in any sense that public schools are or should be irreligious'.[2]

It was with the growth of state collectivism in the present century, and the accompanying huge development in public expenditure, that American Catholics began to increase their demands for state aid to denominational education. During the years of depression, in the 1930s, the expansion of federal aid into many fields previously the preserve of private agencies, suggested to some Catholics that parochial schools might benefit.[3] Their demands have not diminished to the present day. The Catholics put their case upon the same terms they had employed in the mid-nineteenth century: that as taxpayers they had the right to determine how that portion of their tribute given over to educational purposes might be directed, and that it was unjust for their contributions to go towards the maintenance of a system from which they were conscientiously unable to benefit. This was the argument also used by the Irish Catholics of the nineteenth century against

[1] W. G. Katz, *op. cit.* p. 36.
[2] *Religion in the Public Schools. A Report* (Harper Chapel Books, New York, 1964), p. 4.
[3] Paul Blanshard, *American Freedom and Catholic Power* (revised edition, Boston, 1960), p. 113.

the national schools, and it is closely analogous to the case of the English dissenters against the payments of compulsory church rates before 1868. It is, in effect, an argument for concurrent endowment, and would, if actually pursued, resurrect the principle of the old Virginian scheme for a 'General Assessment'. The Catholic case, in this sense, suggests a theoretical proposition quite distinct from the hard constitutionalism in which it is generally expressed: that Catholic freedom of religion, guaranteed by the First Amendment, is infringed by compulsory taxation from which they can receive no benefit. Modern claims for state aid to denominational education are, in practical terms, entirely claims on behalf of Catholics. The tiny minority of Protestant and Jewish private schools have not pressed for public support. Among the surviving indirect aids to religious education in the public school systems, however, there are many which have relieved Catholics. These are at present undergoing review in the courts, and are involving discussion of the most fundamental aspects of the relationship of the state to religious belief.

One arrangement which could be held to imply state support of denominational education is 'released time' in public schools. This began as early as 1913 in Indiana. By 1961 almost 30 per cent of American public schools enjoyed a released time programme.[1] In the typical model, a small portion of the time set aside for regular school instruction is released, so that children can be sent for denominational religious instruction to teachers appointed by the various churches, either in the public schoolrooms or in an outside church building. This could be construed as a means of providing religious instruction within the public school system— and in practice it has often looked like it—including financial support, at least in the sense that where the programme is fulfilled in the public schools themselves, the churches were spared the expense of providing accommodation. It was, indeed, the question of location which proved to be decisive in the courts. In 1948 the Supreme Court ruled, in the case of *McCollum* v. *Board of Education*,

[1] *Religion in America*, edited by Leo Rosten (New York, 1963), p. 271.

that the released time allowed in Champaign County, Illinois, was unconstitutional since the use of a public building for religious teaching was a violation of the First Amendment. Justice Black remarked that the state was affording 'sectarian groups an invaluable aid in that it helps to provide pupils for their religious classes through use of the state's compulsory public school machinery'. He concluded: 'this is not separation of church and state'.[1] In 1952, however, in *Zorach* v. *Clauson*, the same court decided that released time was quite legal in New York City, since there the public schoolrooms were not actually used for the instruction of religion. The children attended external religious centres in the time made available. Therefore the McLaughlin Act of 1940, which had generally permitted released time in the New York schools, was held to be constitutional.

Another form of public aid to denominational education has resulted from state provision of school textbooks in secular subjects. Louisiana, Mississippi and New Mexico have permitted the free distribution of such books to *all* schools, whether private or public. The Supreme Court of the United States upheld the practice in *Cochran* v. *Louisiana State Board of Education*, in 1930, by establishing the principle that it was not the church schools which benefited, but the children who attended them. This helped the state: 'individual interests are aided only as the common interest is safeguarded', as Justice Hughes said in his decision.[2] Yet another form of state support—this time by the federal government—was implied by the School Lunch Act of 1946, which provided free school meals for private-school children in those states whose own laws prevented them from offering the service.[3] It has, again, been the numerically superior Catholic schools which have received assistance here. But the most celebrated

---

[1] J. J. McGrath *op. cit.* p. 175. In this important case, the appellant's petition stated that religious teachers were allowed to visit the public schools weekly, and claimed that this violated the First and Fourteenth Amendments.

[2] *Ibid.* p. 103. The Cochran case was brought by citizens seeking to restrain the state board of education from purchasing textbooks for private schools.

[3] 60. stat. 233.

form of aid to church schools has been public provision of free school-bus transportation. This has been allowed in eighteen states, and 20 per cent of American educational authorities have therefore aided sectarian education indirectly.[1]

The most famous post-war legal decision on the whole question of church and state relations, and certainly one which opened up whole new aspects of controversy, was about school-bus transportation. The Everson case began when a New Jersey taxpayer objected to the use of public funds for transporting parochial schoolchildren, citing it as a violation of the First and Fourteenth Amendments of the American Constitution, and as forming a connexion between the state and religious belief. In 1947 the Supreme Court ruled that the practice, like the Louisiana textbooks case, was an exercise of state welfare—an aid to the child and not to the school—and that it was therefore constitutional. The judgment was not unanimous: four of the nine opinions were dissentient. Mr Justice Black, in delivering the opinion of the Court, explained the position simply;

The First Amendment has erected a wall between church and state. That wall must be kept high and impregnable. We could not approve the slightest breach. New Jersey has not breached it here.[2]

This position explicitly included the doctrine of the state's neutrality in religion. 'We must be careful', Black also said, 'in protecting the citizens of New Jersey against state-established churches, to be sure that we do not inadvertently prohibit New Jersey from extending its general state law benefits to all its citizens without regard to their religious beliefs.'[3] All the opinions delivered in *Everson* v. *Board of Education* involved constructions of the history of the separation of church and state in America, and the four dissentients expressed a very strict separationism.[4] They claimed that, according to the tests originally applied by Madison and Jefferson, indiscriminate school-bus transportation must be

---

[1] Leo Rosten, *op. cit.* p. 271.
[2] J. J. McGrath, *op. cit.* p. 123.   [3] *Ibid.* p. 122.
[4] W. G. Katz, *op. cit.* p. 65.

unconstitutional since it violated the precept 'that money taken by taxation from one is not to be used or given to support another's religious training or belief'.[1]

Some states have had legal cases successfully brought against their provision of free bus transportation for denominational schoolchildren. But the Everson decision has shown the extent to which the American separation of church and state has turned out to be far more flexible, and in some things far more tentative, than Americans had themselves come to imagine. Strict separationists have increased their pressures since 1947 with a large number of legal test-cases. Justice Douglas, who provided the majority of one in the Everson case, has since changed his mind. One of the immediate results of the case was the formation in 1948 of 'POAU'—Protestants and Other Americans United for the Separation of Church and State. This society, with its early anti-Catholic overtones, is a further indication of the close American association between denominational education and Catholic education. Or as Justice Jackson put it, in his dissenting opinion on the Everson case, 'It is no exaggeration to say that the whole historic conflict in temporal policy between the Catholic Church and non-Catholics comes to a focus in their respective school policies.'[2]

2. RELIGION IN THE SCHOOLS—BRITISH NORTH AMERICA

Conflict between the Protestant churches over the issue of state-supported denominational education, the creation of a dual system of church and state schools, the formula of 'common Christianity' in the public schools, and claims by the Catholic Church for a separate grant-aided system of its own—all these appeared in the British North American provinces before the confederation of 1867. As in the United States, educational issues redefined the relationship of church and state as they were debated out by the polemicists. 'On the one side ranged the Church of Rome, the

[1] J. J. McGrath, *op. cit.* p. 138. [2] *Ibid.* p. 127.

High Church party of Anglicanism, and perhaps some Wesleyan Methodists of immediate English extraction, each claiming an exclusive position in Christendom and special privileges from the state'—Dr J. S. Moir has written of the education question in Canada—'on the other side stood all those religious bodies which believed in voluntaryism and the separation of church and state'.[1] The question has remained one of current controversy.

In Upper Canada the govenment had made grants of public land for the maintenance of schools since 1797. These were grammar schools under the exclusive direction of the established Church of England.[2] The funds provided were in fact insufficient, however, and in 1807 it was necessary to enact a provision for a classical and mathematical school in each district. Thus eight district schools (later called grammar schools) were created out of government funds: these were under the direct control of the Governor, and were therefore conducted on Church principles. Opposition had already appeared to the establishment's advantages in the educational field; but the government, in attempting to safeguard the official position of the Church of England, saw its control of education as a necessary security against the diffusion of republican and democratical ideas. Elementary education for the poorer settlers began in 1816, when public funds were provided for the creation of common schools. These also taught the Gospel according to the Church of England.[3] Most of the schoolmasters were brought out from England, at the expense of the Society for the Propagation of the Gospel, and this also tended to enhance the establishment's educational monopoly. In 1823 a General Board of Education, authorized by Sir Peregrine Maitland, assumed direction of both the district and the common schools. Strachan, then archdeacon of York, was its president. By the end of the decade there were 291 common schools, supported by the joint resources of state and church, and ten district schools,

[1] J. S. Moir, *Church and State in Canada West. Three Studies in the Relation of Denominationalism and Nationalism*, 1841–67 (Toronto, 1959), p. 180.

[2] Ernest Hawkins, *Annals of the Diocese of Toronto* (London (for S.P.G.), 1848), p. 183. [3] *Ibid.* p. 187.

self-supporting since they were fee-paying institutions, but under Church management.

Both radicals and dissenters had entered early protests against the establishment's educational privileges. With the rise of dissenting militancy, associated also with the clergy reserves and university controversies, claims were advanced for a share in state aid by dissenting schools. Later this was exchanged for a demand that non-sectarian public schools be created, in which all denominations could share a neutral but distinctly Christian educational system. This second claim came to predominate as weighty sections of dissenting radicalism moved towards absolute voluntaryism through their experience of the establishment's intransigence over the clergy reserves. At the end of the 1820s the Wesleyan Methodists, under the guidance of Egerton Ryerson and the *Christian Guardian*, argued for local taxation to provide a system of public schools in which non-sectarian Christianity would be taught free from the control of the state church.[1] They took the most prominent place in the ensuing Upper Canadian campaign for non-sectarian education. The Presbyterians had inherited the tradition of parochial schools from Scottish practice. The Church of Scotland schools of the Canadas and the Maritimes claimed, and sometimes got, state financial support and even grants from S.P.G. The Church of Scotland therefore tended to side with the Church of England in favour of denominational state education, even though it secured only an inferior allocation of public funds. The Lutherans and Mennonites also established schools of their own, but these were unsupported. The Presbyterian United Synod expressed its voluntaryism by joining the cause of non-sectarian education; so did the Baptists. And so did the Congregationalists in the Canadas, but not in Nova Scotia where they were more immediately soaked in the New England township system with its tradition of state-supported Congregational education.

In Lower Canada the principle of denominational education

---

[1] Goldwin French, *Parsons and Politics. The Rôle of the Wesleyan Methodists in Upper Canada and the Maritimes from 1780 to 1855* (Toronto, 1962), p. 123.

became so entrenched as to become ineradicable. Catholicism and the language question explain this position. The latter produced an almost obvious effect: even had there been interdenominational schools they would—like the national schools of Ireland—have been, in practical terms, largely Catholic parochial establishments, since almost everyone who spoke French was a Catholic. By the start of the nineteenth century the Quebec hierarchy were insistent upon denominational education. It had always been so; only Bishop Bailly, early in the 1790s, had been prepared to sanction a system of non-sectarian schools and mixed universities.[1] He had been on his own.

With the support of Mackenzie and the Canadian radical politicians, the dissenters placed the schools question high in their priority of grievances. The government, for its part, was beginning to recognize that existing educational facilities were inadequate for the growing population of the Canadas—as Charles Buller had pointed out in his section of the Durham Report.[2] Legislation followed the union of the Upper and Lower provinces. Day's Common School Act of 1841 was far less radical as finally passed than its sponsors had originally intended. Designed to create a national, secular system of education, it was in fact amended in response to opposition from the Churches of England and Rome. The Act provided a system of non-sectarian common schools throughout the united Canadian province. The Bible was to be used for religious instruction. Schools were to be endowed out of the sales of Crown lands and by local taxation exacted by municipal boards of education. Under clause 11 of the Act, 'any number of the inhabitants of any Township, or Parish, professing a Religious Faith different from that of the majority' could set up a board of their own and receive the same public aid for schools suited to their convictions.[3] Thus, through this immense concession, the Church of England in Canada West, and the Catholic Church of Canada East, retained both the principle and the reality

[1] H. H. Walsh, *The Christian Church in Canada* (Toronto, 1956), p. 78.
[2] Parliamentary Papers, 1839, xvii, 48.　　[3] J. S. Moir, *op. cit.* p. 132.

of separate denominational education. It now had a reinforced statutory authority. In 1842, when the system was actually begun, Robert Murray became superintendent of the schools in the west, and Jean Baptiste Meilleur in the east: a sensible division of function corresponding to the different linguistic and religious affiliations existing in the united province.

The attempt to graft a single system of common schools onto a very diverse society, and the large number of local compromises which had to result, meant that after two years the administrative machinery had become so intolerably inadequate that Canada West opted out and secured new legislation suited to its greater degree of religious pluralism. As it turned out, this not only broke up the last chance for a cultural assimilation of the Canadas, but gave content to the concept of non-sectarian education. In Hinck's Act of 1843, the denominational separate schools continued to receive legislative recognition and state aid, and were only slightly more restricted in one or two minor particulars. As a protection to the rights of religious minorities—especially the Catholics— children in the common schools were authorized to exempt themselves from the non-sectarian religious instruction on the recommendation of their parents. Thus Upper Canada anticipated the recognition of this principle as it appeared in the Irish 'Stopford Rule' of 1847, the English Cowper-Temple clause of 1870, and the ruling of the New Jersey Supreme Court in the Doremus Case of 1950. It was under the operation of Hinck's Act that Egerton Ryerson, the Methodist minister and propagandist, was appointed superintendent of education for Canada West in 1844.

Ryerson was the real founder of the Canadian public school system. In giving substance to the idea of non-sectarian but Christian education, he was the exact counterpart of Horace Mann in the United States. Like Mann, whose opinions he explicitly endorsed in his 1846 report on Canadian primary education,[1] and

---

[1] C. B. Sissons, *Egerton Ryerson, His Life and Letters* (Toronto, 1947), II, 95. In the same place, he also referred to the advantages of basing the Canadian system on the Irish one.

like the English Lord Stanley, who planned the Irish national schools in 1831, Ryerson was an exponent of 'common Christianity'. He believed that religion must form the basis of educational principle. 'No system of popular education will flourish', he said, 'which does violence to the religious sentiments of the churches.'[1] In 1846 he defined his purpose in a classic statement of 'common Christianity'. It was, he then declared, the object of his schools to promote 'the *general* system of truth and morals taught in the Holy Scriptures'. He believed the 'to inculcate the peculiarities of a Sect, and to teach the fundamental principles of Religion and Morality are equally different.'[2] When in 1849 the Assembly passed the Cameron Act, which completely secularized the schools by prohibiting the use of the Bible and the entry of Christian clergymen to give non-sectarian instruction, Ryerson tendered his resignation—an action which indicated the intensity of his conviction that the compromise of 'common Christianity' could solve the educational problems of a religious pluralism. Ryerson remained in office; his threat of resignation proving enough to make the Act a dead-letter. Lord Elgin correctly characterized Ryerson's endeavours when he described the Upper Canadian school system as established 'in the firm rock of our common Christianity'.[3]

In Canada East the Act of 1841 continued to operate under the superintendence of Meilleur. There, too, modifications occurred, sprung from experience of the actual operation of the common schools. These adjustments, by authorizing separate school boards for Catholics and Protestants, established the system of state-aided denominational education still more firmly in Canada. This was as agreeable to the Protestant minority as to the Catholics. During the debates on the Quebec Resolutions, prior to confederation, in 1865, John Rose told the delegates that in Canada East 'the distribution of state funds for educational purposes was made in

[1] W. H. Elgee, *The Social Teachings of the Canadian Churches* (Toronto, 1964), p. 76.
[2] Goldwin French, *op. cit.* p. 235.
[3] H. H. Walsh, *op. cit.* p. 188.

such a way as to cause no complaint on the part of the minority'. And the restrictions were minor: 'a single person has the right, under the law, of establishing a dissentient school and obtaining a fair share of the educational grant, if he can gather together fifteen children who desire instruction in it'.[1]

Development was not so happy in Canada West. There, where the common schools were non-sectarian, the demands of the Churches of England and Rome for the denominational principle became formidable. In 1846, Ryerson drafted a new Common Schools Act, which again systematized administrative machinery, and paid careful attention to the rights of church schools to public financial support. Protestant non-sectarian schools were to be created where the majority was Catholic and *vice versa*. All clergymen were to become visitors of the common schools in their areas. These concessions reflected Ryerson's increasing conviction that separate education was a necessary cross to bear until such time as the widespread diffusion of the ideals of 'common Christianity' had made it appear redundant. A new board of education was set up by the Act, composed of clergy and laity, and chaired by the Catholic Bishop Power.

Strachan and the High Church party in the Church of England sustained their opposition to the common schools of the provincial system of education. The Low Churchmen, whose leaders were mostly of Irish origin, favoured a scheme of education nearly approximate to the Irish national system. In 1847 Bishop Strachan publicly condemned the Irish system and declared once more for separate, grant-aided denominational schools.[2] In 1847, too, Bishop Power died—an event which was to signal a hardening of sectarian lines, for within a year his successor as Catholic Bishop of Toronto was Armand de Charbonnel. The new prelate was soaked in French Ultramontanism, and like the accession of Archbishop Cullen to the Irish scene in 1850, this led to a change in the Catholic attitude to non-sectarian education in Upper Canada. Earlier

---

[1] *The Confederation Debates in the Province of Canada, 1865*, edited by P. B. Waite (Toronto, 1964), p. 99. [2] J. S. Moir, *op. cit.* p. 139.

toleration and good relations with the government were exchanged for a new emphasis on the exclusive claims of the Catholic Church and the need to protect the faith and morals of Catholic children from Protestant proselytizing. De Charbonnel rejected 'common Christianity' for the same reasons that Cullen and the Irish bishops did, and for those which motivated Hughes in New York: that it was a specious formula which in reality was redolent of Protestantism. Strachan's continued insistence on the educational rights of the Church of England, as an establishment, and his increasing High Church sectarianism, produced effects which were not dissimilar from those wrought by the Catholics. From 1847, indeed, the Church and the Catholics were able, on a number of occasions, to cooperate in their opposition to the provincial school system. Petitions flowed into the assembly praying for a complete scheme of separate schools to replace the non-sectarian ones. In 1851 both Churches worked successfully to defeat Mackenzie's attempt to destroy the denominational schools.[1]

The Catholics were more amply provided with concessions than the Anglicans—a reflexion of the government's willingness to conciliate public opinion in the eastern half of the united province. By the terms of the Separate School Act of 1855, a special superintendent of denominational schools was appointed, and five heads of families were empowered to set up a denominational school. Parents with children at separate schools were exempted from local educational rating, and their schools continued to receive state financial aid determined according to a scale dependent upon the numbers in attendence. But the Act only applied to Roman Catholics. It did not even fully satisfy de Charbonnel; but to Strachan and the Church of England it came as a bitter deflation of their hopes.[2] Many dissenters, and the Grit reformers, regarded the Act as incompatible with the common-school system. They sent in vast numbers of petitions requesting the repeal of all separate school legislation. An increasing tide of anti-Catholicism, exploited by Orange militancy, imparted a quasi-theoretical aspect

---

[1] J. S. Moir, *op. cit.* p. 147.   [2] *Ibid.* p. 161.

to the popular case against the Catholics' educational claims. By the end of the 1850s, the dissenting churches were officially condemning separate schools for the first time. But an Act of 1863 merely reinforced the right of separate denominational schools to public aid. It was received with immense popular dissatisfaction. Under the legal protection afforded them, the denominational schools continued to increase in Upper Canada. The dual system was becoming as firmly established as it was to be in England.

So it was that by the time of the confederation debates, separate schools, existing within a provincial system of education and receiving full state aid, had been created by independent legislative action in both East and West Canada. The united provincial Act of 1841 was their common starting-point. Each of the federal provinces was accorded educational autonomy by the Quebec Conference, and it was stipulated that separate schools must everywhere be maintained as a guarantee of minority rights. The Maritime Provinces, where separate schools also existed, but where the educational battles of church and dissent had been fought out mainly on the university question, were agreeable to join this compromise. At the time of confederation, Nova Scotia had evolved a public school system on a non-sectarian model. But denominational religious instruction was conducted ouside regular teaching periods—an arrangement similar to the later 'released time' programmes of the United States. New Brunswick was without a state school system, and in 1871 the first Governor under the new confederal constitution, Lemuel Wilmot, and George King, a Methodist, created one which entirely replaced denominational education. The schools of the Methodists, Baptists and Presbyterians gladly merged into the new non-sectarian (but Christian) provincial system, happy that the educational imperialism of the Church of England was at last destroyed. The Catholics, however, regarded the non-sectarian principle with the same reservations as their co-religionists in Ontario and Quebec. In a long constitutional contest they were unable to persuade either the Privy Council or the Federal Parliament that the suppression of New Brunswick's state-aided church schools was a contravention of the British North America Act. The provincial government did, however, work out a plan for denominational instruction outside school hours based on the Nova Scotian example. At the present time, the public schools in the Maritime Provinces may even be owned by a religious corporation and leased to the public-school boards. Religious orders run many through this sort of arrangement: a solution also adopted by the Irish Board of Education during the 1860s. Yet despite these qualifications, it is clear that the dual system (of public non-sectarian Christian schools and state-aided Church schools) has survived as part of the Canadian Constitution—in clause 93 of the British North America Act of 1867. In contemporary Canada, a religious minority in the provinces of Quebec, Ontario, Saskatchewan and Alberta can still secure a separate, denominational elementary school, supported by the exclusive direction of their own taxes, and in receipt of direct grants from the provincial governments. In Newfoundland, on the other hand, which only joined the confederation in 1949, all the schools are operated by religious bodies, with full state support. In Canada generally, Indian and Eskimo schools directed by church missions receive government grants, like their nineteenth-century counterparts in the United States. Often these schools are actually built by the government and then handed over to be conducted by individual denominational agencies: a striking modern connexion between church and state.

After the confederation of 1867, the Church of England and the Church of Scotland gradually conformed to the common school system, withdrawing from opposition yet still retaining separate institutions for those who wished to support sectarian education. Opposition to state-aided denominational education had not ceased, but it was now turned almost exclusively against the privileged position of the Catholic schools. In the 1890s the Equal Rights Association sustained a campaign against the Catholic and French language schools of Ontario. The latter were cut off from state aid in 1911, but the Catholic denominational schools have survived. It is, of course, in Quebec that they have survived in the most intimate relation with the state. In the western Canadian provinces, largely settled after the worst of the educational controversies had blown across the east, the legacy of diversity was reflected in the different solutions adopted. Alberta and Saskatchewan now enjoy state aid for separate denominational schools, and provincial systems of non-sectarian Christian education. Manitoba and British Columbia, however, have adopted the American model. There the taxes support only the public schools, and all denominational education is privately financed.[1] In Manitoba this solution was strenuously contested by the advocates of separate schools, but their appeal to the Privy Council to overrule the provincial legislature was unsuccessful.

In Quebec province, the remnants of the non-sectarian school structure were cleared away by the Schools Act of 1875. The Act of 1841 was then finally in abeyance. Following Confederation, the Catholic population was able to enjoy a distinctive government of its own, and French-Canadian society, as de Grandpré remarked, became provincial rather than parochial.[2] Catholic political action revived. Bishop Bourget inspired the 'Programme Catholique'—an attempt to infiltrate conservative politics with the ultramontanist and anti-liberal ideals of the *Syllabus of Errors* and the Vatican Decrees. This divided the Catholics. But the more liberal groups within the Church, led by Archbishop Taschereau, were unable to get any support from Rome, whose influence, in fact, inclined decisively to Bourget's side. The replacement of state-aided church schools by a non-sectarian educational system in New Brunswick directed the energies of the Quebec Programmists to even greater hostility to non-sectarian education. 'Common Christianity', after all, had been condemned in the

---

[1] W. A. Brown, *Church and State in Contemporary America* (New York, 1936), Appendix v, p. 327.
[2] Marcel de Grandpré, 'Traditions of the Catholic Church in French Canada', in *The Churches and the Canadian Experience*, edited by J. W. Grant (Toronto, 1963), p. 11.

The problem of education

Syllabus of Errors under the heading of 'Indifferentism'. It was this renewed excitement and Catholic militancy which provided the context of the Schools Act of 1875; a measure which finally consecrated the confessional principle in Quebec. Under the Act, the Council of Public Instruction appointed two committees, one Catholic and one Protestant, to deal exclusively with the administration of the schools of their own faith. The theory of a single educational system for the province was therefore finally overthrown, and replaced by state-supported denominational schools, conducted by ecclesiastical agencies in cooperation with the provincial government. This is the arrangement which is still in existence. The Protestant schools of modern Quebec are virtually identical with the non-sectarian public schools of the rest of Canada, but in the Catholic schools fully denominational practices and instruction are allowed. Both are supported by taxation; persons of each denomination paying into a fund for the separate use of their own schools, and both drawing on a common fund arising from the taxation of corporations.[1]

Recent developments in Ontario have indicated the continuation of old difficulties, and shown that the existing educational compromise is by no means the final solution. In 1944 the provincial Parliament passed Drew's Education Act, which explicitly provided for religious courses in the public schools. Both the measure itself, and the actual texts prescribed, were based on the English Education Act of the same year—the Butler Act. The Ontario legislation was contested at the time by the Liberal Party, as an infringement of the principle of separation between church and state. This opposition has continued. In 1950, however, the report of a Royal Commission on education (the Hope Report) upheld religious teaching in the schools provided it was non-sectarian. 'Since the inception of a public system of education in Upper Canada, it has been an accepted principle that religion and morality, though not sectarianism, must have a central place in any system of education', the Commissioners remarked: 'It is

[1] Leo Pfeffer, *Church, State and Freedom* (Boston, 1953), p. 44.

166

evident that the spirit of the original statutes still pervades the Acts and regulations regarding religious instruction in our schools'. At the present time, the Ontario Committee on Religious Education in Schools is receiving evidence submitted from church and educational authorities on proposals for re-casting the nature of school religious instruction. Considerable diversity of view appears to prevail, but some liberal Churchmen, while continuing to uphold the need for religious knowledge in education, have moved nearer to the American strict separationist view that teaching *about* religion may be more admissible than straight religious instruction. An opinion submitted by the Anglican diocese of Toronto continues to support religious instruction in the public schools, but suggests changes which would allow appreciations to be made of all religious beliefs. 'It is a pluralistic world', the Anglicans observe, 'variegated in many ways, including religion.'[1]

3. RELIGION AND THE UNIVERSITIES

The question of state-supported higher education in the United States was never so crucial or so bitterly controversial as the schools issue. It never worked its way to the centre of political disagreement as the university question was to do in the British North American provinces. The first American institutions of higher education were under the control of religious bodies. As in Britain at that time, students, teachers and governing councils were subject to exclusive religious tests. These early universities were in fact established as a result of cooperation between church and state, and they received both permanent endowment and occasional grants from colonial legislatures. Charters of incorporation were given by the Crown. Like all British universities, their primary function was the preparation of learned men for the Christian ministry. William and Mary College in Virginia, and King's College in New York, both Church of England institutions, were

[1] *Draft Brief to be Submitted by the Diocese of Toronto to the Ontario Committee on Religious Education in the Schools* (1966), p. 4.

expressions of religious establishment in the educational field. No less so were Harvard, Yale and Dartmouth—provided for the Congregationalist New England establishments. There was already during the eighteenth century, a trend towards the increasing secularization of the colleges. New foundations were slightly less religiously, and slightly more commercially orientated—like the English dissenting academies of the same period. A swelling number of graduates entered secular professions; the rise of scientific studies and freer philosophical thinking added to the decline of theological exclusiveness.[1] With the separation of church and state in the various states during the fifty years following independence, these early colleges were either opened up to students and teachers of all Christian denominations by the abolition of exclusive religious tests and chairs of theology—as in Jefferson's reconstruction of William and Mary College—or else they were allowed to retain a voluntary but independent denominational status.[2]

State universities were established early in the life of the new nation, beginning with Georgia in 1784 and North Carolina in 1789. These were at first Christian, though non-sectarian. The University of Michigan, founded in 1837, was the first to abolish compulsory chapel.[3] Yet the maintenance of religious observance in the new state universities during most of the nineteenth century was an extraordinary testimony to the continuing domination of education by the clergy, in the west as well as in the east of the country.[4] After the mid-century, as the non-sectarian public-school system extended itself, the priority of Christianity in the state universities diminished. There was much variation here. In Georgia all university officers had still to subscribe to Christianity

[1] R. Hofstadter and W. P. Metzger, *The Development of Academic Freedom in the United States* (New York, 1955), p. 186.
[2] R. Hofstadter and Wilson Smith, *American Higher Education* (Chicago, 1961), I, 147–50.
[3] A. P. Stokes, *Church and State in the United States* (New York, 1950), II, 619.
[4] See D. G. Tewksbury, *The Founding of American Colleges and Universities before the Civil War, with Particular Reference to the Religious Influences Bearing upon the College Movement* (New York, 1932).

until 1877, and a South Carolina legislative provision of 1890 that the President of the University should not be an atheist is still in existence.[1] Public opinion supported the view that learning and religion were related: the American 'establishment' of non-sectarian Protestantism during the nineteenth century prevented any rapid departure from the recognition of some sort of religious affiliation. Most of the attacks which were made upon religious influence in higher education were not inspired by convictions about the impropriety of connexions between the churches and state institutions: they generally arose out of professional awareness that the clergy were ill-qualified to teach or plan scientific subjects.[2] The academic controversies over evolution and philosophic theology weakened religious authority in the universities, as they did in Britain and Canada.

After the establishment of state universities, it was the huge proliferation of denominational higher education which really characterized the first half of the nineteenth century. Indeed. Henry Caswall—admittedly a not quite impartial observer—noticed in 1839 that 'the institutions which have been endowed and are sustained by the state seldom prosper equally with those which have been established by the efforts of some Christian denomination'.[3] The militant dissenters of the United States, having succeeded in the formal separation of church and state, turned their abundant energies not so much against the existence of religious tests at the older colleges (as their counterparts did in Britain and Canada), for those tests had largely been rendered innocuous, but to a competition in higher education. A rapid multiplication of denominational colleges and theological seminaries was the result. Between 1780 and 1860 the total number of colleges increased from 9 to 173, all permanent foundations, with perhaps a substantially larger number which proved unsuccessful and have disappeared.[4] The Protestant denominational colleges usually ad-

[1] A. P. Stokes, *op. cit.* II, 621.   [2] R. Hofstadter and W. P. Metzger, *op. cit.* p. 353.
[3] Henry Caswall, *America and the American Church* (London, 1839), p. 201.
[4] C. E. Olmstead, *Religion in America, Past and Present* (Englewood Cliffs, New Jersey, 1961), p. 72.

vertised themselves as offering non-sectarian instruction, but despite the absence of religious tests and direct ecclesiastical control, most of them were distinctly partisan, especially when it came to the appointment of teaching staffs.[1] Most of the theological seminaries did not grant degrees, but they were incorporated by the state legislatures. All the denominations took a part in the expansion of theological education. In 1791 the Sulpicians founded a college in Baltimore to train Catholic clergy. In 1807 the first Congregationalist seminary was established at Andover in Massachussetts. In 1812 came the first Presbyterian venture (Princeton); the first Lutheran in 1816; in 1817 the first Episcopalian (General Theological Seminary in New York City); in 1825 the first Baptist; and in 1839 the first Methodist. Harvard founded its Divinity School in 1816, with Yale following in 1822. In the west the Churches were equally quick to set up theological colleges: the Episcopalians in 1824 and the Presbyterians in 1827.

The pattern of state and independent universities and colleges has survived to the present. Some of the independent institutions are secular, but most have some sort of religious affiliation, though almost nowhere are actual religious tests applied. Probably the Catholic University of America, founded at Washington in 1884 by the Third Plenary Council of the Church, is the most strictly denominational. By the start of the present century, the various states' governments were advanced in removing financial aid from denominational colleges. In Massachusetts aid was explicitly prohibited by law in 1917. But there are still traces of confessionalism: in Maryland, Maine, Pennsylvania and Vermont, state legislatures continue to allocate annual grants to colleges which have denominational affiliations.[2] There are wide variations, too, in the different states' interpretation of the separation of church and state in the public universities. In some southern states voluntary chapel services are permitted on the campus.[3] Illinois and New York have state scholarship programmes which allow their recipients

[1] R. Hofstadter and W. P. Metzger, *op. cit.* p. 294.
[2] A. P. Stokes, *op. cit.* II, 621.   [3] *Ibid.* p. 622.

to use them at church-related institutions.[1] This is certainly a connexion of church and state, and has, as such, been contested in the
courts.[2] The creation of Departments of Religion is not, perhaps,
a state support of religious belief, since the teaching and research
conducted in them are frequently *about* religion, rather than confessional teaching, and anyway the Departments, where they exist,
are not usually integrated faculties of the universities concerned,
though credits may be obtained towards an honours degree in
many of them.[3] But there are some states, like Wisconsin, where
even the affiliation of a Department or School of Religion is
thought to violate the strict separation of church and state in the
field of higher education.[4]

Second only to the clergy reserves controversy, it was the university question which most sharply focused the clash between
religious pluralism and the estalishment principle in British North
America. In almost every respect this clash either anticipated or
reproduced the experience of Britain itself. The critics of religious
discrimination in higher education were for a time placated, in the
Canadas and the Maritimes, by the acceptance of state concurrent
endowment, and by the removal of religious tests at the existing
Church colleges. Their agitation to secure the latter was strikingly
similar to that of the English dissenters' movement for the opening
of Oxford and Cambridge. It was in 1854 that British Parliamentary action first began to undermine the Church of England's
exclusive position at the two ancient universities. The need for
administrative reforms and the dissenters' demand for religious
equality were responsible for the resulting modifications, and ultimately for persuading Gladstone. In 1871 his administration passed
the University Test Act: by its provisions no academic office-

[1] J. J. McGrath, *Church and State in American Law* (Milwaukee, 1962), p. 113.
[2] W. G. Katz, *Religion and American Constitutions* (Northwestern, 1964), p. 69.
[3] See Harry H. Kimber and Milton D. McLean *The Teaching of Religion in State
Universities: Descriptions of Programs in Twenty-five Institutions* (University of
Michigan, 1960); and Stanley W. Thomas, 'Studying and Teaching Religion
at State Universities: Developments, 1958–65', in *Religion, The Bulletin of
Kansas School of Religion at The University of Kansas*, vol. 3, no. 2 (January, 1966).
[4] A. P. Stokes, *op. cit.* II, 621; and W. G. Katz *op. cit.* p. 52.

holder was to be required 'to subscribe any article or formulary of faith, or to make any declaration or take any oath respecting his religious belief or profession, or to conform to any religious observance'.[1] Yet it was again Ireland which provided the most obvious parallel to Canadian experience. In Ireland the Catholics prompted a long campaign for the abolition of the exclusive control by the religious establishment of the endowments of Trinity College, Dublin. The Catholic dissenters also founded a denominational university of their own (Newman's) for which they demanded both a charter and an endowment from the state. The Irish Catholics were unsuccessful with these claims, and the solution finally adopted—the creation of a secular examining university by the state, with affiliated denominational colleges, similar to the model provided by the University of London—was the solution tried in Upper Canada with the secularization of King's College, Toronto, in 1849, and which also failed to satisfy denominational interests. The parallel was clear at the time: when Bishop Strachan met Sir Robert Peel in London, during June 1850, they actually discussed the similarities between Irish and Canadian university problems in detail.[2] The Canadian experiment in secularization was in fact deeply unpopular, and a pattern of denominational higher education became more typical instead. But during the mid-nineteenth century, most of the colleges surrendered strict confessionalism by the voluntary removal of religious tests.

At the start of the nineteenth century, the main function of higher education continued to reside in the training of clergy for the Christian ministry. In Upper Canada this alone suggested not only the need for a university, but also the need for confessionalism in any proposed institution, especially as this would accord well with the government's policy of giving substance to the Church establishment by placing all provincial education under its control. The Wesleyan Methodists, the Church of Scotland, and the Roman Catholics also favoured the idea of denominational higher

[1] 34 Vict, c. 26, clause 3.
[2] A. N. Bethune, *Memoir of the Right Reverend John Strachan* (Toronto, 1870), p. 247.

education: their aim was to smash the establishment's exclusive rights at King's College, Toronto, and secure shares in its endowments for their own use. Should this scheme fail, they were prepared to seek an impartial endowment of denominational higher education directly from the state. But there were also the more militant dissenters, marked off by their complete voluntaryism and their unambiguous support of secular education as the only fair guarantee of real religious equality. There were the denominations who also sought the secularization of the clergy reserves, rather than their re-apportionment. They were the Baptists, the Congregationalists, the members of the Presbyterian United Synod, and the various Methodist splinter-groups: each refusing, in principle, to countenance state endowment of denominational colleges, because they regarded any connexion between the state and religious belief with repugnance.

There was a good deal of variation in the experience of the various provinces over the question of higher education, just as there was over other religious issues. But everywhere a coherent theme became apparent: the clash of the establishment principle with voluntaryism. The classic model was Upper Canada, where King's College had been founded by the Church of England at Toronto in 1827. There had been earlier state plans for such an institution, and it had always been assumed that the university, once established, would be under clerical control. Strachan procured a royal charter, and in 1827 King's College fulfilled those aspirations. Yet compared with English colleges of its period, the actual degree of religious control was slight and the religious tests surprisingly liberal: a clear sign that at least in this venture Strachan recognized the need to temper the establishment principle in the face of Canadian religious pluralism. Indeed the religious tests at King's went further than Strachan wished. Even so, they applied only to members of the governing Council, and only undergraduates in divinity were required to subscribe to the Thirty-nine Articles of the Church of England. The College was plainly intended to provide Church education, however, and to furnish candidates for holy orders. It received a large endowment from the Crown lands—over 200,000 acres; and it was this state support which drew dissenting objections. In 1837 the Charter was amended to require only a simple Trinitarian religious test for membership of the Council, but this further liberalism came too late. By that date radical and dissenting opposition to King's had already decided to satisfy itself with nothing less than total religious equality in the field of higher education. In 1843, when the College finally started its teaching functions, the dissenters' agitation flowed out onto the platform of provincial politics.

The Methodists were the first to raise their objections to the religious exclusiveness of King's in a political context. In 1828 they had petitioned the provincial assembly against the Charter. In 1830 the 'Friends of Religious Liberty' demanded the removal of all religious tests at the college.[1] Other dissenting bodies soon joined in. Like the Methodists, they also began to establish separate colleges of their own in an endeavour to satisfy the urgent need for more trained ministers. The Methodist institution, Upper Canada Academy, was opened at Cobourg in 1835. There were no religious tests, and the college was open to students of all denominations; but it was Methodist discipline which was practised and theological instruction was in the hands of Methodist teachers. State aid was given, as well as quite large sums subscribed by radical political groups. These radical contributions soon ceased, as the Methodists withdrew from general adherence to reform politics.[2] The Academy was incorporated by the provincial legislature in 1841 as Victoria College. A permanent state grant was then given, and this sealed the Methodists' commitment to the principle of state aid for denominational higher education. Apart from the doctrinal instruction of its theological school, the religious teaching at Victoria comprised a generalized statement of faith: a university equivalent of the 'common Christianity' of the schools. The Church of Scotland, failing in an attempt to get a

[1] Goldwin French, *Parsons and Politics* (Toronto, 1962), p. 124.
[2] *Ibid.* p. 152.

Religion and the universities

Presbyterian professor of theology appointed at King's College—an attempt aimed at clarifying its rights as a co-establishment in the educational field—created a university of its own as well. This was Queen's College at Kingston; essentially an institution for the training of ministers. Religious tests were far more rigorous than at King's. The Westminster Confession had to be subscribed to by all professors, theological students, and members of the board of trustees. A state endowment was promised, but was never in fact given due to a protracted controversy between the Church and the provincial assembly over the actual amount. The Roman Catholics founded Regiopolis College which, in 1837, though not incorporated, was authorized to hold land titles and received small sums from the government. It was not until 1860 that the Baptists opened a Literary Institute at Woodstock, for the training of ministers, and not until 1887 that it was incorporated as McMaster University.[2]

This creation of separate denominational institutions of higher education with measures of state support, did not, however, lessen the clamour of radical and dissenting groups against the Church of England's exclusive rights at King's College, Toronto. Together with the clergy reserves and the common-schools question, the abolition of the religious tests and the Church's control at King's became a central element in the campaign for religious equality in the province. But there the unanimity of the militants ceased. For the extreme voluntaryists and radical politicians sought the complete secularization of King's, whereas others, like the Methodists and Presbyterians, looked merely for a fair share of its ample endowments and believed in the retention of Christian principles—non-sectarian ones—as part of the foundation of the university. During the 1840s both groups were roughly united in opposition to the Anglican religious tests, and this was enough to enable a legislative opening.

[1] J. S. Moir, *Church and State in Canada West* (Toronto, 1959), p. 84.
[2] Stuart Ivison, 'Is there a Canadian Baptist Tradition?' in *The Churches and the Canadian Experience*, edited by J. W. Grant (Toronto, 1963), p. 59.

The problem of education

Robert Baldwin's University Bill of 1843 was an attempt at compromise. The endowments of King's were to be appropriated by the state and re-allocated to a 'University of Toronto'. Denominational colleges—King's, Queen's, Victoria and Regiopolis—each in receipt of £500 a year from the University endowment, were to be affiliated. The University itself was to be entirely secular, and only an examining body, like London University in England. The affiliated colleges were to give theological instruction on sectarian lines, and were to retain their own religious tests. Baldwin's proposals were attacked by King's College as a spoliation of Church property. Strachan, as President of the College, pointed out that, if adopted, the Bill would lead to the overthrow of all property titles everywhere.[1] This argument was one he had taken straight out of the book of the English opponents of Church reform. The Church of Scotland and the Methodists supported the Bill, however. Yet it was not to pass. A political crisis over the Governor-General's refusal to allow an Act suppressing the Orange Order led to an election in which the Liberal administration of Baldwin and Lafontaine was defeated.

The university question, once raised to political importance, could not be left on one side. In 1845 W. H. Draper followed the earlier Bill by also attempting legislation to create a secular provincial university with affiliated denominational colleges. Although it was to enjoy the appropriated endowments of King's, this 'University of Upper Canada' was to make rather more generous payments to its constituent colleges than Baldwin's plan had envisaged. All students were to be required to join colleges appropriate to their own confession: a striking concession to the denominational principle.[2] Opposition came from the Church of England—for the same reasons which Strachan had put two years previously—and from both sides of the provincial assembly. Militant voluntaryists attacked the Bill for not going far enough; for continuing to uphold the supremacy of state-aided denomina-

[1] A. N. Bethune, *Memoir of the Right Reverend John Strachan* (Toronto, 1870), p. 237.   [2] J. S. Moir, *op. cit.* p. 92.

tionalism. After a second-reading, the Bill was withdrawn. The voluntaryists were not conciliated in Macdonald's two Bills of 1847 either. King's College was to remain exclusively Anglican, and was to receive a public grant twice as large as that to be given to any of the other denominational institutions. The idea of a secular university was abandoned, and instead Macdonald proposed a board to administer endowments composed of representatives from King's, Queen's, Victoria and Regiopolis. But the denominational colleges were to remain separate Universities in their own right. This was, therefore, a plan to give the denominational principle in higher education a very decided legislative sanction. Accordingly, the Baptists, Congregationalists, and other voluntaryist groups petitioned against the Bills, and repeated their point that a secular university would alone fulfil their idea of religious equality. Since those churches had no institutions of higher education of their own, this was an understandable point. In the assembly, the Liberals and Radicals united against the Bills and also demanded a secular university. The Methodists, on the other hand, welcomed Macdonald's proposals and approved of the principles they were to embody;[1] so did the Catholic hierarchy, grateful at the prospect of receiving generous financial aid for Regiopolis; and so did the Church of Scotland But the King's College Council, and the High Church party in the Church of England, were steadfastly hostile, still refusing, even on such relatively favourable terms, to countenance the appropriation of any part of their original state endowment. To this attitude a large majority of the Tories in the provincial assembly joined their votes. Macdonald abandoned the Bills. In the elections of 1847, fought very largely on the allied questions of the clergy reserves and the universities, the Liberals were returned to form an administration.

Baldwin reverted to his earlier plans, this time with success. The Act of 1849 created a single university, completely secular, and enjoying the appropriated endowments of King's. There were

[1] Goldwin French, *op. cit.* p. 260.

no religious tests, and in fact the offices of Chancellor and President were explicitly closed to clergymen. Affiliated denominational colleges were to receive no grants, and as there was to be no chair of divinity in the university their main function was clearly to provide theological education. One member from each college could sit on the Senate, and this was the only recognition of religious opinion in the entire scheme. The university was to be a teaching, as well as an examining body.[1] Strachan and the High Church party opposed the Act with all their old arguments against 'spoliation'; now also being able to add that a blow was made at *all* religious belief. Division from the Low Church party was marked: Baldwin was himself a churchman, and a majority of the Low churchmen favoured his plan.[2] The Church of Scotland Kirk and the Methodists once again stood together in opposition. The Wesleyan *Christian Guardian*, in a phrase borrowed from the opponents of the Irish Queen's Colleges of 1845, described Baldwin's venture as 'the Godless University'.[3] The voluntaryist denominations, predictably enough, welcomed the Act. The Catholics assumed a position of some ambiguity. Opposed in principle to secular education, yet finding that many lay members, especially the Irish elements, were allied with radical political interests in favour of the secularization of the King's endowments, the Church spoke with a faint voice. There were familiar features in the position: during the 1860s the Catholics of Ireland allied with English radicals and voluntaryist dissenters in a largely successful attempt to overthrow the endowments of the established church in Ireland and alienate them to secular purposes.

The Canadian Churches of England and Scotland petitioned the Crown to disallow the 1849 Act. The British government, whatever its view on the merits of their case, would not upset the practice of Canadian Responsible Government, and therefore refused to interfere. Queen's and Victoria Colleges declined to affiliate to the 'godless' University of Toronto, and Strachan, bereft of a Church institution after the affiliation of King's, decided to start

[1] J. S. Moir, *op. cit.* p. 102.   [2] W. H. Elgee, *op. cit.* p. 55.   [3] *Ibid.* p. 73.

again from scratch. Trinity College, Toronto, which he founded with a Royal Charter in 1851, was distinctly denominational. Established entirely by private subscriptions raised in Britain and Canada, it was a paradoxical monument to the efficacy of the voluntary system of endowments.[1] Its incorporation by the Crown broke the monopoly of the new secular university, and encouraged the Presbyterians and Methodists to retain autonomous institutions. Indeed, the widespread unpopularity of 'irreligious education' among most groups except the extreme voluntaryists, was leaving Baldwin's Toronto University without much support anywhere. The numbers of students fell off. In 1852 yet another denominational venture came into existence when the Basilian Fathers founded St Michael's College in Toronto. Contrary to the principle of Baldwin's Act, it managed to get a state grant.

A legislative recognition of the relative failure of the 1849 attempt at secular education came with Hinck's Act of 1853. The secular university was reconstructed as a mere examining body, and teaching functions were left to loosely affiliated denominational colleges. Through clause 54 of the Act it was possible for surplus incomes from the University endowment to be applied in support of these denominational colleges, but since, in reality, no surplus ever accrued, the Act left the colleges without additional financial assistance.[2] Under the new arrangements, Queen's and Victoria Colleges affiliated, and so did Knox College, a recent Free Kirk establishment. A dual system in higher education had thus evolved in Canada West. On the one hand were denominational colleges affiliated to a secular university; on the other were the Church of England Trinity University, and the Catholic St Michael's, both of which were fully independent. During the 1850s ten new colleges were founded, and only one of these was not denominational.[3] Even the Baptists, Episcopal Methodists and Congregationalists, who had campaigned with such fervour for a secular university, were sufficiently disenchanted with the result

[1] J. S. Moir, *op. cit.* p. 112.   [2] Goldwin French, *op. cit.* p. 269.
[3] J. S. Moir, *op. cit.* p. 116.

of their labour to set up denominational colleges of their own. But in these new creations, no state aid was given.

The university question continued to provoke occasional political excitement. In 1863 there was a report by a public commission which proposed the division of the endowments of Toronto University between its constituent colleges. This was opposed; but the popularity of denominational over secular education continued. And the number of sectarian institutions multiplied. Anglican Evangelicals, who found Trinity's mild Tractarianism unconducive, established Huron College in 1863 and Wycliffe in 1877. In 1868 the state discontinued the remaining financial grants to independent colleges, and this resulted in the necessary absorption of some of them into the University of Toronto. Under an Act of 1887 the University received a new federal structure, and this facilitated the entry of those denominational institutions prepared to surrender their charters. This led to the affiliation of Victoria in 1890, of Queen's in 1903 and of St Michael's shortly afterwards.

Lower Canada's experience in the university question differed as much from that of the upper province as it had over the schools issue. Despite the early efforts of the Jesuits and the Sulpicians to foster educational institutions in French Canada, the standards attained were modest and the diffusion of learning slight. But Laval's Quebec Seminary, founded in 1663, had survived to the nineteenth century, and was fast transforming itself into the Catholic university of the province. In 1851 the Seminary was formally incorporated. This implied the development of higher education on denominational lines—like the Quebec schools. It was the only way of protecting the minority rights of the Protestants, quite apart from doing justice to the Catholic majority. As elsewhere, higher education was still primarily intended for the preparation of clergymen. In 1801 the Lower Canadian assembly had created a 'Royal Institution for the Advancement of Learning'. Unable to operate in the field of primary education because of the opposition of the Catholic prelates, the Institute did oversee the establishment of McGill University. This venture, opened in 1835, had actually sustained a shadowy existence since 1823. In 1830 it had been incorporated as a distinctly Church of England university. Its endowment came, after some litigation, from the bequest of James McGill. Although there were no religious tests for the teachers or students, the former were in fact named by the Bishop of Montreal, and the teaching of theology was in the hands of the Church. The Church of Scotland pressed its claims as a co-establishment, as it had done in Upper Canada, and sought to open the McGill faculty of divinity to Presbyterianism. These efforts succeeded in 1848, but only at the cost of removing *all* denominational content from the theological instruction at the University. Yet by then the recognition of the denominational principle in the province's higher education was advanced. Bishop Mountain, deciding to create a new and exclusively Church college, just as Strachan had had to do in similar circumstances, had founded Bishop's University at Lennoxville in 1845. The Baptists had opened a college of their own at Montreal in 1838, which lasted only a decade. Other denominations sent their students to the flowering sectarian institutions of Canada West. State aid to both the Catholic and Protestant universities has continued in Quebec province.

The battle for either non-sectarian, or wholly secular higher education was even fiercer in the Maritime Provinces than in Upper Canada. There the Church establishment had originally acquired a monopoly. King's College at Windsor had been created by a Nova Scotia statute in 1789 and provided with a state grant. Permanent endowment and a Royal Charter came from England in 1802. The College was strictly under the control of the Church of England: all students, as well as the professorial body, were obliged to subscribe to the Thirty-nine Articles. Government support reflected a belief, echoed in the Canadas, that higher education controlled by an established Church would deflect republicanism and foster loyalty.[1] This belief led to the creation of King's College at Fredericton, New Brunswick.

Dissenting demands for a share in the state grants allocated to

[1] W. H. Elgee, *op. cit.* p. 154.

higher education, and an end to the establishment's exclusive control, got early support in the legislatures of the Maritime provinces. The Church stood firm, and it was not until 1831 that King's College, Windsor, declared itself open to students of other denominations by the modification of its religious tests. By that date the leading dissenting churches had established institutions of their own, and these were all in receipt of state grants: a concurrent endowment solution to the claims of religious equality in the field of higher education. Pictou Academy was founded by Secession Presbyterians in 1808, as a deliberate attempt to break the Church of England's monopoly. In 1816 it received a permanent grant from the Nova Scotian legislature—but not without sustained opposition from the establishment; opposition which, joined with attacks from the Church of Scotland, led eventually to its closure. The work of Pictou's founder, Thomas McCulloch, was revived in Dalhousie College,. This had been founded in 1817 and opened in 1823. In 1838 the provincial assembly appointed McCulloch to its presidency and provided financial support. It became a non-sectarian but Christian college. The Baptist Association set up a college of its own in 1828: Horton Academy in Nova Scotia, which received a state grant for several years before it was discontinued—not due to the delicacy of Baptist voluntaryism, but because of Church of England pressures in the legislature.[1] The Wesleyan Methodists, who had projected an institution of their own since 1830, finally established Mount Allison in New Brunswick during 1839. State financial support was given by the legislatures of both New Brunswick and Nova Scotia. Another Baptist College, at Fredericton, also received state aid.

With the major denominations providing denominational state-supported higher education for themselves, the idea of a single, provincial, non-sectarian or even secular university, was slow to acquire adherents. But those churches which were militantly voluntaryist on the general question of state endowment of religion did begin to combine with political radicalism in a campaign

[1] *Ibid.* p. 64.

against the disproportionately large share of the state funds flowing into the Church of England's colleges. The Baptists were hardly in a position to lead this campaign, since they had compromised on higher education in the Maritimes. During the political conflict over the university question, in fact, they found themselves in unlikely alliance with the Tory party, especially in Nova Scotia. They pointed to a distinction between receiving state aid for their ministers, which they still eschewed, and public aid for education, in which they participated. But the Free Presbyterians, Congregationalists and the independent Methodist bodies unreservedly supported the principle of non-sectarian university education. In the New Brunswick legislature, L. A. Wilmot, who was a Methodist, managed to curtail Anglican control of King's College, Fredericton, in 1845. In 1859 it became the University of New Brunswick, as a non-sectarian institution. But state aid to the denominational colleges continued.[1]

In Nova Scotia the movement for a non-sectarian (but not secular) university was led in the provincial assembly by two Liberals, Joseph Howe and William Annaud. The latter envisaged the ending of all state support for denominational institutions and the creation of a single non-sectarian university. He made concrete proposals in 1843. These passed the assembly, but amidst so much public controversy that a general election was precipitated. The issue at the polls turned almost entirely on the university question, and resulted in a narrow victory for the Tories. The principle of denominational higher education therefore achieved security. When the Liberals returned to office in 1847 it had become clear that a substantial majority of the public favoured denominationalism. No serious attempts were made, after this time, to press a non-sectarian solution to the problem of higher education in Nova Scotia. The pattern of state-aided denominational higher education has survived. The movement for religious equality, at least as expressed in the university question, had halted at the compromise of concurrent endowment.

[1] Goldwin French, *op. cit.* p. 206.

CONCLUSION

Redefinitions in the relationship of religious belief and public life in North America and Britain largely arose out of the growth of religious pluralism in society, and from necessary adjustments of function as the state came to accumulate welfare machinery of its own. The campaigns for actual disestablishment were almost entirely the work of Christian agencies. The same was true of Australia and New Zealand, where the duplication of British institutions correspondingly allowed the forces of religious diversity to produce similar modifications to the confessional office of the state. Altogether, these countries form a unique area of experience. Continental European separations of church and state, in contrast, have mostly indicated hostility between the religious and governmental spheres, and the determination of the state to destroy the power of ecclesiastical interests. The only trace of a comparable feeling in Britain and North America was to be found in the small circles of advanced secular radicalism in the nineteenth century. As a force making for a redefinition in the relationship of church and state in those countries, this secular tradition was negligible.

It is clear that the modifications in the relationship of church and state suggest three stages of development. From its beginnings in public confessionalism (however incongruously that may have been expressed in practice), the state moved towards the 'establishment' of non-sectarian Christianity. The educational counterpart of this phase, in which its theoretical basis became apparent, was the formulation of 'common Christianity'. This position has in some things been gradually broadened to include Judaism. Finally, amidst much deceptive discussion about 'secularization', the state has begun to advance towards a stricter neutrality; a condition in which belief and unbelief are equally allowed a protected existence, but without official preference of one over the other. Now it would appear that Britain, Canada, and the United States are still very largely in the second stage of development—the stage where non-sectarian religious opinion is accorded a sort of established status. The laws and customs of all three nations continue to be shot through with supports for religious belief and actual aids, direct and indirect, to the churches. It is clear that Britain retains strong vestiges—in the shape of surviving if rather anomalous state churches—of original confessionalism; that the United States, on the other hand, has made some slight advances into a fuller practice of stage three neutrality; and that Canada is pretty centrally in the middle zone. Yet taking the broadest view, it is evident that even the increased neutrality of the United States is frequently a technicality. Where public opinion continues overwhelmingly to subscribe to the proposition that a nation is indelibly religious in character, then only a real decline of religiosity will alter the prevailing belief that the state has a discriminating religious conscience. At the present time, the United States enjoys a numerically superior quantity of personal religiosity—at least as far as church affiliation is any indication.

The loosening of ties between church and state is one aspect of the larger decline of political exclusiveness. As a wider representation extended to the legislatures and to public office—as persons, and not interests were admitted to a public voice—the older groups who maintained exclusive state churches were persuaded, through a sense of political justice, or forced, by numbers, to conciliate the demands prompted by the existence of religious diversity among the newly enfranchised. And intellectual endeavour, released progressively from the dominion of the churches, was no longer contained within the concepts of universal truth which revealed religion had sought to establish as the immutable reference to right conduct in human society. Expressions of political theory have increasingly tended to describe the modern state without reference to religious sanction. Yet practical political thinking in these three countries has not, with minor exceptions, been militantly secular. While side-stepping religious issues, it has also avoided larger questions concerned with the origins of the state's own moral authority. This pragmatism, however, in reality assumes whole series of popular ethical value-judgments, the vast majority of which are decidedly drawn from traditional Christian teaching, or at the very least transmitted through Christian precepts. But these judgments are allowed to remain vaguely defined; for to advertise the problem would be either to reveal the Christian moralism lying at the root of so many contemporary political values, and so vitiate the state's pracitical endeavours to secure neutrality, or else would prompt a search for independent and secular *a prioris*—which would project the state beyond neutrality, and leave it in the position of propagating values of its own and necessarily in opposition to the competing religious beliefs of its subjects, whether these beliefs were articulate or latent.

Thus the movement of these three countries towards a measure of state neutrality, though real enough, has in many things been arrested. Modern America is now again entering something of a critical phase. But, once more taking the broadest view, it must be apparent that it was a *common* series of adjustments, responding to essentially shared conditions and pressures, which has led to alterations in the relationship of church and state amongst the members of the Atlantic community. The chance survival of religious establishments on one side of the ocean is in reality a minor feature of a larger development sustained by all. The separation of church and state, of religious belief and public life, was programmed at the outset, when the three countries still enjoyed a constitutional relationship. It has been realized, though imperfectly; it is still in the making, despite the chronological disparities. And in all this—though frequently unrecognizable and perhaps largely imperceptible—is expressed a transcendent providence beyond the present terms of reference.

BIBLIOGRAPHY

Reference

Burr, N. R. *A Critical Bibliography of Religion in America.* Princeton, 1963.

Mode, P. G. *Source Book and Bibliographical Guide for American Church History.* Menasha, Wisconsin, 1921.

Smith, H. S., Handy, R. T. and Loetscher, L. A. *American Christianity.* New York, 1960–7.

Stanton, F. M. and Locke, G. H. *A Bibliography of Canadiana; items in the Public Library of Toronto relating to the early history and development of Canada.* Toronto, 1934.

Works mentioned in this book

Bacon, L. W. *A History of American Christianity.* London, 1899.

Baird, Robert. *The Progress and Prospects of Christianity in the United States of America.* London, 1851.

—— *Religion in America.* New York, revised edition, 1856.

Baldwin, A. M. *The New England Clergy and the American Revolution.* Duke University, 1928.

Beaver, R. Pierce. 'Church, State and the Indians: Indian Missions in the New Nation', in *A Journal of Church and State*, May, 1962.

Bethune, A. N. *Memoir of the Right Reverend John Strachan.* Toronto, 1870.

Billington, R. A. *The Protestant Crusade, 1800–60, A Study of the Origins of American Nativism.* New York, 1938.

Blanshard, Paul. *American Freedom and Catholic Power.* Boston, second edition, 1960.

Bowden, H. W. 'Philip Schaff and Sectarianism: The Americanization of a European Viewpoint', in *A Journal of Church and State*, vol. VIII, no. 1, 1966.

Brady, W. Maziere. *The Episcopal Succession in England, Scotland and Ireland, 1400 to 1875.* Rome, 1876.

Bridenbaugh, Carl. *Mitre and Sceptre. Transatlantic Faiths, Ideas, Personalities, and Politics, 1689–1775,* New York, 1962.

Brown, S. W. *The Secularization of American Education.* New York, 1912.

Bibliography

Brown, W. A. *Church and State in Contemporary America*. New York, 1936.

Bryce, James. *The American Commonwealth*. New York, 1913 edition.

Butts, R. Freeman. *The American Tradition in Religion and Education*. Boston, 1950.

Carrington, Philip. *The Anglican Church in Canada*. Toronto, 1963.

Caswall, Henry. *America and the American Church*. London, 1839.

Channing, W. E. *Memoir, with Extracts from his Correspondence and Manuscripts*. London, 1851.

Clark, E. T. *The Small Sects in America*. New York, revised edition, 1959.

Clark, S. D. *Church and Sect in Canada*. Toronto, 1948.

Clarkson, J. Dunsmore. *Labour and Nationalism in Ireland*. New York, 1925.

Cobb, S. H. *The Rise of Religious Liberty in America*. New York, 1902.

Cogley, John (ed.). *Religion in America. Original Essays on Religion in a Free Society*. Cleveland and New York, 1958.

Conant, J. B. *Education and Liberty. The Role of the Schools in a Modern Democracy*. Harvard, 1953.

Considine, Bob. *It's the Irish*. New York, 1961.

Cousins, N. '*In God we Trust*': *The Religious Beliefs and Ideas of the American Founding Fathers*. New York, 1958.

Creighton, Donald. *John A. Macdonald, The Young Politician*. Toronto, 1956.

Cubberley, E. P. *Public Education in the United States*. Boston, 1919.

Culver, R. B. *Horace Mann and Religion in the Massachusetts Public Schools*. Yale, 1929.

Daly, G. T. *Catholic Problems in Western Canada*. Toronto, 1921.

Dignan, P. J. *A History of the Legal Incorporation of Catholic Church Property in the United States (1784–1932)*. New York, 1935.

Dunham, Aileen. *Political Unrest in Upper Canada, 1815–36*. Toronto, new edition, 1963.

Eastman, Mack. *Church and State in Early Canada*. Edinburgh, 1915.

Eckenrode, H. J. *The Separation of Church and State in Virginia*. Richmond, 1910.

Elgee, W. H. *The Social Teachings of the Canadian Churches, Protestant, The Early Period, before 1850*. Toronto, 1964.

Ellis, J. Tracy. *American Catholicism*. Chicago, 1955.

Engels, Frederick. *The Condition of the Working Class in England in 1844*. Blackwell, Oxford, 1958 edition.

Bibliography

Foster, C. I. *An Errand of Mercy. The Evangelical United Front, 1790–1837.* University of North Carolina Press, 1960.

French, Goldwin. *Parsons and Politics. The rôle of the Wesleyan Methodists in Upper Canada and the Maritimes from 1780 to 1855.* Toronto, 1962.

Geary, G. J. *The Secularization of the California Missions, 1810–40.* Washington, 1934.

Gladstone, W. E. *The State in its Relations with the Church.* London, 1838.

—— *The Vatican Decrees in their Bearing on Civil Allegiance; A Political Expostulation.* London, 1874.

Gohdes, Clarence. *American Literature in Nineteenth Century England.* Carbondale, Ill., 1944.

Grant, J. W. (ed.). *The Churches and the Canadian Experience.* Toronto, 1963.

Greene, E. B. *Religion and the State. The Making and Testing of an American Tradition.* Ithaca, New York, 1959 edition.

Hawkins, Ernest. *Annals of the Diocese of Toronto.* London, 1848.

—— *Annals of the Diocese of Quebec.* London, 1849.

Herberg, Will. *Protestant-Catholic-Jew. An Essay in American Religious Sociology.* New York, revised edition, 1960.

Hofstadter, R. and Metzger, W. P. *The Development of Academic Freedom in the United States.* New York, 1955.

Hofstadter, R. and Smith, W. *American Higher Education. A Documentary History.* Chicago. 1961.

Hinton, J. M. *The Test of Experience; or The Voluntary System in the United States.* London, 1851.

Hudson, W. S. *The Great Tradition of the American Churches.* New York, 1963 edition.

Humphrey, E. F. *Nationalism and Religion in America, 1774–89.* Boston, 1924.

Inglis, K. S. *Churches and the Working Classes in Victorian England.* London, 1963.

Irish Position in British and Republican North America. (Anonymous), Montreal, 1866.

Journal of Visitation to a part of the Diocese of Quebec by the Lord Bishop of Montreal in the Spring of 1843. The Church in Canada, no. II (published for S.P.G.) London, third edition, 1846.

Journal of Visitation to the Western Portion of his Diocese by the Lord Bishop of Toronto. The Church in Canada, no. I (published for S.P.G.) London, third edition, 1846.

Bibliography

Katz, W. G. *Religion and American Constitutions*. Northwestern University Press, 1964.

Kenyon, C. M. 'Men of Little Faith: The Anti-Federalists on the Nature of Representative Government,' in *The William and Mary Quarterly*, third series, vol. XII, no. 1 (1955).

Kimber, H. H. and McLean, M. D. *The Teaching of Religion in State Universities: Descriptions of Programs in Twenty-five Institutions*. University of Michigan, 1960.

Lathbury, D. C. (ed.). *Correspondence on Church and Religion of William Ewart Gladstone*. London, 1910.

Lewis, A. H. *A Critical History of the Sabbath and the Sunday in the Christian Church*. New York, 1886.

Littel, F. H. *From State Church to Pluralism*. Doubleday Books edition, New York, 1962.

Loder, J. E. *Religion and the Public Schools*. New York, 1965.

Mackay, Alexander. *The Western World, or Travels in the United States in 1846–7: Exhibiting them in their latest development, social, political and industrial*. Philadelphia, 1849.

Manross, W. W. (ed. and comp.). *The Fulham Papers in the Lambeth Palace Library. American Colonial Section, Calendar and Indexes*. Oxford, 1965.

Martin, John. *A Brief Survey of Popery*. London, 1875.

Maynard, Theodore. *The Story of American Catholicism*. New York, 1946; and a paperback edition, 1960.

—— *Great Catholics in American History*. New York, 1962.

Mays, D. J. *Edmund Pendleton, 1721–1803*. Harvard, 1952.

McDonald, Forrest. *We The People, The Economic Origins of the Constitution*. Chicago, 1963 edition.

McGrath, J. J. *Church and State in American Law. Cases and Materials*. Milwaukee, 1962.

McIllwain, C. H. *The American Revolution: A Constitutional Interpretation*. New York, 1923.

Mecklin, J. H. *The Story of American Dissent*. New York, 1934.

Miller, Perry. *The Life of the Mind in America*. London, 1966.

Miller, W. L. 'Religion and Americanism', in *A Journal of Church and State*, vol. V, no. 1, 1963.

Mode, P. G. *The Frontier Spirit in American Christianity*. New York, 1923.

Moir, J. S. *Church and State in Canada West, Three Studies in the Relation of Denominationalism and Nationalism, 1841–67*. Toronto, 1959.

Bibliography

Monk, Maria. *The Awful Disclosures*. Consul Books edition, London, 1965.

Montgomery, John. *Popery as it exists in Great Britain and Ireland, Its Doctrines, Practices and Arguments*. Edinburgh, 1854.

Morris, B. F. *Christian Life and Character of the Civil Institutions of the United States, Developed in the Official and Historical Annals of the Republic*. Philadelphia, 1864.

Morrow, E. Lloyd. *Church Union in Canada: Its history, motives, doctrine and government*. Toronto, 1923.

Nelson, W. H. *The American Tory*. Oxford, 1961.

Newman, J. H. *Lectures on the Present Position of Catholics in England*. London, 1892 edition.

Niebuhr, H. Richard. *The Social Sources of Denominationalism*. New York, 1929.

Norman, E. R. *The Catholic Church and Ireland in the Age of Rebellion, 1859–73*. London, 1965.

Oaks, D. H. (ed.). *The Wall between Church and State*. Chicago, 1963.

O'Laverty, James. *The Bishops of Down and Connor*. Dublin, 1895.

Olmstead, C. E. *Religion in America, Past and Present*. Englewood Cliffs, N.J., 1961.

Orangeism in Ireland and Throughout the Empire, by a Member of the Order. [by R. M. Sibbeth], London, 1942.

Past and Present Policy of England Towards Ireland. [by Charles Greville], London, 1845.

Pfeffer, Leo. *Church, State and Freedom*. Boston, 1953.

Reed, Andrew and Matheson, James. *A Narrative of a visit to the American Churches by a Deputation from the Congregational Union of England and Wales*. London, 1835.

Reid, N. S. *The Church of Scotland in Lower Canada; Its Struggle for Establishment*. Toronto, 1936.

Religion in the Public Schools, A Report by the Commission of the American Association of School Administrators. New York, 1964.

Riddell, W. R. *The Constitution of Canada in its History and Practical Working*. Yale, 1912.

Rosten, Leo (ed.). *Religions in America*. New York, 1963.

Saunders, Leslie. *The Story of Orangeism, Its Origin and History for more than a century and a quarter in Canada*. Toronto, 1960.

Schaff, Philip. *America. A Sketch of the Political, Social and Religious Character of the United States of America*. New York, 1855.

Bibliography

Schaff, Philip. *Church and State in the United States.* New York, 1888.

Senior, Hereward, *Orangeism in Ireland and Britain, 1795–1836.* London, 1966.

Sissons, C. B. *Egerton Ryerson, His Life and Letters.* Toronto, vol. I, 1937; vol. II, 1947.

Sperry, W. L. *Religion in America.* Cambridge, 1945.

Stephens, W. R. W. *The Life and letters of Walter Farquhar Hook.* London, third edition, 1879.

Stimson, E. R. *History of the Seperation of Church and State in Canada.* Toronto, second edition, 1887.

Stokes, A. P. *Church and State in the United States.* New York, 1950.

Stokes, A. P. and Pfeffer Leo. *Church and State in the United States.* (a revised and abridged edition of the above); New York, 1964.

Sweet, W. W. *The Story of Religion in America.* New York, 1939 edition.

—— *Religion in the Development of American Culture, 1765–1840.* New York, 1952.

—— *The American Churches, An Interpretation.* London, 1947.

Taylor, P. A. M. *Expectation Westward. The Mormons and the Emigration of their British Converts in the Nineteenth Century.* Edinburgh, 1965.

Tewksbury, D. G. *The Founding of American Colleges and Universities before the Civil War, with Particular Reference to the Religious Influences Bearing upon the College Movement.* New York, 1932.

Thomas, S. W. 'Studying and Teaching Religion at State Universities: Developments, 1958–65', in *Religion, The Bulletin of Kansas School of Religion at The University of Kansas,* vol. 3, no. 2, January, 1966.

Thorpe, F. N. *The Federal and State Constitutions, Colonial Charters and other Organic Laws of the United States of America.* Washington, 1909.

Thurston, Herbert. *No Popery. Chapters on Anti-Papal Prejudice.* London. 1930.

De Tocqueville, Alexis. *Democracy in America,* (1835–40). Oxford edition, 1955.

Trisco, R. F. *The Holy See and the Nascent Church in the Middle Western United States, 1826–50.* Rome, 1962.

Tussman, Joseph (ed.). *The Supreme Court on Church and State.* New York, 1962.

Van Deusen, G. G. 'Seward and the Schools Question Reconsidered', in *The Journal of American History,* vol. LII, no. 2, 1965.

Bibliography

Van Tyne, C. H. *England and America, Rivals in the American Revolution* Cambridge, 1927.

Waite, P. B. (ed.). *The Confederation Debates in the Province of Canada, 1865.* Toronto, 1964.

Walker, Williston, *A History of the Congregational Churches in the United States.* American Church History Series, New York, 1894.

Walsh H. H. *The Christian Church in Canada,* Toronto, 1956.

Warburton, A. B. *A History of Prince Edward Island.* St John, 1923.

Weigel, Gustave. *Churches in North America.* Baltimore and Montreal, 1961.

Welter, Rush. *Popular Education and Democratic Thought in America.* New York, 1962.

Werline, A. W. *Problems of Church and State in Maryland during the Seventeenth and Eighteenth Centuries.* South Lancaster, Mass., 1948.

Whately, Richard. *Essays [Third Series] on the Errors of Romanism.* London, fifth edition, 1856.

Wilberforce, Samuel. *A History of the Protestant Episcopal Church in America.* London, 1844.

Williams, Michael. *The Shadow of the Pope.* New York, 1932.

Wilson, D. J. *The Church Grows in Canada.* Toronto, 1966.

Wogaman, Philip. 'The Changing Role of Government and the Myth of Separation', in *A Journal of Church and State,* vol. v, no. 1, 1963.

INDEX

Aberhart, William, 15
Act of Union, between Britain and Ireland (1800), 9
Act of Union, between England and Scotland (1707), 54
Adams, John, 110
adoption laws, 86
Affirmation Act (Britain, 1888), 12
Alline, Henry, 69
American Association of School Administrators, 151
American Protective Association, 90, 101
American Protestant Association, 99
American Revolution, influence on religious organizations, 9, 36, 37, 38–45, 49
Annaud, William, 183
Anti-Catholic agitations: in Britain, 90–8; in British North America, 25, 90, 96, 97, 101–3, 131, 162; in United States, 75, 90, 96, 97, 98–101, 111, 125, 141, 142
Anti-Clergy Reserves Association, 63
Anti-Communist oaths, (United States), 79
Anti-State Church Association (Canada), 63, 64
Arkansas, religion in the state of, 82, 148
Asbury, Francis, 108
Attwood, Thomas, 55

Backus, Isaac, 44
Bailly, Bishop Charles, 158
Baird, Robert, 22, 25, 30, 76, 83, 87, 93
Baldwin, Robert: University Bill (Canada, 1843), 176; University Act (1849), 177–8, 179
Baltimore, provincial and plenary councils, 126, 143, 170
Baptist Church: relations with the state, 6, 7; in British North America, 51, 54, 56, 63, 68, 69, 70, 72, 118, 157, 163, 173, 175, 177, 179, 181, 182, 183; in United States, 27, 33, 39, 41, 42, 43, 44, 107, 112, 144, 170
Beecher, Lyman, 23
Bedini, Cajetan, Cardinal, 126
Bible-reading in schools, 133, 139, 142, 146, 147, 148, 158
Binney, Bishop Herbert, 114
bishops of London, jurisdiction in America, 38
Bishop's University, Lennoxville, 181
Blaine Amendment (United States, 1875), 145
blasphemy laws, 20, 82, 83, 88

Blomfield, Bishop C. J., 17
Bolster, Sarah, case of, 102
Bourget, Bishop Ignace, 165
Bowers, H. F., 101
Bradfield v. *Roberts*, (United States, 1899), 86
Bradlaugh case, 12
British and Foreign School Society, 132
British colonial churches (other than North American), 10, 12, 98, 184
British Columbia, church and state relations, 74, 165
British North America Act (1867), 9, 73, 164; *see also* Confederation of Canada
Broadcasting religious, 85, 89
Bryce, Viscount, 2, 22, 30
Buller, Charles, 158

Calhoun, John C., 144
Canada Company, 52, 53, 56
California, secularization of missions, 45
Cameron's Schools Act (Canada, 1849), 160
Carby, Fr. Thomas, 125
Carroll, Bishop John, 112, 124
Cartwright, Richard, 50
Caswall, Henry, 77, 138, 169
Catholics, Roman: in British North America, 64, 66–9, 70, 101–3, 115, 116, 129, 130, 158, 160, 161, 162, 163, 165, 166, 172, 177, 178, 180, 181, *see also* Lower Canada; in United States, 36, 80, 98–101, 111, 112, 119, 120, 121–6, 138, 140–3, 144, 148, 151–2, 155, 170.
Catholic Emancipation: in Britain, 11, 52, 93; in United States, 80
Catholic University of America, 170
census of religion (Britain, 1851), 11
Chalmers, Thomas, 10, 57
Channing, William Ellery, 138, 139
chaplains, military: in Britain, 14; in British North America, 88; in United States, 77, 85
Charbonnel, Bishop Armand de, 161, 162
Charleston Constitution, 126
Chiniquy, Charles, 93
Christian Examiner, The, 56
Christian Guardian, The, 25, 60, 157, 178
Christian Science, 28, 87, 89
Christian Statesman, The, 77
Christian Witness, The, 25
Church, The, 57

195

Index

Church of England: reforms of, 6, 11, 12, 13, 105, 128, 176; Constitutional position in Britain, 9, 104, 132; in British North America, 8, 25, 49, 51, 52–66, 66–74, 104, 113–15, 130, 131, 156, 157, 158, 161, 162, 163, 164, 172, 173, 174, 175, 176, 177, 178, 179, 181, 182, 183; in American colonies, 7, 32, 33, 35, 36, 37, 39, 41, 42; in United States (Episcopal Church), 25, 46, 104, 106, 108–11, 113, 126–8, 170

'Church of God and Saints of Christ', 28

Church of Scotland: in Britain, 9, 105; in British North America, 54, 57–8, 59, 60, 62, 63, 64, 67, 68, 71, 72, 117, 157, 164, 172, 174–5, 176, 177, 178, 181, 182; in American colonies, 41

Church of Wales, 10, 60, 64, 128

Church Missionary Society, 74

church rates: in Britain, 33, 152; in British North America, 70, 71; in American colonies, 33

church societies (Canada), 113, 114, 115

Clergy Corporations (Canada), 53, 58, 60

Clergy Reserves Acts: 1840 (Imperial Parliament), 62; 1853 (Imp. Parl.), 64; 1854 (Canadian Parl.), 64

clergy reserves question, 26, 48, 50, 52–65, 67, 68, 157, 171, 173, 175

Cochran v. *Louisiana State Board* (United States, 1930), 153, 154

Coke, Thomas, 108

Colborne, Sir John, 58, 61, 66

collectivism, influence on relations of church and state, 16, 17, 18, 19, 81, 86, 184

Colonial Advocate, The, 54, 60

Colonial America, relations of church and state, 5, 31, 32–45

Colonial Bishopric question, 37, 38, 39, 107

'Common Christianity' in education, 137, 138, 139, 140, 141, 145, 146, 148, 155, 160, 162, 165, 184

concurrent endowment, 20; in Britain, 132; in British North America, 49, 56, 64, 72, 171, 183; in United States, 41

Confederation of Canada (1867), 65, 68, 73, 135, 155, 164, (see also British North America Act)

confessionalism of the state, general points relating to, 6, 20, 75 ff., 184; in Britain, 14, 75; in British North America, 88, 89; in United States, 7, 34, 76–87

Congregational Church: in New England, 5, 6, 7, 32, 34, 43–5, 107, 112, 135, 168, 170; in British North America, 51, 56, 63, 69, 71, 72, 118, 157, 173, 177, 179, 183

Connecticut, religion in the state of, 44, 79, 80

conscientious exemption from military service, 86

Continental Congress (of 1787), 45

Constitutional Act (Canada, 1791), 49, 50, 51, 57, 58

Constitution, British, 6, 31, 34

constitutions, ecclesiastical, 103; in Britain, 104, 105; in British North America, 113–18, 127, 128, 129; in United States, 106–13, 126, 128–9

Constitution, Federal, of the United States, 4, 7, 31, 45–7, 79, 150, 154; First Amendment (1791), 47, 86, 137, 148, 150, 153, 154; Fourteenth Amendment (1868), 8, 48, 134, 150, 154

Conwell, Bishop Henry, 124

Corrigan, Robert, 102

Craig, Sir James, 129

Crown v. *Ramsey and Foot* (Britain, 1882), 83

Cullen, Paul, Cardinal, 161, 162

Dalhousie College, 182

Dalhousie, Lord, 130

Dartmouth College, 168

Davis v. *Beason* (United States, 1890), 87

Day's Common School Act (Canada, 1841), 158, 160, 163

Deism, influence in America, 7, 39

Delaware, religion in the state of, 5, 32, 79, 108

Denault, Bishop, 129

departments of religion in American Universities, 171

Disciples of Christ, 28

Dissenting Deputies of London, 11

Doremus v. *Board of Education* (United States, 1950), 147, 148, 159

Draper's University Bill (Canada, 1845), 176, 177

Drew's Education Act (Canada, 1944), 166

Dubois, Bishop Jean, 125

Durham Report (1839), 9, 26, 62, 114, 158

Dutch Reformed Church in America, 36, 112

Eastern Townships (Quebec), 66

education: British schools, 13, 132, 133, 135, 137; Education Act (1870), 18, 133, 138, 147, 159; Education Act (1944), 133, 166. Denominational Schools: in Britain, 132, 133; in British North America, 68–9, 133, 156, 157, 158, 159, 160, 162, 163, 164, 165, 166; in United States, 81, 85, 134, 135, 136, 137, 140–3, 145, 151, 152, 153, 154, 155. State nonsectarian schools: in Britain, 133; in British North America, 8, 54, 73, 133, 157, 158, 159, 161, 163, 164, 166, 167;

Index

in United States, 85, 134, 136, 137, 138, 139, 140, 141, 146, 147, 148, 149, 150
Edwards, Morgan, 44
Engel v. *Vitale* (United States, 1962), 75, 78, 149–51
Engels, Frederick, 94
England, Bishop John, 125
Episcopal Church, *see* Church of England
Equal Rights Association, 164
European ecclesiastical organizations, 98, 184
Evangelical Alliance, 23
Everson v. *Board of Education* (United States, 1947), 21, 140, 154–5

Federalist Party (United States), 44
Fenianism (Canada), 101, 103
Florida, religion in the state of, 79
'Friends of Religious Liberty' (Canada), 61, 174
Fulford, Archbishop Francis, 115

Galway, ecclesiastical irregularities of, 120, 129
Gano, John, 44
Gavazzi, Alessandro, 96
'General Assessment' (Virginia), 41, 42, 44
Georgia, State University of, 168
Gladstone, W. E., 1, 12, 75, 90, 93, 171
Glasgow Colonial Society, 58
Glebe lands: in British North America, 52, 70; in American colonies, 39, 42
'Great Awakening' revival, 5, 107
Greville, Charles, 48

Haliburton, T. C., 73
Harden v. *State* (United States, 1948), 87
Harvard University, 168, 170
Hawkins, Ernest, 52
Hinck's Schools Act (Canada, 1843), 159; Hinck's University Act (1853), 179
Hinton, John Howard, 2, 24, 77
Hobart, Bishop J. H., 25
Hogan, Fr. William, 124
Hope Report (Canada, 1950), 166
Horton Academy, 182
Howe, Joseph, 183
hospitals under religious control, 81, 86
Hudson's Bay Company, 74
Hughes, Archbishop John, 125, 141, 142, 162
Hume, Joseph, 26, 55
Huron College, 180

Idaho, religion in the state of, 87
Illinois, religion in the state of, 148, 153
immigration, effect on the churches: in British North America, 94, 102; in United States, 29, 45, 94, 122, 124, 136

incorporation of ecclesiastical property, 128, 129, 131
Independence, Declaration of in America (1776), 7, 32, 35, 40, 46
Indian missions, 85, 89, 130, 143, 144, 164
Indiana, religion in the state of, 152
industrial revolution, effect on the churches, 17, 29, 39, 140
Inglis, Bishop Charles, 70, 130
Inglis, Sir Robert, 48
Ireland, Archbishop John, 134, 142
Irish Catholic Church, 10, 32, 68, 120, 121, 130, 151, 162
Irish Educational System, 132, 133, 138, 147, 158, 159, 161, 162, 164, 172, 178
Irish Protestant Church, disestablishment of, 10, 32, 60, 64, 66, 128
Irish religious influence in America, 95, 96, 122, 134

Jefferson, Thomas, 41, 42, 47, 154, 168
Jehova's Witnesses, 89
Jews, religious freedom for, 11, 80, 148, 149, 184

Kansas, religion in the state of, 28
Kelly, Bishop Patrick, 125
Kenmare, Lord, 121
Kenrick, Archbishop F. P., 142
Kentucky, religion in the state of, 129
King, George, 163
King's College, Fredericton (N.B.), 181, 183
King's College, New York, 167
King's College, Toronto, 172, 173, 174, 175, 176, 177, 178
King's College, Windsor (N.S.), 181, 182
Klein, Fr. Felix, 97
Kneeland, Abner, 82
Knights of Columbus, 101
Know-Nothing Party, 90, 99, 101, 125
Knox College, 179
Ku Klux Klan, 101

Laval, Bishop François de M., 129, 180
Leo XIII, Pope, 97
'Liberal Church' (United States), 78
Liberation Society, of Great Britain, 11, 63
Liberal Party (Britain) and church reform, 11
'Liberty of Worship Act' (Britain, 1855), 12
Lindenmuller v. *the People* (United States, 1861), 84
literature, translatlantic, 25
London Missionary Society, 118
Louisiana, religion in the state of, 153
Lower Canada, Catholicism of the Province, 8, 9, 10, 15, 49, 66–9, 88, 101–3, 115, 116, 129, 130, 131, 133, 158, 159, 165, 180, 181

197

Index

loyalists in American Revolution, 35, 36; loyalist exiles in Canada, 8, 69

Lutheranism in North America, 28, 36, 72, 107, 112, 118, 143, 157, 170

Macdonald, John A., 64, 177; Macdonald's University Bills (1847), 177

Macdonnell, Bishop Alexander, 56

Mackay, Alexander, 14, 24, 28, 140

Mackenzie, William Lyon, 54, 55, 158, 162

Maclay Act (New York, 1842), 142

MacMullan, Bishop of Down, 121

Madison, Bishop James, 111

Madison, James, 36, 47, 154

Maillard, Abbé, 70

Maine, higher education in, 170

Maitland, Sir Peregrine, 156

Mann, Horace, 137, 138, 139, 159

Manning, President, Rhode Island College, 44

Maréchal, Bishop Ambrose, 125

Maria Monk (and the *Awful Disclosures*), 99, 100

Maritime Provinces: anti-Catholicism, 103; Church and state relations, 8, 49, 51–2, 69–73, 114, 115, 116, 118; education question, 157, 163, 164; revivalism, 27; university question, 181–3

Marriage Acts: Canada (1793), 51; England (1836), 12, 18; Virginia (1784), 41. Agitations on the marriage question: Lower Canada, 68; Maritimes, 72, 73

Maryland, religion in the state of, 42, 43, 80, 108, 111, 112, 128, 170

Massachussetts, religion in the Commonwealth of, 32, 44–5, 80, 82, 99, 136, 138, 139, 170

Maynooth Grant, 12, 68, 75, 90, 99

McCloskey, John, Cardinal, 143

McCollum v. *Board of Education* (United States, 1948), 141, 147, 152, 153

McCulloch, Thomas, 182

McGill University, 180, 181

McLaughlin Act (New York, 1940), 153

McMaster University, 175

Meilleur, J. B., 159

Mennonites, 86, 157

Methodism: in Britain, 5, 11, 23; in British North America, 54, 55, 56, 58, 59, 60, 61, 62, 64, 71, 116, 117, 157, 163, 172, 173, 174, 175, 176, 177, 178, 179, 182, 183; in Colonial America and United States, 27, 33, 35, 40, 107–8, 144, 170

Methodist Episcopal Church (in Canada), 26, 61, 63, 116, 117, 179

Michigan, religion in the state of, 79, 136, 145; University of, 168

Micmac Indians, 70

Militia Acts (United States, 1792, 1903, 1916), 86

Mississippi, religion in the state of, 148, 153

Missouri Synod, 118, 143

Mormonism, 23, 28, 87, 89

Morris, B. F., 76, 77, 80

Morris, William, 58

Morse, S. F. B., 99

Mount Allison College, 182

Mountain, Bishop George, 68, 181

Mountain, Bishop Jacob, 58, 67

Murray, Sir George, 58

Murray, Robert, 159

National Catholic Welfare Conference (United States), 15

National Education Association (United States), 134

National Reform Movement (United States), 78

National Society (Britain), 132

nativism, in America, 75, 125, 142; (*see also* Know-Nothing Party)

New Hampshire, religion in the state of, 44, 79, 80, 136

New Jersey, religion in the state of, 79, 80, 137, 147, 154

New Mexico, religion in the state of, 153

New York city and state, religion in, 80, 82, 98, 100, 109, 110, 124, 125, 149, 153

New York Public School Society, 141

Newlight Revival, 27, 69, 71, 72, 118

Newman, John, Cardinal, 75, 91, 92, 97, 172

North-west Ordinance (1787), 45

North Carolina, religion in the state of, 34, 43, 79, 80, 168

oaths, confessional, 79, 85

O'Connell, Daniel, 102

Oklahoma, religion in the state of, 87

Ontario, *see* Upper Canada

Orange Order, 95, 96, 101, 102, 103, 162, 176

Oregon, religion in the state of, 145

Oxford movement, influence in North America, 25, 97, 101, 114

Paley, William, 41

Papacy, 90, 106; Papal Infallibility, 91, 93, 165

patronage, lay ecclesiastical: in Britain, 10; in British North America, 126, 127, 130; in the United States, 122, 124; *see also* Trusteeship question

Peel, Sir Robert, 172

penal laws, against dissenters: in British North America, 103; in American colonies, 38, 39, 40, 121; in Ireland, 120

198

Index

Pennsylvania, religion in the state of. 5, 32, 79, 82, 109, 112, 148, 170
People v. Ruggles (United States, 1811), 82
pew-rents, 126, 127
Philadelphia Convention (1787), 46
Pictou Academy, 182
Pierce v. Society of Sisters (United States, 1925), 145
Pittsburgh Synod, 118
Pius IX, Pope, 92, 102
Plessis, Bishop Joseph-Octave, 67
pluralism in religion, general effects, 4, 5, 8, 29, 32, 73, 131, 136, 184
plural marriage, see Mormonism
Poughkeepsie Plan, 143
Power, Bishop Michael, 161
Presbyterianism, in British North America, 54, 57-8, 60, 68, 71, 72, 117, 157, 163, 175, 179, 183; in United States, 27, 36, 39, 41, 44, 46, 107, 112, 113, 170; see also Church of Scotland
Priestley, Joseph, 35
Princeton University, 170
'Programme Catholique', 165
Protestant, The, 99
Protestants and Other Americans United for the Separation of Church and State (POAU), 15, 155
Provoost, Bishop Samuel, 110
Putnam Act (New York, 1855), 98, 99, 125

Quakers, views on Church and state relations, 5, 6, 86, 107, 112
Quebec Act (1774), 49, 51, 66, 111, 115, 131
Quebec Province, see Lower Canada
Quebec Resolutions (1865), 160, 163
Quebec Schools Act (1875), 165, 166
Quebec Seminary, 180
Queen's Colleges (Ireland), 178
Queen's College, Kingston, 175, 176, 177, 178, 179, 180

radicalism, political, in alliance with religious dissent, 15, 33, 34, 39, 51, 53, 55, 157, 174
rebellions of 1837 (Canada), 55, 56, 62
rectories, endowed (Canada), 50, 61, 66
Regents' Prayer, see Engel v. Vitale
Regiopolis College, 175, 176, 177
Regium Donum, 12
'Released Time' in schools, 152, 153, 163
Religious Disabilities Removals Act (Britain, 1891), 12
Religious Freedom Act (Massachussetts, 1811), 44
republicanism, in British North America, 55, 59, 70, 116, 118
Revenue Act (United States, 1916), 81

revivalism, 27, 28, 69; see also Great Awakening, Newlight and Ulster
Reynolds v. United States (1878), 87
Rhode Island, religion in the state of, 5, 32, 79, 128
Rose, John, 160
Royal Supremacy in religion, 37, 49, 66, 113
Russell, Lord John, 56, 64, 105, 132
Ryerson, Egerton, 8, 54, 55, 60, 61, 157, 159-60, 161; Ryerson's Schools Act (1846), 161

Saint Michael's College, Toronto, 179, 180
Saint Paul's Church, Halifax (N.S.), 130
Schaff, Philip, 2, 79
Schempp v. School District of Abington (United States 1959), 148
School Lunch Act (United States, 1946), 153
Scopes, John, 149
Seabury, Bishop Samuel, 109, 110
sectarianism, 28, 104-6, 123, 136, 148
secularism, 4, 21, 86, 137, 147, 176, 179, 185, 186
Select Vestries, 39, 41, 122
Selwyn, Bishop G. A., 22
Separate Schools Acts (Canada 1855), 162, (1863), 163
Seton, Mother Elizabeth, 142
Seward, W. H., 141
Simcoe, Governor John, 50
slavery agitation, effect on the Churches, 23, 27, 29
Social Credit (Canada), 15
Society for the Propagation of the Gospel, 52, 61, 67, 156, 157
South Carolina, religion in the state of, 46, 79, 80, 125, 126, 128; University of, 169
Stimson, E. R., 65
Strachan, Bishop John, 25, 52, 53, 57, 58, 60, 62, 65, 102, 104, 114, 115, 156, 161, 162, 172, 173, 176, 178
Sunday Observance, laws and agitations, 14, 20, 77, 78, 83, 84, 88
Supreme Court (United States), rulings on church and state, 75, 80, 84, 85, 86, 87, 129, 140, 144, 145, 147, 148, 149-51, 152, 153, 154
Syllabus of Errors (1864), 91, 165, 166
Synods of the Church of England, 65, 114, 115

Talbot, Bishop James, 111
Taschereau, Elzéar, Cardinal, 165
tax-exemption for Church property, 80-2, 89, 137
temperance agitations, 20, 55, 88
Tennessee, religion in the state of, 87, 148, 149

Index